Out of the Ordinary

Out of the Ordinary

Folklore and the Supernatural

Barbara Walker
editor

UTAH STATE UNIVERSITY PRESS
Logan, Utah

Typography by WolfPack
    Cover design by Michelle Sellers
Copyedited by Michelle Sanden Johlas

Library of Congress Cataloging-in-Publication Data

Out of the ordinary : folklore and the supernatural / Barbara Walker, editor.
    p. cm.
    ISBN 0–87421–191–3 (cloth)
    ISBN 0–87421–196–4 (paper)
    Includes bibliographical references and index.
    1. Folklore. 2. Supernatural. 3. Folklore—United States. I. Walker, Bar-
bara, 1946– .
GR81.O98 1995
398'.4—dc20   95–4422
                                                              CIP

To my daughter, Becky,
who for many years
lived with the ghost of Mrs. Carson
and my disbelief.

Contents

Preface

THIS BOOK IS AN OUTGROWTH OF UTAH STATE UNIVERSITY'S 1991 FIFE CONference on folklore and the supernatural, with some of the articles stemming from lectures presented during the conference by guest faculty members—specifically, David Hufford, Barre Toelken, Timothy Lloyd, and James McClenon. The conference was well received and highly successful, and a book on the topic seemed a worthwhile undertaking. In addition to obtaining these essays from conference faculty, I solicited manuscripts from other scholars working on various issues of belief.

It would be close to impossible to assemble a complete, comprehensive volume on folklore and the supernatural. But this book offers a useful selection of topics, ranging from Barre Toelken's examination of Native American communication systems (which confound non-Natives) to Kenneth Pimple's account of the ramifications of possible hoaxes, the Fox sisters, and the advent of Modern Spiritualism in America; from Timothy Lloyd's interviews with Lloyd Farley about fundamental belief systems that rely on zodiac signs for determining agricultural practices to Erika Brady's exploration of exorcism and the role of Catholic priests; from David Hufford's intellectual discussion of how belief as a concept is defined and regarded to Joyce Hammond's look at tourists, Hawaii's goddess Pele, and the desire to experience "Other." As a whole, the book offers a spectrum of writing that invites questions, generates discussion, and engenders reflection.

My sincere appreciation goes to each of the authors for their industry and patience. Many of them are long-time scholars of the supernatural and have published other stimulating works on parallel topics. This project, which encouraged my own thinking about the supernatural, particularly about belief itself as a general concept, has been mentally fun and personally gratifying. It also created an opportunity to work with old friends and a framework for meeting new ones, which has been an unexpected serendipitous benefit of the book.

I am grateful to my colleague Barre Toelken, who, as director of the folklore program at Utah State University, allowed me time to converse and gather, to think and write. Without his generosity and encouragement there would be no book. We share a multitude of impromptu discussions at work and many longer, more memorable conversations in homes, restaurants, automobiles, airports, and planes. Through tears, laughter, and even disagreements, we have a caring friendship.

It would be an oversight not to mention William A. "Bert" Wilson, who is a good friend to many of us who have written here. Although he is not a direct contributor to this book, Bert and I have worked, walked, talked, and argued together for several years over many ideas that skirt these pages, and I deeply value his keen intelligence and his great heart.

I want to thank my former and present workmates Karen Krieger, Randy Williams, and Michele Casavant, who cheerfully toast the good times and unfalteringly soothe the bad. They make Monday through Friday especially good-humored and productive.

I am indebted to Michael Spooner and John Alley of Utah State University Press for their careful and helpful insights, their skilled editorial and production know-how, their unwavering encouragement and calming influence, and for being both professionally and personally kind and supportive. Also, I am grateful for the warmth and hard work of their office-mates at USU Press, Anna Furniss and Cathy Tarbet. Finally, I thank copyeditor Michelle Sanden Johlas, who amazed me with her expertise and editing memory, kept our scholarship scrupulously clear and honest, gave straightforward feedback, and generally rescued me from passive voices of all kinds.

BARBARA WALKER
Logan, Utah, 1995

Introduction

THE ESSAYS IN THIS VOLUME CALL INTO QUESTION THE IDEA THAT THE SUPER-
natural is something strange or even extraordinary, and reading them as a
whole brings attention to the fact that aspects of the supernatural are comfort-
ably incorporated into everyday life in a variety of cultures (even in those
"advanced" communities that emphasize formal education and technological
sophistication). These assimilated aspects of the supernatural act as an integral
part of belief constructions and behavior patterns, and, in many instances, have
significant cultural function and effect.

The realm of the supernatural is inextricably connected to belief, and belief
is rooted near human cognition itself, starting with a simple trust in words as
symbols that allow thoughts to be communicated, ranging to polished and
often complex systems of belief on which we may establish meaning and motivation for our lives.

As much as we may prefer to think otherwise, we live in an imprecise and
ambiguous world, which in its inexactitude allows for the awesome, the inexplicable, the wondrous. Consider a circle drawn on a page: In your early algebra lessons, you were taught that to find the circumference of a circle you
multiplied the diameter by pi, which represents the ratio between the diameter
and the circumference of a circle. But pi is an irrational number (which means
it is infinite, it has no end), and when a rational number is multiplied by an
irrational one, the resulting number is also irrational. What that meant to me
in eighth-grade algebra, and still does, is that either the ratio of the diameter
to the circumference (pi) is inexact—perhaps because our mathematical system is inadequate for dealing with circles—or that circles have an inherent
infinite quality about them. Either way, this phenomenon is pretty astounding, considering circles, our mathematical system, and how our society relies
on both. Think how we believe in our circles and in our numbers: think of
wheels and gears and things that turn round; think of one (unity, uniqueness),

two (dualities, bilaterals, opposites), three (wishes, examples, strikes and you're out), four (seasons, compass points, humors), ten (numerical and monetary systems), and twelve (inches, hours, months). Think how irrational and infinite our belief is when using pi.

What I want to suggest here is that even—or perhaps especially—in areas where we have come to think of our world as rational and stable, there are elements of belief and acceptance that are equally as astonishing as belief in the supernatural. There are more than 225 languages spoken by at least one million speakers each; the speed at which the earth rotates on its axis intermittently varies, with those variations classified as secular, irregular, or periodic. These two simple facts alone leave amazing latitude regarding how the people of Earth consider space, time, and the nature of the universe. And regardless of how these conceptualizations are formed, they are by nature, at best and always, limiting, compromising, and accepting of a particular way of thinking. There is a leap of faith necessary whenever we adhere to any system of thought, whether it means relying on pi or some other unknown.

Identifying the Inexplicable

Referring to something as "supernatural" is not to call it unreal or untrue—on the contrary. The existence of the term itself is a linguistic and cultural acknowledgment that inexplicable things happen which we identify as being somehow beyond the natural or the ordinary, and that many of us hold beliefs which connect us to spheres that exist beyond what we might typically see, hear, taste, touch, or smell.

For some the supernatural is a natural part of life, and supernatural experiences not only are considered "normal" but, in some instances, are expected to occur, with personal attitudes and behaviors shaped and acted out on the basis of those expectations. No matter how we consider the supernatural, it exists in belief systems throughout the world, and examples abound:

from visionary encounters with the holy, such as a deity, to tangible confrontations with the unholy, such as a practitioner of black magic;

from contact with beings who come from far away, such as inhabitants of other planets, to those who might live in hiding among us, such as Sasquatch;

from interactions with supernatural entities who are alive, such as shapeshifters, to those who are dead, such as ghosts;

from entering structures that are consecrated, such as religious temples, to avoiding those which are fearsome, such as haunted houses;

from employing objects to keep the supernaturally powerful away, such as garlic to ward off vampires, to those which invite the supernaturally powerful into one's home, such as Ouija boards;

from participating in customs that curse an individual, such as the evil eye, to those that heal, such as a Blessing Way ceremony or prayer;

from sacred foods that connect believers to their gods, such as bread or wine used as sacrament, to mundane foods that connect people to prodigious forces in the universe, such as vegetables planted according to zodiac signs;

from sacred places that are intimate and private and shared within the family, such as the home hearth where a religious icon is placed, to those that are cloaked and mysterious and shared only with the initiated, such as sacrificial altars hidden in deep woods, to those which are somewhere in-between, such as cemeteries.

The span of the supernatural in our lives, both invited and uninvited, has wide boundaries: sometimes cyclical or everyday or ordinary and sometimes so unique that the supernatural experience occurs once in a lifetime; sometimes it is an event or occurrence that is only believed to have happened to someone else and never really is witnessed by the individual holding the belief at all. For some, the supernatural is disclaimed so unequivocally that beliefs are held because they discount or somehow disqualify the supernatural as a legitimate option—an *anti*-supernatural system of belief.

One belief system may incorporate more of the "supernatural" as "natural" than another. For example, among Asian populations, it is not unusual to believe that honoring dead ancestors is mandatory for avoiding disharmony in one's earthly life, or among Mormons, to believe that spiritual interaction between people in this world and souls in heaven is an almost daily occurrence through ritual enactments in Mormon temples. Basically, when regarding the supernatural, what is agreeable within one group may seem superstitious, primitive, uneducated, or ignorant to another.

If you belong to a religious congregation that believes the world of the living and the world of the dead openly interact for the overall good of humankind, then another member telling of a wakeful encounter with a dead loved one may not seem startling or even out of the ordinary; it might, in fact, be an enviable distinction or evidence of worthiness or holiness. If, however, this same person were to say that last night creatures from outer space made a housecall, you might apply "loony" as an appropriate appellation. If you gather with those who believe in extraterrestrial visitations and indeed feel you have experienced such an exchange, then you might share a sense of close camaraderie with someone describing a personal account of alien abduction, but maybe less so if that person were to relate a first-person confrontation with the Devil.

So what becomes defined as *super*natural is, in many respects, relative to the individual or the society. Within some communities a supernatural event is not necessarily an extraordinary event, but most likely it has an "other-worldly" quality about it. And whether or not we belong to groups who actively and openly embrace and incorporate the supernatural, we nevertheless can find it in our lives. In my family, my grandmother read palms and tea leaves, one aunt consulted the Ouija board, another aunt (one of the most level-headed ones, I might add) had dead relatives appear to her at various times, an in-law cleansed his house of menacing spirits, and I myself (beyond my own incredulity) am certain of having lived in a house also inhabited by a female ghost. I have friends and acquaintances who have been "hag-ridden" by a paralyzing presence, who have participated in various kinds of ritual healing ceremonies, who have suffered the consequences of telling Coyote stories out of season, who have had out-of-body experiences, one who has lived out specific events that were carefully predicted in detail by an African holy man, one who claimed to be a warlock and was hounded by an evil spirit living in him, one who has the power of water-witching, and one who saw an ancient Oriental master emerge from a blank wall. I have had students tell me of sighting Bigfoot, of living and communicating for several years with a ghost who adopted the family, of first-person interactions with vanishing hitchhikers. The valley that is my home also shelters water-witches, folks who plant by the signs, a weeping cemetery statue, a canyon ghost, a haunted bridge, a house cursed by gypsies, Three Nephites, a temple where Christ has appeared, a coven of witches, and a cluster of UFO watchers. I highly suspect my experience is not unique, and whether I'm skeptical or not really doesn't matter because these things are a part of my immediate world regardless.

Acknowledging the supernatural is one thing, but studying it is another, and one might ask, "Why bother with a closer examination of the supernatural at all?" For one thing, if the supernatural is seriously considered, the events and phenomena reported or described within a group give us evidence of a particular way of perceiving the world. It provides insight into cultural identity and a greater awareness of the breadth and quality of human experiences and expressions. How groups regard the supernatural contributes to thought and behavior, and by attending to those patterns, we gather a fuller understanding of what is meaningful to the group, what gives it cohesion and animation, and thus we develop a rounder perspective of cultural nuance, both within the group and cross-culturally.

The Supernatural as a Transcendental Force

In mainstream American society (and perhaps in other societies, too), which prides itself on scientific advancement, technological know-how, educational superiority, and computerization of almost everything, the supernatural functions as a transcendental element. It goes beyond the mechanical, the empirical, the quantifiable, the provable, and beyond the immediate and practical. It resonates with the idea that even though we have advanced technologically, there still are elements and concerns that rest outside our arena of control or conscious understanding. Some New Age literature (which often is tenuously derivative of ancient beliefs) appears in mass America as a symptomatic response to a pendulum that has swung too far in one direction; it suggests an attempt to believe in and connect with a "larger" universe in a world that has become increasingly sophisticated and objective on the one hand and abysmally narrowed and single-focused on the other. It is possible that as the infiltration and complexity of technology increase so does our longing for a network attaching us to something beyond; it seems that belief in the supernatural is not discouraged by scientific advancement nor by formal education, and that the more we feel dispossessed the more significant become our connections to the things that on a mundane level identify us as human.

In his recent book *Technopoly,* Neil Postman[1] examines the relationship between technology and culture, and concludes his discussion by stating that one of the most relevant fields to study is religion, because to do so is to study "how different people . . . have tried to achieve a sense of transcendence" (p. 198). Although technology is a human endeavor, for most of us the intricacies of things like microcircuitry or fiber optics or even grocery-store barcode readers are essentially outside of our immediate understanding. In such a world, where the individual may sense a certain loss of control, belief in the supernatural (itself quite possibly outside of our control) ironically returns more direct power to humans: We may feel powerless before the juggernaut of technology, but technology is powerless and perhaps irrelevant when juxtaposed with the supernatural; and beyond it all, humans still have access to their supernatural realms. Some occurrences cannot be explained through logical or scientific thought.

In a way, believing in the supernatural is conceding and submitting to a universe that extends further than human understanding or control or empirical observation, and such belief imbues that universe with possibilities that surpass ordinary human devices. Yet when supernatural powers are tapped or extraordinary events occur, we in some respects are empowered, because then the limitations of any sphere repudiating the magical or the miraculous are outdistanced. We successfully broaden and deepen our world and perhaps open ourselves to a greater reality. In this regard, and in the best senses of the words, belief in the supernatural is primal, is uncontrollable, is subversive.

Human identification, understanding, and expression of any kind are never arrived at lineally through a single source or cause. We acculturate in response to a matrix of influences, and in the process, each society generally maintains a homeostasis—something that is dynamic and changing, yet generally in balance. As modern advancements infiltrate most aspects of our lives, we continue to preserve and stretch our frontiers of multiplicity and texture and riddles. When technology speeds most of us along faster than our capacity to grasp, when it collapses generational gaps into increasingly shorter spaces of time, when we find our lives glutted with an overabundance of available information—then the supernatural acts as a balance. In a strange way, it becomes comfortable and acceptable to not "know it all" (because the supernatural is based less on facts and more on faith), and the puzzles themselves—still enigmatic and unsolved but nevertheless familiar—can be defined or incorporated by our cultural groups, be made acceptable in a world of limited understanding, act as a stabilizer in modern society, and defy our sensation of feeling overrun and perhaps out of control.

Attitudes and experiences regarding the supernatural often are manifested through folklore. Vernacular culture conveys such things as beliefs about preworlds, the afterlife, and exchanges between those worlds and this one; relates humans to gods, devils, and their emissaries; identifies people, creatures, symbols, places, actions, or words as having supernatural powers and defines what those powers mean and how they function; provides a rationale for the unexplainable; gives direction and purpose to individual lives and enhances the experience of living itself. Supernatural aspects of any community can fall inside or outside the confines of formal or institutionalized belief, although the distinctions between what is vernacular and what is "official" can overlap and often be hazy. For instance, you may belong to a religion which officially believes in direct revelation from God through a prophet or minister or pope, and the revelations might be written down or otherwise canonized; on the vernacular level, you may have heard a legend about an individual member of your church successfully being healed through prayer. One is institutionally sanctioned and codified doctrine, the other is folklore—but this is not to say that one is true and one false, one somehow better and one worse. Both align with a particular position regarding the nature of God and powers that extend beyond daily life, and not only are they compatible but they are supportive of the same belief system. *Folklore*, for the purposes of this book, generally should be thought of as those expressions of vernacular culture within a group that provide it with identity, cohesion, and perpetuation. Some of the essays deal with formalized parts of a religion or with broader culture, but even within standardized institutions it is possible to study folk dynamics.

The folklore of the supernatural can be evidenced in all aspects of our lives: the things we say (ghost stories, creation myths, tales of skinwalkers, prayers), the things we do (what we wear, what we eat, how we bury our dead, how and when to plant and harvest crops, avoiding bad luck and encouraging good), the things we create (religious symbols, charms, amulets, foods), the things we believe in (gods, devils, spirits, ghosts, interplanetary travelers, healing rituals, life after death), where we go (to church on Sunday, to the cemetery at midnight, to the Bermuda Triangle), and who our friends and associates are (Catholics, shamans, witches, Navajos, the religious, the irreverent). Even if we personally might not claim any belief in the supernatural, we will rub shoulders with people who do.

This book naturally can present only a limited sampling of some examinations of folklore and the supernatural—it is not exhaustive, by any means. But we hope that what it offers will stimulate thought, discussion, and maybe even controversy.

Each essay in the book was developed independently. As mentioned earlier, any discussion regarding the supernatural also inevitably examines the parallel issue of belief. How is belief defined? On what basis are beliefs formed? Does belief influence perception and experience, or do perception and experience engender belief? To what extent does the relationship between belief and skepticism form a necessary balance within a culture? How do we handle the mysteries? Indeed, are there any mysteries? No matter what position readers of this volume take on the issues presented here, it is our hope that this work will help to stimulate and expand the conversation encompassing culture, folklore, belief, and the supernatural.

Endnote

1. Neil Postman, *Technopoly: The Surrender of Culture to Technology* (New York: Vintage Books, 1992).

I

Perception, Belief, and Living

From the moment we are born, our world is patterned by our culture, and this includes not only what we eat or wear or say or do, but also to some extent our ability to perceive, what we know or believe, and how we think. These things are basic and instilled so early that it is as though the world were actually created in the image our culture provides. Cradled in language and human interaction, a way to live is unfurled and becomes the standard for defining and evaluating life's experiences.

But some experiences exist independent of culture, and these experiences also help to give us definition and insight and to engender belief.

The three essays included in this section all deal with perception, belief, and experience, and consequently how life is lived on the basis of these elements. In Chapter 1, David Hufford examines definitions of belief and knowledge and relates those concepts to "core experiences." He discusses how some events take place regardless of any societal constructions, and although those happenings might be culturally interpreted or integrated, they nevertheless can happen independently of cultural boundaries. This idea seems obvious when dealing with circumstances that are inherent to being human—puberty or childbirth, for instance. But what happens when the experience falls into the realm of the supernatural, as in an out-of-body interlude or during an encounter with a supernatural power or force? Hufford makes a strong case in support of the concept that sometimes a supernatural incident precedes belief, even in spite of cultural conditioning.

In Chapter 2, Barre Toelken sensitively discusses his encounters with the "improbable" in Navajo culture, giving personal examples of episodes that fall outside his own set of cultural assumptions and expectations. Essentially, Toelken states that one's understanding of the world is determined in part both by experience and culture, but different cultures have different ways of decoding experience and of interpreting life events. What one culture might identify as a cause–effect relationship another might consider coincidental; what seems supernatural to one group is quite natural to another. Therefore, one of the important aspects of intercultural exploration, especially in terms of the "supernatural," is exposure to other ways of organizing information and thus to stretching the limits of our understanding.

Timothy Lloyd's essay in Chapter 3 insightfully reexamines traditional definitions of the supernatural and offers a glimpse of how a few individuals actively incorporate it into their everyday lives. For some, the supernatural is not necessarily something mysterious, but rather is a specialized kind of practical knowledge that can be tapped, allowing a positive interaction between commonplace procedures, like butchering or planting crops, and the influences of universal power. Lloyd discusses how certain signs or symbols have cultural functions and experiential validity, acting not only as expressions of belief but as elements that directly connect humans with the supernatural.

In combination, these three essays invite reevaluation of our own perceptions of the world and perhaps encourage a less strident adherence to our own sociocentric values and a more open-minded approach to concepts of knowledge, belief, and how the universe might work.

1

Beings Without Bodies:
An Experience-Centered Theory of the Belief in Spirits

David J. Hufford

THIS ESSAY CONCERNS A PARTICULAR SET OF "FOLK BELIEFS," THAT IS, UNOFFI-cial beliefs. The meanings and implications of this definition are discussed at some length below. Most academic theories have assumed that folk belief—especially beliefs about spirits—is false or at least unfounded, "non-rational" and "non-empirical." Because my experience-centered theory is contrary to this very powerful and old intellectual tradition, the following exposition must be somewhat complex. It will, therefore, be helpful for the reader to know where we are going right at the start: the "bottom line" of my experience-centered theory is the proposition that much folk belief about spirits *is reasonable*, that it is rationally developed from experience. That is to say, the reasoning involved in many such beliefs utilizes methods of inference, based on observations, which are commonly accepted as valid. Such reasoning does not show neurotic defenses or other overwhelming biases that lead to obvious fallacies, such as post hoc reasoning, equivocation, or *consensus gentium*.

Granting such reasonableness does not entail accepting any such beliefs as true, but it does call into very serious question the academic grounds for holding that spiritual folk beliefs are false. Neither does my theory suggest that *all* spiritual belief is rationally derived from experience. Obviously such a claim would be false. Faith, which is usually understood as belief in the absence of evidence, is of enormous importance in religious belief. But I do mean to argue against the common assumption that *all* spiritual belief relies entirely on faith.

A final disclaimer: I do not suggest that my experience-centered theory conflicts with or should replace all current approaches to the study of spiritual beliefs—but it does have important implications for most of them.

Two Preliminary Illustrations

In the early 1970s, while studying folk belief in Newfoundland, I found a tradition about what was locally called the "Old Hag," an experience said to have the following features:

> (1) waking up during the night (or occasionally the experience occurs before falling asleep); (2) hearing and/or seeing something come into the room and approach the bed; (3) being pressed on the chest or strangled and therefore feeling suffocation; (4) being unable to move or cry out until . . . finally breaking through the feeling of paralysis. . . . The victim is almost invariably lying on his back during the experience and is convinced that he has been awake throughout.[1]

Despite the local term "Old Hag," the attacker could be either male or female, and when a male carried out such an attack through witchcraft, he was said "to hag" his victim.

In *The Terror That Comes in the Night: An Experience-Centered Study of Supernatural Assault Traditions* (1982), I extended my analysis of this experience and its cross-cultural distribution. I was able to show that what Newfoundlanders call the Old Hag comprises a cross-culturally stable experiential pattern underlying many belief traditions in widely separated places. I also documented the occurrence of the same pattern among subjects with no prior cultural knowledge about such attacks, as in the following case, which comes from a young man who thought he was the only one to ever have this experience:

Example 1: Newfoundland's "Old Hag" in a Pennsylvania College Dormitory

What woke me up was the door slamming. "OK," I thought, "It's my roommate. . . " I was laying on my back just kinda looking up. And the door slammed, and I kinda opened my eyes. I was awake. Everything was light in the room. My roommate wasn't there and the door was still closed. . . .

But the next thing I knew, I realized that I couldn't move. . . . I kind of like gazed over to the door and there was no one there. But the next thing I knew, from one of the areas of the room this grayish, brownish murky presence was there. And it kind of swept down over the bed and I was terrified! . . . It was like nothing I had ever seen before. And I felt—I felt this pressing down all over me. I couldn't breathe. I couldn't move. And the whole thing was that—there was like—I could hear the stereo in the room next to me. I was wide awake, you know. It was a fraternity house. I could hear everything going on all over the house. It was a pretty noisy place. And I couldn't move and I was helpless and I was really—I was really scared. . . . And this murky presence—just kind of—this was *evil!* This was evil! You know this is weird! You must think I'm a . . . This thing was *there!* I felt a pressure on me and it was like enveloping me. It was a very, very, very strange thing. And as I remember I struggled. I struggled to move and get out. And—you know, eventually, I think eventually what happened was I kind of like moved my arm. And again the whole thing—just kind of dissipated away. The presence, everything. But everything else just remained the same. The same stereo was playing next door. The same stuff was going on.[2]

This medical student had never heard of anyone else having such an experience, but his description corresponds perfectly to accounts of supernatural assault found all over the world—not only the "Old Hag" tradition in Newfoundland, but also the *da chor*,[3] *dab coj, poj ntxoog*,[4] or *dab tsog*[5] in Southeast Asia; the sitting ghost or *bei Guai chaak*[6] in China; the *Mara*[7] of Sweden; even the "witch riding" in Salem, Massachusetts, during the witchcraft trials.[8] Each of these traditions and many more also correspond to the category "sleep paralysis" found in the tradition of modern medicine. Although medical knowledge about the experiential *contents* of this experience is quite impoverished compared to folk traditions, sleep physiologists do seem to have located the physical source of the temporary paralysis.[9] However, because sleep paralysis theories do not account for the consistent subjective pattern of the experience, sleep paralysis cannot be said to "explain" or *reduce* the related folk beliefs.

Each traditional term for this frightening experience carries a great deal of theoretical baggage, from theories of witchcraft and the inaccurate gender implications of "Old Hag" to the physiologic reductionism of "sleep paralysis." To avoid these difficulties, I have chosen to use the old Anglo-Saxon word for the experience, *Mara*.[10] By this term I refer simply to the experience of finding oneself awake and paralyzed in the presence of a frightening being. Nothing more—neither interpretation nor cause—is implied. In 1982 I estimated that this event has a prevalence ranging from about 16 percent to 25 percent in the general population, regardless of prior knowledge or belief. That estimate has now received a good deal of confirmation.[11]

Since complete and recognizable Mara experiences—loaded with the same experiential details reported within traditions that describe such attacks—occur in the *absence* of such traditions, it seems fair to infer that the Mara experience itself has given rise to a variety of similar beliefs in different cultures. The conventional expectation has long been that folk belief creates experience (and the illusory appearance of experience) in a self-fulfilling process, as when the believer dreams of a ghost and afterward believes the event to have been real.

But on the contrary, here a host of traditional beliefs actually seem to be produced by a particular kind of experience, the details of which are independent of prior belief or knowledge. That realization immediately raised for me the question of whether the Mara stood alone, or whether there might be other experiential categories with a similar cross-cultural distribution and interpretations showing great similarity from one tradition to another? The answer has turned out to be "Yes."

I am pleased to report that very positive spiritual experiences are even more common than horrific ones. The following is an account told to me by a surgical nurse in Harrisburg, Pennsylvania, concerning events that occurred in 1976.

Example 2: A Nurse's Near-Death Experience

I was having fluorescein angiography for my heart . . . I was having a great deal of coronary spasm . . . and the pain was incredible. . . . And when the pain became the most intense I had a horrible ringing noise . . . and I was rushing . . . through sort of a black tunnel . . . and then the ringing seemed to diminish . . . the pain was gone . . . and I realized I had floated right out of . . . the top of my head. . . . And I was looking down, I was somewhere over my knees, and I could see Dr. Smith and Dr. Thompson . . . working on me. This seemed of almost no importance to me . . . I just observed it. . . .

I felt like I was swimming or floating in a lovely . . . I don't know . . . if you could imagine swimming in champagne, that's what it was like, it was lovely. [And as I floated upward I became aware of a light, and then] I found that I was a *part* of the light, the light was enveloping me. . . . I could see the [operating room] clock . . . [and] I knew that in a given amount of time there would be brain damage. [But] the feeling I had besides the pleasurable one was one of—just unconditional love is the only thing I can think of. . . . I've never had a feeling like it before, so it's really difficult to describe, but unconditional love comes as close as anything. And I was in communication [with] a . . . being . . . who read my mind and I just read his mind, which I say as an afterthought, because at the time I just knew that we weren't speaking. And the whole time I was in communication with this person, there was like a Greek chorus in the background . . . multiple presences that I was aware of as I watched them resuscitate me. . . .

Now the communication I had with the presence was one simply of—we discussed my life. But I also felt that I never had to say anything . . . and he didn't say anything, and he understood my motivation if I did something that I thought might have been questionable. . . . and [then] he said to me . . . it's time [to go back]. And I was so happy, I wasn't even sure that this was a good idea to go back to the body. But he said . . . everything's fine and you should . . . return, so I did.

And as I regained consciousness [I was aware] of this immense grin on my face. And Dr. Smith who's been my physician for years and is a dear friend, said . . . "Do you know what happened?" And I said, "Yes, I died." And he said, "You sure as hell did."[12]

The experience reported by this nurse occurred in 1976, years before she had heard the term "near-death experience" or knew that anyone else had ever had a similar experience. But her description corresponds perfectly not only to the pattern described by Raymond Moody in the 1975 book *Life after Life*,[13] in which he coined the term *near-death experience* (NDE), but also (for just a few examples) to beliefs and accounts from Pure Land Buddhism in China,[14] medieval European Catholicism,[15] and an account of a visit to the land of the ancestors during a Chant Way healing ceremony, as told to me by a Navajo woman.

Belief That Spirits Exist

What is it that is believed in the Buddhist, Catholic, and Navajo traditions just noted? Are there elements that traditions around the world have in common, as well as distinct elements that make each tradition unique? There is a common core, and it consists in the belief that there exists an order

1. that is objectively real, (i.e., not "all in the mind");
2. that is qualitatively different from the everyday material world (e.g., invisible at times);
3. that interacts with this world in certain ways (e.g., answers to prayer, visits from deceased loved ones); and
4. that includes beings that do not require a physical body in order to live (e.g., God, souls of the deceased, angels, evil spirits).

In different traditions, this order is variously called "the spirit world," "the supernatural," "land of the ancestors," and so on.

These four elements are held in common by folk belief traditions and religions around the world.[16] How this spiritual order is different, when and how it interacts with the mundane world, and who the persons in it are, constitute major differences in cultural and religious traditions, and frequently between institutional religious tradition and folk belief.

Scholars have generally called such a belief in spirits *supernatural* belief. I rather like that term myself, but it has been so problematized by long academic misuse that now it has been given up even by many religious speakers.[17] Here, to avoid confusion, I will instead use *spiritual belief* to refer to the belief that spirits and a distinctly spiritual domain exist. Even this term can be confusing, because it has been metaphorically extended to mean *ideas* (as in "the spirit of democracy"), and *spiritual* is often used as a rough equivalent to *psychological*.

I shall use the term in its narrowest sense:

> *spiritual* refers to *spirits* (i.e., extra-corporeal beings)

This definition has the added advantage of calling attention to the important relationships between folk belief and institutional religious belief, where the word *spiritual* still has a comfortable home. In this use, spirits are sentient beings not requiring bodies in order to live. They may use bodies (as human souls do during Earthly life), or they may possess some kind of non-physical body (resurrection body, subtle body, astral body, etc.), but they are conscious beings whose life is not absolutely dependent on a flesh-and-blood body for existence. This definition is derived from the observation of beliefs in such beings held in cultures all over the world. Accepting the usefulness of the *definition,* and its accuracy in summing up widespread belief, has nothing to do with either accepting or rejecting associated *beliefs.*

Spiritual Belief in the Modern World

By the 1950s, intellectuals were broadly proclaiming the death of spiritual belief. Granting that belief in God was the slowest of these to go, belief in angels, ghosts, and other lesser spirits was thought to be rapidly disappearing.

In 1953 Rudolf Bultmann, a famous theologian, laid groundwork for the anti-theological "God Is Dead" school of theology. He stated:

> Now that the forces and the laws of nature have been discovered, we can no longer believe in *spirits, whether good or evil.* . . . It is impossible to use electric light and the wireless and to avail ourselves of modern medical and surgical discoveries, and at the same time to believe in . . . spirits.[18]

In 1966 anthropologist Anthony F. C. Wallace said:

> Belief in supernatural beings and in supernatural forces that affect nature without obeying nature's laws will erode and become only an interesting historical memory. . . . [A]s a cultural trait, belief in supernatural powers is doomed to die out, all over the world, as a result of the increasing adequacy and diffusion of scientific knowledge. . . . [T]he process is inevitable.[19]

And in 1971 historian Keith Thomas began his magnum opus *Religion and the Decline of Magic* with the statement that in contrast to the past, belief in ghosts is now "rightly disdained by intelligent persons."[20]

It has been widely assumed that something about modern knowledge, particularly scientific knowledge, is antithetical to spiritual belief. This is the basis for the secularization thesis that has guided the social sciences since their very beginnings in the mid-nineteenth century. Auguste Comte, the father of sociology, in his writings specifically described a natural and inevitable route of cultural evolution from supernatural belief to an entirely materialistic view that he called positivistic. In 1922 Max Weber, the pioneer sociologist of religion, called this allegedly inevitable secularization process the disenchantment of the world.[21]

Apparently most folklorists have accepted such conclusions about the demise of spiritual belief, and they have studied "folk belief" or "superstitions" by going to remote areas, isolated rural communities, or people recently immigrated from less modern settings to gather up the remnants of spiritual belief—that is, when folklorists have paid any attention at all to the topic. Gillian Bennett, who—along with the other contributors to this volume—is among a growing band of folklorists who do take spiritual belief seriously, neatly sums up the problems of most modern folklorists regarding these beliefs:

> No one will tackle the subject because it is disreputable, and it remains disreputable because no one will tackle it. Secondly, because no one does any research into present-day supernatural beliefs, occult traditions are generally represented by old legends [leaving] published collections of supernatural folklore . . . stuck forever in a time-warp.[22]

Given all of this scholarly certitude that spiritual beliefs must and should die out in the face of growing modern knowledge, the ease with which I have been able to find people in all walks of life who not only hold spiritual beliefs but who cite their own spiritual experiences as their reason has always seemed anomalous to me. I might have begun to doubt my own findings were it not for the growing body of empirical evidence, gathered primarily by sociologists doing quantitative survey research.[23] The Gallup organization has been documenting the spiritual beliefs of Americans for several decades, and their data most decidedly do not conform to the secularization view sketched above. In 1990, for instance, a Gallup poll found that 25 percent of Americans believe that "ghosts or . . . spirits of dead people can come back." If this 25 percent were made up of the least educated and most isolated Americans, it might not necessarily contradict the secularization thesis. But this is not the case. For example, in 1982 Gallup related the belief that it is "possible to contact the dead" to educational background. He found that the belief was held by 9 percent of those with only grade school education, 25 percent of those who had graduated from high school, and 28 percent of those with college educations.[24] All of the best empirical data from the past several decades shows that modern education does *not* eradicate spiritual belief.

I am convinced that a fundamental reason that spiritual beliefs have been able to resist the enormous social pressures toward secularization is that they are, in part, rationally founded on experience (that is, empirically grounded). This assertion often elicits a howl of protest from those committed either to the falseness of such beliefs or to the proposition that the issue of truth or falseness cannot (or should not) be addressed by belief scholars. So I hasten to add the following commonplace from epistemology: The rationality and empirical grounding of a belief are separate from its "truth"; many false beliefs are rationally held on empirical grounds (e.g., the belief that the sun went around the earth, as held in antiquity), and many true beliefs are held without rational or empirical grounds. A very common example of the latter are those beliefs accepted on the basis of *cultural authority*. Cultural or epistemic authority is the power or right to make "judgments about the nature of the world," and it therefore "entails the construction of reality through definitions of fact and value."[25] For example, young children accept many beliefs (many of them true, others false) simply on the cultural authority of their parents, without doing their own reasoning about the beliefs, just as laypeople accept the statements of "experts" in general, largely on cultural authority.

It is not that the acceptance of cultural authority is *ir*rational. Authority is itself subject to reasoning, and one may have more or less rational grounding for the acceptance of a particular authority or authoritative statement. But that is different from having rational grounds for particular statements themselves. When one subjects oneself to authority, one yields personal judgment and reasoning in favor of some expert who is believed to "know better."[26] The acceptance of authority is an essential part of knowledge-making, but it is evaluated primarily on the grounds of the validity of claims to have expertise, the claim that underlies cultural authority. Technical experts, government personnel, parents, oral tradition, and many other sources of authority exist in society, and the claims of these sources may either conflict or harmonize with one another. Cultural authority is contrasted with social (executive) authority—the right or power to do certain things, including to give commands. The two are often, but not always, found together.

Having said that rational and empirical grounding do not prove a belief to be true, I must add that finding such a basis for spiritual beliefs does show that such beliefs are sometimes held for better reasons than most academics have granted. Rationality and empirical grounding do not settle truth claims, but they certainly don't hurt those claims, either!

The two cases given at the beginning of this chapter are examples of experience on which certain spiritual beliefs were based, rationally and empirically, by those who had the experiences. My conclusion about the rational and empirical elements of spiritual belief—its reasonableness—grows out of my experience-centered study of beliefs about supernatural assault, mystical experience, miraculous healing, consoling visits by the deceased to the grieving, near-death experiences, and haunted houses, among others. This claim about spiritual belief and experience is both radical and complex, and it requires a good deal of explanation. I shall begin this explanation with some basic discussion of the relationships of belief, experience, and culture.

Inferring What Is Believed

Belief is the certainty that something is true. (This is belief in the cognitive sense; *belief* also has important emotional meanings that associate it with such terms as faith, but those aspects are beyond the scope of this paper.) *Knowledge* is a particular kind of belief, that is, belief that has met customary criteria of justification; this is the basis for the strong distinction between the two terms—that knowledge is justified true belief.[27] However, different criteria for justification are customary in different cultural settings, so this distinction does not serve us well in examining belief in a cultural way. In cultural terms, *knowledge* is what particular people call the beliefs that they consider to be most justified and true. This usage relies on local values and does not require the outside observer either to impose alien criteria or to enter into local debates. Under this usage we may determine which beliefs are knowledge simply by asking those who hold them, rather than by attempting to finally determine matters of truth.

For fieldwork, however, we must remember that in ordinary conversation people choose the strongest term that conforms to their own level of certainty.[28] Therefore, if we ask for *belief* our field consultants may omit what they *know*, and if we use *belief* to describe their *knowledge*, they are likely to be insulted. As is often the case, good sense dictates that our use of terms in analysis must be different from our use of the same terms in fieldwork and in ordinary conversation. My discussion in this paper uses *belief* to include knowledge.

Holding a belief—believing—is an active process that refers to ideas. "The Earth goes around the Sun" and "People have souls that survive death" are statements of ideas. Some people hold the belief that one or both of these are true, and others do not. Belief is found in the process of "holding," but it can only be described by reference to the ideas held. The ideas held are most easily expressed as propositions, although they are not necessarily "held" in that form. Yesterday I believed "that the sun would rise again" (and it did). However, not once did I articulate that proposition, even mentally, although I "acted on that belief," and if asked I would have approved the proposition as something "I believed." I use this example to demonstrate that the cognitive definition does not imply that people hold their beliefs as a list of articulated propositions, as some critics have suggested.[29]

In fact, I assume that most people believe a large number of things that they never explicitly state as propositions, even to themselves. The natural vehicle of folk belief, perhaps of most belief, is stories that show what is true by what is said to have happened. This process combines beliefs with some of their reasons and some of their implications. But for tacit and embedded beliefs to be described and understood, the investigator must infer them and state them as propositions. The investigator must also ensure that the propositions as stated are agreeable to those who are said to hold them. In the cognitive sense it is wrong to attribute to someone a belief they disagree with or do not understand.[30]

Beliefs in propositional form are to be understood as constructed by the investigator in an attempt to refer to the truth ideas of the people from whose speech and behavior they have been inferred. These beliefs in propositional form have the same status as the values, symbols, and other abstract entities that scholars infer from the behavior and statements of people.

Inevitably, *belief* is also used as a shorthand reference to the ideas themselves, the believed propositions, as in "the belief that ghosts exist." This seems unavoidable in conversation, but the distinction between the proposition itself and the belief that a proposition is true must be kept in mind. Otherwise one falls into the habit of referring to beliefs that are not believed: for example, many know the "belief" that breaking a mirror will result in seven years of bad luck, but not all who know of this proposition believe it.

Belief, Culture, and Experience

Belief is a fundamental and profoundly powerful part of culture. *Culture* refers to the entire human heritage apart from biological inheritance. We receive our skin pigment from our parents through genetic transmission. We may receive some immunity to disease through our mother's milk. These are not culture, although culture can influence such transmission, as in social mores surrounding the selection of mates, and values and attitudes toward breastfeeding.

We receive our language, our moral code, and most of our beliefs from communication with other human beings. Biology is involved, since, for example, we could not hear and speak language without the biology of audition and speech. But although the potential for speech may be genetically acquired, our language is culturally transmitted. Even if our biological parents had spoken nothing but Mandarin, we would have no extra difficulty learning English if we were raised in an English-speaking family.

I have said that we obtain *most* of our beliefs from culture. But not all beliefs are acquired in this way. This sets beliefs apart from most language and many other features of our mental life, and herein lies a central feature of my theory of folk belief. It has been common for scholars to argue over whether belief-inspiring experiences, such as near-death experiences, arise from biology or from culture (the "nature–nurture" debate).[31] But such arguments assume a false dichotomy. While believing always involves both biology and culture, most belief also at least claims to involve the rest of the environment. Beliefs are claims about the world in which humans live, and they arise from many different kinds of interactions—not only social interactions. For example, many beliefs about solar eclipses are rooted in *cultural* tradition, and the perception of an eclipse cannot be understood without a consideration of the *biology* of vision. But neither can beliefs about and perceptions of eclipses be understood without reference to the sun and the astronomical events involved. Eclipse beliefs are not only about dragons who swallow the sun. They are also about "that bright light that moves across the sky during the day." An understanding of *any* belief must recognize this implicit claim of reference to the "objective" world (that is, "the world out there").

Many beliefs about the world are acquired through culture. For almost all modern people, the belief that the Earth goes around the Sun is culturally acquired. Many are told the basics of this by their parents. In school, most Americans are taught about the role of Galileo and Copernicus in the great historical shift away from the belief that the Earth is the center of the universe. We have also seen charts of the solar system, and so forth. But most of us have never made a personal observation that could show us that the Earth goes around the Sun. (Such observations are a great deal harder to make than most realize.) For this *we* rely on our culture, but Galileo and Copernicus managed to make observations that actually contradicted what *they* had learned from their culture. It is certainly true that they could never have made those observations without the benefit of a great deal of culturally acquired knowledge, including language. Neither could they have done so without their biology: eyes, brains, and so forth. But, nonetheless, their new belief was not given to them by cultural transmission, nor did it originate in their biology. Their belief in a solar-centric system arose primarily out of particular experiences, observations of the environment. Modern astronomers make many such observations, building both on their cultural inheritance (all of their astronomical training) and new observations made within the context of that tradition.

The work of modern astronomers illustrates a central function of culture: to allow humans to learn from each other's experiences. The number of things that can be learned from experience of the world is vast; many of them require special training, and the opportunities of individuals are limited. Culture allows us to build on an enormous treasury composed of the experiential learning of others. This is also a central function of cultural authority, as discussed earlier.

It is not only scientists who learn from both culture and the environment. A simple example is that many people come to recognize poison ivy, and to hold the belief that touching it can cause a rash, blisters, and intense itching. Some people are fortunate enough to learn this through culture (whether from parents, friends, or a Scout handbook) without ever having the experience of a poison ivy rash themselves. Others learn about poison ivy through direct experience of that aspect of their environment. Culture, experience, and biology intermingle constantly in life, and the variety of life experiences helps to account for the great diversity of beliefs and views found within a single society.

Folk Belief and Official Culture

Unlike the solar-centric belief, which requires sophisticated mathematics and instrumentation, the belief that poison ivy causes itching can arise from non-technical experiences of the environment. Through the life experiences of people with no technical training in either botany or toxicology, knowledge of poison ivy has entered folklore. Technical investigation can add to that knowledge, and official culture (such as dermatology textbooks) can transmit technical information about poison ivy reactions. But such information does not necessarily displace or invalidate most folk beliefs about poison ivy, many of which are derived from firsthand experience.

When I say *folk* belief, I mean *un*official belief. Official beliefs are those that are promulgated through social structures invested with executive authority, while the beliefs themselves are generally based on claims to cultural authority. An example is the U.S. Surgeon General's statement that "cigarette smoking can cause lung cancer." In some societies, social and cultural authority are largely invested in elders and priests. In modern Western society such authority tends to be concentrated in secular institutions.

Folk beliefs—unofficial beliefs—are those that develop and operate outside powerful social structures. This is an inherently political definition, but it conforms to the most common general definitions of folklore. This definition is *relative*: a belief that ghosts visit the living is a folk (that is, unofficial) belief in most Christian denominations (it is not promulgated in catechisms or endorsed by church governing bodies), while most *official* Christian belief is *un*official (that is, folk) in the United States because of the separation of church and state. (Do not confuse pervasiveness, salience, or influence with officialness. For example, simply because many Christian images and beliefs, such as those relating to Christmas, are very pervasive and influential in the United States does not make them official.) So, when calling a belief a "folk belief," one must specify the context about which one is speaking. We should not get bogged down in this relativity, though. For many of the beliefs that I will discuss here, there are very few settings in the United States, even within churches, where they are in any sense official. And *all* of them are unofficial, folk, in the national context. The belief that "ghosts of dead people can come back" is decidedly not an official belief in modern American culture. Not only is it not *required* to be taught in public schools, its teaching would not be *permitted* there. The National Science Foundation and the National Institutes of Health have no position on ghosts. Explicitly the subject does not exist at the national level of official culture. Implicitly it is understood to have been settled negatively long ago. This belief is, nonetheless, culturally transmitted through unofficial channels. It is an example of a spiritual folk belief.

My definition also refers to *process*, so it is entirely possible for the same belief statement to be both folk and official at the same moment for different people. The poison ivy example can illustrate this. The simple belief that touching poison ivy can cause an itchy rash is received through folklore by some and through medical textbooks (official medical tradition) by others. Some people receive both communications. Since we are discussing the *process*, not two contrasting lists of propositions, the question of whether poison ivy belief ceased to be folk when it entered medical texts is a meaningless question. The belief is not "out there" leading a unitary existence. There are as many poison-ivy-causes-a-rash beliefs as there are people who hold them.

The official–unofficial distinction has major practical implications. Because official structures involve power, official belief operates with access to greater power and, therefore to resources, than does folk belief. Those resources and power make it possible for official culture to establish and maintain many beliefs—some of which may be true and some of which may not—that are actually contrary to the experience of most people. Because the Sun *appears* to go round the Earth, a constant communication effort is required to disseminate and stabilize the opposing belief that the Earth really goes around the Sun. School, books, magazines, TV programs, movies, all communication channels are saturated with references to the solar-centric and other official views, references which do not so much argue or demonstrate that the view is true but rather *assume that it is true*. This is official cultural authority in operation.

When folk beliefs appear in such communication channels, they are usually either debunked or at least shown as deviant views that contend with consensual reality. Those media that explicitly propagate some folk beliefs, such as tabloid newspapers and TV shows, serve to stigmatize them even as they promote them. Spiritual beliefs and related experiences are placed alongside Elvis sightings and pictures of the president conferring with aliens. This illustrates the advantage enjoyed by official beliefs over folk beliefs. As a result of competition from official sources, many folk beliefs have been destroyed, or their influence has been reduced. And yet many spiritual folk beliefs do manage to flourish.

Folk Belief and Experience

Most features of life are open to more than one interpretation. The choices made among interpretive possibilities are influenced by many factors in addition to observation. For example, the belief that the Sun goes around the Earth seemed to many medieval people to fit better with their theology than did the theory presented by Copernicus. Not only did the naked eye suggest that the Sun goes round the Earth, but the belief that human beings are central to God's creation seemed to suggest the same thing. Culturally sanctioned values and attitudes exert a powerful influence on beliefs about the world. That is why observation—experience—must constantly compete with other forces that shape belief. The cultural history of alcoholism as it has gradually been reconstructed from moral weakness to disease provides a good example, as does the continuing struggle to culturally construct AIDS. In both cases there are crucial biological facts, though in neither case are all of these biological facts known. But the facts themselves are never simple, and they never "speak for themselves." Again, experience (whether scientific observation or the life experiences of ordinary people) mingles with culture. This powerful influence of societal attitudes and values on the shaping of belief has been central to the academic prediction that spiritual beliefs would wither and die in the modern world. That just seemed to follow from the increasing social pressures against spiritual beliefs.

As my examples from astronomy and medicine suggest, the crucial elements of official culture tend to rest on experiences and interpretations that are not possible for ordinary people. Telescopes and microscopes, computers and laboratories, years of training—all are necessary to make officially authoritative statements about the world. This reflects a shift in the construction of cultural authority that really crystallized at the end of the nineteenth century and beginning of the twentieth: the change from life experience to technical experience as the source of authority. Developments throughout science were showing that one could not "trust one's own eyes" in making judgments about reality. Microbes, X-rays, higher mathematics, Freud's concept of the unconscious—all of these undercut the idea that living long and well and reflecting on your life could yield authentic knowledge. Unschooled life experience seemed inadequate for understanding the complexities of such a misleading world. At the same time, communities of professional experts were developing, experts with the equipment, the knowledge, and the desire to re-create the modern worldview. The resulting process of renegotiating cultural authority has proceeded at an accelerating pace, until now there are highly trained experts to interpret and explain every facet of life, from economics to marriage and the family to medicine to parenting to agriculture to literature to folklore! All of this expertise is based on the general idea of using technical skills to pierce the constantly misleading appearance of the world. By contrast, intuitive understandings of the world, drawn from ordinary life experience, are treated as naive and illusory.

In the latter part of the twentieth century, a variety of factors, including a slowing of technical payoffs (cancer has not been cured, electricity is not as cheap as water, and the weather is still serenely in control of itself) coupled with the still-accelerating cost of technical development, has caused some to question whether the shift toward technical expertise may have gone too far. In medicine this has resulted in a reexamination of the doctor–patient relationship and the reinvention of "patient-centered care." In economics it has led to the idea that workers and people in business need to join economists in developing economic policy. In a similar vein, people with spiritual experiences are seeking to be heard despite an expert modern theology that is abstract and remote.

In all of these developments, folk tradition has served as a repository of the cultural knowledge acquired from day-to-day living. And it is from folk tradition that the current challenge to official, expert knowledge comes. To some this may sound like an anti-intellectual scenario, but I disagree. This is a rebalancing in which the intellectual work and insights of ordinary people must be acknowledged, and in which the excesses of a powerful, self-regulated intellectual elite require some accountability and reform. The result should be a reinvigoration of intellectual life.

As I noted earlier, official culture in the Western world has been increasingly opposed to spiritual beliefs of all sorts, at least since the Enlightenment. In the eighteenth century, philosopher David Hume asked the question, "Can we ever have rational grounds for the belief in miracles?" In his essay, which became a classic of disbelief, he claimed to demonstrate conclusively that no supernatural belief could ever be considered rationally founded.[32] By the mid-nineteenth century, theologians had come to consistently condemn most cognitive spiritual beliefs as superstitious.[33] These trends sometimes made exceptions for religious belief, on the condition that God was not conceived of as currently acting directly in the world. In the twentieth century, Freudian psychoanalytic theory—an enormously popular belief system that has affected every aspect of American intellectual life—identified all spiritual belief as a neurotic defense mechanism, an illusion based on infantile wish fulfillment.[34] At the same time, Marxism explained spiritual belief in political terms as an instrument of the powerful used to maintain an unjust status quo. By the 1960s theology seemed to have completely capitulated on spiritual matters and declared that "God is dead."[35] Through all of these historical changes, spiritual folk belief has been under even greater official pressure than institutional religion, because folk belief consistently refers to spiritual events erupting into the everyday world: ghostly visits, angelic assistance, answers to prayer. It was the expectation that such straightforward spiritual beliefs could not be sustained in the face of hostility from the official worldview that led scholars, as illustrated by the quotes given above, to anticipate the ultimate secularization of modern society.

With spiritual folk belief under escalating official pressure, its persistence is an anomaly. The further discovery that its persistence involves all segments of modern society, even showing some positive association with educational attainment as documented repeatedly by the Gallup polls, is little short of astonishing. Folk tradition has not only survived, it has given rise to a successful revival of spiritual beliefs within modern institutional religion. In Christianity, for example, the Charismatic revival began as a folk movement with roots in Pentecostalism and Neo-Pentecostalism, and it has had enormous impact in Christian churches since the 1960s. That is, the Charismatic movement originated in unofficial religious tradition but has forced its way into the institutional church, producing remarkable changes in belief and practice in all Christian denominations during the past thirty years. As sociologist Margaret Poloma put it in her book *The Charismatic Movement,* this new "emphasis on the reality and power of the supernatural might be termed the resacralization of religion."[36] With its highly spontaneous and informal style, this spiritual revival retains a strongly folk aspect even as it revises late–twentieth-century Christianity.

Similar revivals of the supernatural aspects of religion are occurring in other American religious traditions, and worldwide. This is often treated simply as a rise of "fundamentalism" and associated with religious intolerance and interfaith violence. For example, Eleanor Munro, criticizing sociologist Peter Berger's *A Far Glory* (a book on religious believing in the modern world), comments that "hunger for personal immortality still gives rise not only to new philosophies and arts but also to holy wars and 'ethnic cleansings.'"[37] Such loose generalization and stigmatization characterize the intellectual defenses that have suppressed cognitive spiritual belief throughout modern times.[38] But spiritual belief can be either socially helpful or destructive, moral or immoral. Belief in the existence of souls, spirits, angels, or God can move one to compassion and love—or to fear and hate—just as can devotion to family and clan, commitment to a political theory, or a host of other ideas. It is the cultural context of belief that largely determines its social consequences. And particular social consequences of a belief are not logical grounds for determining its truth.

The Experiential Theory

What accounts for the universality of spiritual folk belief *and* for its refusal to wither and die in the modern (and postmodern) world? Certainly many very complex theories have been suggested. I have no doubt that many factors are involved, but I propose that there is a single basic reason that must be taken into account, a reason without which other theories will consistently fail to fit the data. This reason has to do with the relationship of belief to experience and the *kinds* of experience that are most crucial to spiritual belief.

The conventional view has assumed that spiritual beliefs are one kind of interpretation of *the same sets of experiences to which secular interpretations refer.* That is, the conventional view assumes that there is no distinctively "spiritual" set of experiences, that there are, rather, spiritual interpretations of ordinary experiences that vie with secular interpretations of the same things. One person's miracle is another's coincidence, one person's mystical experience is another's sense of awe at the beauty and majesty of the universe, one person's visit from the dead is another person's dream.

There is no doubt that spiritual and secular interpretations of ordinary experience compete in society, often over the same observations. But we cannot entirely separate the discussion of what is observed from how it is interpreted. It is now widely recognized that every observation description is laden with some interpretation. Every interpretation has some impact on what is observed, so that one's belief has the capacity to shape one's experience. But for most topics it is also accepted that observations vary in their *ambiguity*—the ease with which they can be shaped by what is expected and the variety of interpretations they seem to fit. An ink blot is quite ambiguous: we tend to see in it what we expect, and individual interpretations can vary widely. On the other hand, an ordinary wooden pencil sitting on my well-lit desk, viewable from many angles and available to be picked up, is relatively difficult to construe as anything else under normal circumstances. The conventional view explains dramatic accounts of spiritual experience by asserting that they refer to ambiguous observations that have been shaped by prior belief, such as hearing the sound of a house settling as ghostly footsteps. Visual experiences are often explained by reference to special circumstances that increase ambiguity, such as poor lighting (and other environmental factors) or fatigue (and other characteristics of the perceiver, such as intoxication or mental illness). In *The Terror* I summarized these conventional explanations as "the cultural source hypothesis," because they each rely on a culturally provided model in the production of tradition-confirming accounts of experience.

Based on such experiences as the Mara, the "near-death experience," and a growing list of others, however, I propose that while the conventional view is useful for many experience–belief linkages—because cultural sources do influence experience—it is flawed by the omission of a large quantity of instances in which neither interpretive bias nor perceptual ambiguity appear to be adequate explanations. There are classes of experience that give rise to spiritual beliefs among practically all who have them, regardless of their prior beliefs. The perception and interpretation of such experiences are similar among persons with very different backgrounds and expectations. Those who have had such experiences form a minimum core of "believers," a substantial fraction of any population below which certain basic spiritual beliefs will not drop regardless of cultural and social pressure. It is then the extent to which the experiences and beliefs of these individuals affect those of others that is primarily governed by cultural mechanisms.

I call this the experiential source theory. Its basic points may be simply stated as follows:

1. Many widespread spiritual beliefs are supported by experiences that:
   A. Refer intuitively to spirits without inference or retrospective interpretation, and
   B. Occur independently of a subject's prior beliefs, knowledge, or intention (psychological set).
2. These experiences form distinct classes with stable perceptual patterns. I call experiences meeting these criteria *core experiences*.
3. Such experiences provide a central empirical foundation from which *some* supernatural beliefs develop rationally.

Stating that these experiences refer "intuitively" is *not* a naive claim that such experiences are unmediated,[39] but rather that, like many ordinary perceptual experiences, *they are not necessarily mediated by the concepts to which they give rise.* One who has never heard of a hummingbird, and therefore lacks the concept, can still perceive a hummingbird if it flies into the garden. Although not experiencing the percept "as a hummingbird," one will still have a perceptual experience. Further, if one observes closely, one will subsequently have a concept similar to the consensual concept of hummingbird—to the extent that one sees clearly, reasons well, etc. The experience will "refer intuitively" to a little bird that can hover by moving its wings so fast that they are a blur, and that seems attracted to flower blossoms. Granted, to get that far one would have to start with the concept *bird.* By the same token, core supernatural experiences require the prior concept of "beings" or persons. But it seems reasonable to assume that such a general concept is ubiquitous among intact humans above the age of infancy. The specifics by which concepts such as *person* vary from culture to culture are not relevant to the ability to have a core experience, anymore than whether one's concept of bird has been developed around parrots or robins is relevant to having a perceptual experience of hummingbirds. *In their independence from the concepts to which they give rise, core experiences are like any novel perception of the environment.*

I call these classes of experience *core experiences* and the basic beliefs that inevitably arise from them *core beliefs.* For example, I consider "near-death experiences" to be core experiences, and the belief in a soul that will survive death is one associated core belief. The paralyzing Mara attack is another core experience, and the belief that some spiritual encounters are threatening is an associated core belief.

Core experiences and related core beliefs do not logically conflict with each other or with established scientific knowledge. Space does not permit a full treatment of this important issue, but I can note two points. First, very few widespread spiritual beliefs and scientific claims actually do contradict each other; for example, creationism and evolutionary theory do so. Those beliefs are not core in my experiential sense (though widespread, they do not follow necessarily from widespread spiritual experiences). Currently recognizable core experiences do not contradict each other or established scientific knowledge, nor are they contradicted by scientific knowledge. Mara beliefs and sleep paralysis knowledge are not contradictory; in fact, they harmonize very easily. NDE beliefs and neurobiological knowledge are not contradictory, and so on. Further investigation might conceivably establish some contradictory relationships with either new core experiences or new scientific knowledge, but to assert that now would be entirely speculative.

Second, core experiences and related core beliefs show the inadequacy of the skeptical view that spiritual experiences are just a form of biased interpretation of ordinary experience, that such experiences are easily accounted for by established scientific knowledge. This is the argument from parsimony or Occam's Razor. This claim arises from the nineteenth-century notion of supernatural belief as primitive explanations for observations of natural phenomena. I know of no core experiences that inherently offer an account of any natural phenomena. What they do offer is an account of the nature of spirits and their relationship to humans. All conventional theories of such experiences treat them as hallucinations or illusions and rely on assumptions of cultural sources to account for patterning, because no psychological theories exist that could explain complex hallucinations having a complex, cross-cultural, perceptual stability. (This is not to say that such a theory is impossible, only that no such well-established theory currently exists. The closest would be the Jungian psychology idea of the "collective unconscious," but this is not generally accepted as scientifically established, and even it does not predict the kind of perceptual stability actually found.) Therefore, even on grounds of parsimony, modern knowledge does not conflict *at all* with core supernatural beliefs.

The experiential theory is limited to the reasons for which spiritual beliefs are held and why they are so persistent and prevalent. It does not address the question of whether these beliefs are true, although it does show that many such beliefs are held for good reasons.[40] That is, these beliefs are *not* obviously or self-evidently false even in view of modern knowledge.

This is a radical theory. It runs counter to most academic accounts of spiritual belief, as already noted, and it also runs counter to the prevailing ideas within folklore scholarship about experience. When experience is noted by students of culture, it tends to be in broad terms, as in "the American experience." I use *experience* to refer to particular, datable episodes in peoples' lives, their perceptions of events.

The common folklore approach to experience focuses on life stories, and is based on a model of those stories as conventionalized fictions. As Jeff Titon said in his 1980 article "The Life Story," "life storytelling is a fiction, a making, an ordered past imposed by a present personality upon a disordered life."[41] More recently, Elaine Lawless, drawing on the work of Titon and of Sandra Stahl, has argued for personal experience and life stories as folklore on the basis that "the actual, personal experience and the shared, group tradition (that is, in terms of form, content, structure, language) fused in these stories which, if closely examined, often sounded remarkably similar from one narrator to another."[42] Lawless goes on to speak of the "spiritual life stories" of Pentecostal women preachers, saying, "I hear the recollections to a very large degree as 'fictions' which draw on an understanding of *facio*, not a lie but a 'making.' The stories are creations."[43] The interests of folklorists in personal accounts are strongly influenced by literary ideas, and similarity from one account to another is taken as evidence of traditional borrowing, the imposition of culture on an alleged experiential report. This is similar in principal to the interpretation of "urban legends" in which, ironically, the greater the quantity of testimony that accumulates, the more certain it is that the accounts are fiction rather than fact. This can be a fruitful approach for some purposes. But as a basis for the study of belief narratives it is hopeless. It dismisses all of the teller's claims, in advance, without the need for evidence. That cannot help us to understand why widespread beliefs are held.

In my theory I am suggesting that *some* spiritual beliefs show not only persistence but remarkable similarity from one tradition to another because they accurately recount observations which are themselves remarkably similar. This is a standard rational technique for assessing the reliability of experiential reports: do the witnesses agree? For the limited set of core experiences, my interpretation holds that independent witnesses do show remarkable agreement. And, because that independence extends to individuals from very diverse traditions, the agreement cannot be explained as mere conformity to cultural expectations. I do not wish to defend the truthfulness of urban legends nor to argue that when people tell their life stories they "tell the truth" (I think sometimes they do, but I'll leave that for another time). But I do intend to argue that at least *some* accounts of spiritual experiences have characteristics that strongly suggest that they are accurate reports. *All* reports are constructed, but that does not make all reports fiction. Accurate reports are constructed and evaluated differently from fictitious or inaccurate reports.

It is crucial to understand that the experiential theory does *not* suggest that all or even most stories of spiritual experience are accurate, nor that all spiritual beliefs are based on specifiable sets of extraordinary experience. I have no doubt that there are widespread spiritual accounts that, like urban legends, never had a first-person version, and that many spiritual beliefs are powerfully shaped by psychological and social forces. The experiential theory simply holds that scholars have been mistaken in their failure to seriously consider the possibility that spiritual belief traditions might have some of the same empirical and rational characteristics that other folk traditions display. Folklife scholars have long been aware that folk traditions concerning architecture, food preparation, agricultural practice, botany, the making of textiles and pottery, and so forth, constitute impressive bodies of valid knowledge rooted in experience. This experiential theory of spiritual folk belief suggests that folk belief traditions, including spiritual beliefs, may have more in common with the practical traditions of folklife than with folktales and folksongs. The belief in spirits seems to relate to experience in much the same way as do beliefs that salt preserves meat, that the south side of a hill is a warmer place for a house than the north side, or that there is a plant called poison ivy that causes an itchy rash. *Core spiritual experiences* stand in relation to *spiritual beliefs* in much the same way that other encounters with the environment relate to traditional knowledge about it. This relationship of spiritual experience to culture, and the way that it varies in different cultural settings, is presented schematically in Figure 1.

In Figure 1, *X* represents any core experience. Remember, a core experience will occur in all populations regardless of cultural references. The use of *X* does not suggest that all instances of a core experience are identical. Rather, it refers to the experiential theory's core experience categories, all members of which fall within a specifiable range that is independent of cultural factors. The use of arrows pointing from *X* to "Cultural Accounts" represents the experiential theory's assertion that core experiences are not dependent on (determined by) culture, but that cultural accounts are in part, shaped by core experiences.

With those things in mind, the three examples given in the figure represent the following cultural possibilities:

Figure 1

Varieties of Enculturation of "Core Spiritual Experiences"

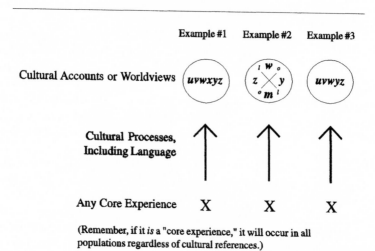

(Remember, if it *is* a "core experience," it will occur in all populations regardless of cultural references.)

Example 1 (shown on the left) is an account that is relatively "experience near" with regard to X. The experience category X is represented with little embellishment. The representations of Mara attacks in Mormon, Charismatic, or Jehovah's Witness traditions illustrate this. The experiences are heavily interpreted, but the experiential elements are usually given in fairly straightforward, recognizable fashion.

Example 2 (shown in the center) is a highly embellished account in which X is central, but so highly ramified and tightly integrated with other elements (other experiences, descriptions, interpretations, etc.) that X is only recognizable and discrete to the observer who is fully familiar with X—and even then, some effort is required. The representation of Mara attacks in UFO abduction accounts illustrates this. The interpretation enters into ramified descriptions of the perceptual category X (e.g., "an alien entered the bedroom and paralyzed me") and that experience is presented as continuous with and causally connected to several others (such as "transport to the UFO").

Example 3 (shown on the right) is an account in which X is absent. I still represent X as associated, because its suppression is an active process. Since core experience X occurs in the population that uses this worldview, mention of X cannot be merely omitted from that culture. If it were, anomalous claims of X would constantly surface in public.

I have suggested that the removal of the Mara and NDE (near-death experience) categories from public knowledge in modern society has required a great deal of effort, and currently engages a variety of institutions (e.g., psychiatry, CSICOP [Committee for the Scientific Investigation of Claims of the Paranormal, a major debunking organization], anti-cognitivists in theology, etc.) and individuals (famous members of CSICOP—including Carl Sagan and James Randi—many clergy and therapists, and legions of local workers) in "policing" the official worldview. The representation of NDEs as delirium is one good example of this. If X is the NDE and w in Example 3 is delirium, then one basic process for omitting X is to state: "That event of which you speak [which I call X but this account does not name; it is anomalous] is just one of a great variety of forms that w takes."

One of my reasons for including these examples for reference is to clarify the following methodological issues: First, no X (core experience) can be derived from any single worldview. Even a comparison of worldviews can only hypothesize X, because some suppress reference to X (as in Example 3). Cultural documentation must be supplemented by the inquiry into experiences. Second, no worldview can be derived from X or even several Xs. Even though X suggests and constrains the experiencer's interpretation, social and cultural processes always enter into enculturation, resulting in very diverse accounts from similar experiences. Therefore, worldviews must be described through ethnographic methods. Core experiences must be described through phenomenological methods. Understanding each and the processes linking them requires both.

Conclusion

Because my experiential theory is so contrary to conventional wisdom, it is also very easy to misunderstand. I do not claim that all spiritual beliefs are experientially grounded, nor that all beliefs that flow from core experiences are properly inferred. I only point out that many spiritual beliefs do appear to be experientially grounded and to be supported by the experiences from which they arise. I have already noted that this does not prove that these beliefs are *true,* but I do not have a new interpretation that can show reasons to believe that they are false. Those interpretations that do purport to show all such beliefs false, or at least baseless, generally have two flaws: (1) poor descriptions of the beliefs actually held, and (2) lack of rigorous attention to experiential reports.

My position has also been misunderstood, occasionally, as being hostile to culture and cultural interpretations. For example, Carol Burke recently called my view of culture "deeply reductive" and "positivistic," claiming that I was "repudiating culture, the discursive production of knowledge."[44] This is no more true of my theory than of folklife approaches that include information about plants and soils in the study of traditional agriculture. Unfortunately, this kind of bombastic rhetoric is often used in an effort to mark off particular topics as the exclusive property of a particular disciplinary view.[45] But reductionism—whether cultural, biological, or other—*always* underestimates the complexity of real situations. The purpose of the experiential theory is not to remove culture from the discussion of belief. Rather, it is to inform and clarify that discussion and to ground our understanding of the role of culture in sound and systematic observation. It is very important to note that such a grounding has the effect of protecting traditional beliefs and accounts from mere translation into the cultural idiom and tacit beliefs of scholars.

Possible Classes of Core Experience

I have noted two classes of experience that seem to meet my criteria for *core experiences* (those criteria being intuitive reference to spirits; independence from a subject's prior beliefs, knowledge, or intention [psychological set]; and a stable perceptual pattern). I do not claim to know all of the varieties of experience that might meet these criteria. Twenty years ago no one could have said that the Mara and the NDE would qualify as core experiences. And until serious attention is paid to the experiential spiritual claims of ordinary people, and those claims are subjected to rigorous cross-cultural comparison, we will have only a very incomplete view of this aspect of human life. Even now, however, I can suggest several likely core candidates.

The visits of deceased loved ones were once considered a pathological symptom of disordered grieving. But within the past twenty years these experiences have come to be considered a common and normal aspect of bereavement, and they have been documented in many different cultural settings.[46] In fact, there is reason to believe that this experience can have a strongly positive effect in the resolution of grief.[47]

"Omens of death"[48] and deathbed visions[49] may be a part of the NDE class, or they may constitute a distinct class.

Visits by unidentified loving presences constitute one or more additional classes of widely reported experience. For example, after completing *The Terror* I had the pleasure of working with Genevieve Foster on a project to publish her memoir centered on an intensely positive mystical experience she had in 1945. That experience changed her life but remained a personal secret until she was in her seventies. In 1985 *The World Was Flooded with Light* was published with her description of her experience and its meaning to her, and my commentary on the mystical experiences of people without mystical training or contemplative lifestyles.

Example 3: A Medieval "Intellectual Vision" in Suburban Philadelphia

> I saw nothing unusual with my outward eye, but I nevertheless knew that there was someone else in the room with me. A few feet in front of me and a little to the left stood a numinous figure, and between us was an interchange, a flood, flowing both ways, of love. There were no words, no sound. There was light everywhere. . . . [T]he world was flooded with light. . . . The vision lasted five days . . .[50]

Perhaps the most surprising thing about this experience is the religious background of its subject. Gen Foster said that it "was so far from my expectation, so far from anything that I had thought in the realm of the possible, that it has taken me the rest of my life to come to terms with it" (p. 36), and "occurring as it did to one reared in the most staid and unemotional branch of Protestantism, taught to believe that such things were truly impossible, or if not impossible then certainly abnormal—such an event was truly overwhelming" (p. 42). Medieval Christian mystics described such an event as "an intellectual vision."[51] But Gen is not a medieval mystic. Here is another stable perceptual pattern that seems to occur independently of the kind of cultural context that conventional explanations treat as necessary and causal. Some describe this kind of experience as angelic, and I suspect that it does partially underlie the widespread belief in guardian angels and the continuing interest in angels, represented by the enormous number of current popular books on the subject. Recent popular works about angels, however, also document the process by which arguably ordinary experiences are interpreted as spiritual and mingle with more extraordinary and direct spiritual experiences.[52]

Experiences of healing constitute several possible sets of core experience. In particular, healing accompanied by an overwhelming perception of energy passing into and through the sick person has a very wide distribution. The following illustration comes from a man who was healed of a hiatal hernia following an ecumenical healing service in Harrisburg, Pennsylvania:

Example 4

[Later] on the way to my car I thought, 'I wonder if I got healed? How are you supposed to feel when you get healed at one of these things?' And then I thought, 'Well, it doesn't matter. Whether I get healed or not, I won't lose faith in God.' . . . Then suddenly, I felt like high voltage touched me on my head and I had a feeling that I can only describe as like bubbling, boiling water rolling to my fingertips and back up. . . . And I felt the presence of God right there on the street. . . . I knew I had been healed.[53]

Such experiences of healing energy are reported from all over the world. They are part of the basis for the modern alternative healing technique of "therapeutic touch."[54] Richard Katz's *Boiling Energy: Community Healing among the Kalahari Kung* describes similar perceptions of healing energy in the healing rituals of the Kung in the Kalahari Desert of southern Africa.[55] The conceptions of life energy that the Chinese call *ch'i* and the Japanese *ki,* which form the basis for such healing practices as acupuncture and Shiatsu, may be based on such perceptions also.

Ian Stevenson, a psychiatrist who has studied reincarnation belief all over the world, has documented many cases of claimed past life memories among children. Most pertinent to the experiential theory, Stevenson has shown that, surprisingly, these memories occur even in populations in which belief in reincarnation is not only not held, but is actively discouraged.[56] Such recollections, independent of a prior concept of reincarnation but intuitively suggesting a previous life, would constitute core experiences.

This is not an exhaustive list, but it should demonstrate that there already is a substantial body of description from which the investigation of the relation of spiritual belief and experience can proceed. I am pleased that even in the area of religious studies and philosophy of religion such a serious reexamination seems to be starting. For those interested in the complex connections of religious belief with experience, I strongly recommend Caroline Franks Davis's *The Evidential Force of Religious Experience.*[57]

Misinterpretation

I have noted that the experiential theory does not suggest that *all* folk belief is strongly founded on experience. Furthermore, culture can operate to suppress experiential knowledge as well as to highlight it; I expect the suppression of discussion about spiritual experience to produce frequent confusion, in both folk and official culture, as people try to make sense of experiences about which they lack traditional, experience-based knowledge. The current UFO debate will serve as a brief illustration. UFO beliefs provide an excellent example of the way that experience refuses to be silent, even when official culture insists. Modern UFO beliefs are entirely unofficial, and official efforts to "stamp them out" have been vigorous and repeated. UFO reports are subject to a spiritual interpretation by many investigators and experiencers,[58] but to physical, high-tech interpretation by many others. That very ambiguity, along with its insistent claims of an experiential basis, should make UFO belief a prime subject for students of folk belief. In fact, though, only a few have given it serious attention.[59] I find the subject fascinating, and I grant that the general claim that "something is going on" seems to be experientially based. This makes UFO beliefs similar to the beliefs I have discussed earlier.

Recently, however, UFO belief has developed a new aspect, one that has gained great notoriety and that illustrates the problems of misinterpretation that can arise when culturally shared knowledge about experience is suppressed. This is the UFO abduction phenomenon—the idea that extraterrestrials are repeatedly abducting humans and subjecting them to bizarre experiments aboard spaceships. Having listened to many who have memories of these terrifying events, I have no wish to dismiss or debunk the subject. I do not pretend to have a clear idea of what lies behind all of these reports. However, within the past two years I have had it repeatedly called to my attention that many accounts of abduction begin with "waking up paralyzed with a sense of a strange person or presence or something else in the room."[60] This quote is taken from a recent, privately funded poll of the American population carried out by the Roper Organization, a highly respected survey group. This survey was intended to assess the prevalence of alien abduction, and such waking paralysis events are very common in alien abduction accounts. Even before that poll was done in 1991, I had received letters from members of abduction support groups, asking help in understanding the connection between what I had reported in *The Terror* and what had happened to them. As a result, I have become involved in the debate.

In *The Terror* I had noted that when a Mara attack occurred in the life of a person interested in UFOs or who had recently seen a UFO, the experience was frequently interpreted, understandably, as UFO-related—usually meaning that the "strange presence" was taken to be an alien. This is entirely consistent with the general range of variation in the interpretations of this event across cultures: subjects take it as real and involving a force with extraordinary power. In most cultural settings this suggests a spiritual force that may be variously considered a ghost, a witch, a skinwalker, a demon, and so forth. Since an extraterrestrial might conceivably have mysterious powers, such beings fit within the intuitive implications of the event.

In the present abduction debate, however, a group of primary investigators, including those who funded the Roper poll, are attempting to distinguish genuine alien bedroom paralysis attacks from those that are "merely the Old Hag–sleep paralysis thing." In their poll they found that 18% (± 1.4 percent margin of sampling error, p. 21) of the population admits to "waking up paralyzed with a sense of a strange person or presence or something else in the room" at least once. This rate is essentially the same as that which I had documented ten years earlier.

In the abduction scenario, the bedroom paralysis attacks are often followed by being floated helplessly out of bed, out through a ceiling or closed window, and on to an alien ship. As I had reported in *The Terror,* Mara attacks that persist for more than a few minutes often culminate in unpleasant out-of-body experiences. Further parallels could be elaborated, but space will not permit.[61] The idea that such experiences are "not sleep paralysis" has been encouraged by the total absence of attention to the experiential contents of sleep paralysis by sleep researchers. Given that absence, it is not correct to say that any of these other categories *is* sleep paralysis, because sleep paralysis is the cultural construction of one tradition. Although it is constructed in a manner that overlaps with related categories in other traditions, *as a category, it is not the same.* And making sleep paralysis the same by adding good descriptions of the experiential contents would provide a major challenge to the explanatory options of sleep research. It would be a good thing to try, but it is impossible to know in advance what they could come up with. So when scientist Carl Sagan, in a recent *Parade* magazine identified these experiences as just sleep paralysis not alien abduction,[62] he engaged in the same kind of labeling without explaining that UFO investigators do when they say that *their* accounts are of authentic alien abductions and "not just 'Old Hag' attacks" (several investigators have actually adopted the Newfoundland term).

The terrifying paralysis attacks have caused serious confusion before, each error caused largely by a general ignorance of the prevalence and consistent subjective features of the Mara event—an ignorance characteristic of modern culture. For example, investigators of sudden unexpected nocturnal death syndrome (SUNDS) among Southeast Asian refugee immigrants, especially the Hmong from Laos, discovered that a number of these refugees had experienced terrifying awakenings characterized by paralysis and an evil presence. Not knowing of the universal distribution of such experiences and related beliefs, investigators took these events to refer to the experience of surviving a SUNDS attack[63] (an oxymoron, since SUNDS is definitively diagnosed only by autopsy!), and SUNDS was then interpreted as a kind of culture-bound post-traumatic stress disorder related to the refugee experience. Actually the incidence and nature of the paralysis attacks in this population is very similar to that described elsewhere, while the distribution of SUNDs cases, which occur among young adult men, is entirely different. Furthermore, such unexpected deaths in sleep, specifically among young men, are well-known in Southeast Asia and the western Pacific (for example, *bangungot*[64] in the Philippines and *pokkuri*[65] in Japan), and they have been documented in Southeast Asia among the Hmong in refugee camps.[66] Unfortunately, this kind of confusion is typical of the culture-bound syndrome literature, where exclusive cultural and psychological explanations compete with exclusive biological explanations.[67] The terror associated with the paralysis attacks may be an occasional contributing cause that interacts with more basic causes, such as cardiac conduction defects,[68] a much more reasonable interpretation supported by the work of folklorist Shelley Adler,[69] who in Chapter 10 of this volume examines how the Hmong themselves interpret both the nightmares and the unexpected deaths. But the argument that the paralysis attacks alone cause the deaths is contradicted by the cross-cultural distribution and prevalence of those attacks, and the strikingly distinctive and localized patterns of SUNDS. Even some shamans in these groups are aware that SUNDS and *dab tsog* are two different events, but some Western investigators have made a disastrously wrong connection—a sort of cultural reductionism. This kind of erroneous association is very similar to the common pathological reductionism that assumed NDEs must be symptoms of delirium, an error only recently being corrected.[70]

Finding Balance

Repeated confusion about the meaning of spiritual experiences arises from the exclusion of knowledge and discussion of them from public discourse. The stigma and the suggestion of mental disorder have served very effectively to either prevent any sharing at all or to keep the sharing very localized. Now the current in this process seems to be shifting. More and more people are speaking openly about their beliefs and experiences. I hope that this will continue, and I further hope that interested parties will resist simple explanations from experts. This discourse, like the discourse over medical and other technical issues, will have to be opened beyond what experts can offer.

Life experience must coexist and share authority with technical expertise in order for a society to develop and maintain a rich and human view of itself and the world in which it lives. Folk belief traditions are an enormous and invaluable resource for this process. With the wisdom that they offer, we have the capacity to enrich our lives without rejecting the benefits that have come with scientific and technical progress. The usefulness of knowing the relationship of the Mara attack to dreaming sleep, of being able to distinguish near-death experiences from delirium, the necessity of distinguishing the consoling visits of bereavement from the hallucinations of insanity—all of these show the value of balance.

Today many are frustrated by facile dismissals of spiritual belief and experience by self-proclaimed experts wrapped in the mantle of science. They often assert that our understanding of spiritual matters has been corrupted by "too much science and reliance on rationality." But the problem of the modern world is not too much intellectual activity and reasoning, and science and rational analysis do not contradict basic spiritual beliefs. The problem is a too-narrow view of what intellectual activity is and who has the capacity to reason soundly. Folklore as a field has the capacity to help our society find more democratic ways of sharing cultural authority.

Endnotes

1.   David J. Hufford, "A New Approach to 'The Old Hag': The Nightmare Tradition Reexamined," in *American Folk Medicine,* ed. Wayland D. Hand (Berkeley and Los Angeles: University of California Press, 1976), 74.
2.   Interview with medical student in Pennsylvania, as cited in Hufford, *The Terror That Comes in the Night: An Experience-Centered Study of Supernatural Assault Traditions* (Philadelphia: University of Pennsylvania Press, 1982), 58–59.
3.   Joseph Jay Tobin and Joan Friedman, "Spirits, Shamans, and Nightmare Death: Survivor Stress in a Hmong Refugee," *American Journal of Orthopsychiatry* 53 (July 1983): 439–448.

4. Ronald G. Munger, "Sleep Disturbances and Sudden Death of Hmong Refugees: A Report of Fieldwork Conducted in the Ban Vinai Refugee Camp," in *The Hmong in Transition*, ed. Glenn L. Hendricks et al. (Staten Island: Center for Immigration Studies of New York, 1986), 379–398.

5. Shelley R. Adler, "Sudden Unexpected Nocturnal Death Syndrome among Hmong Immigrants: Examining the Role of the 'Nightmare,'" *Journal of American Folklore* 104 (Winter 1991): 54–71.

6. Charles F. Emmons, *Chinese Ghosts and ESP: A Study of Paranormal Beliefs and Experiences* (Metuchen, NJ: Scarecrow Press, 1982), 144.

7. Carl Herman Tillhagen, "The Conception of the Nightmare in Sweden," in *Humaniora: Essays in Literature, Folklore, and Bibliography Honoring Archer Taylor*, ed. Wayland D. Hand and Gustave O. Arlt (New York: J. J. Augustin, 1969), 317.

8. Hufford, *The Terror*, 220–222.

9. For an extensive discussion of sleep paralysis and the mechanisms and stages of sleep, see Hufford, *The Terror*, Chapter 4.

10. For a discussion of the etymological history of the terms for this event, see Hufford, *The Terror*, especially 53–56 and 125.

11. The percentage of affirmative response depends on the context of the question; see Hufford, *The Terror*, 50. Corroborating results can be found in Carl C. Bell, "Prevalence of Isolated Sleep Paralysis in Black Subjects," *Journal of the National Medical Association* 76 (1984): 501–508; Bell, "Further Studies on the Prevalence of Isolated Sleep Paralysis in Black Subjects," *Journal of the National Medical Association* 78 (1986): 649–659; Budd Hopkins et al., *Unusual Personal Experiences: An Analysis of Data from Three National Surveys Conducted by the Roper Organization* (Las Vegas: Bigelow Holding Corp., 1992); and James McClenon, *Wondrous Events: Foundations of Religious Belief* (Philadelphia: University of Pennsylvania Press, 1994).

12. Hufford, "Commentary: Mystical Experience in the Modern World," in *The World Was Flooded with Light: A Mystical Experience Remembered*, Genevieve Foster (Pittsburgh: University of Pittsburgh Press, 1985), 137.

13. Raymond A. Moody, *Life after Life: The Investigation of a Phenomenon—Survival of Bodily Death* (Atlanta: Mockingbird Books, 1975).

14. C. B. Becker, "The Centrality of Near-Death Experiences in Chinese Pure Land Buddhism," *Anabiosis: The Journal of Near-Death Studies* 1 (1981): 154–170; W. Y. Evans-Wentz, trans., *The Tibetan Book of the Dead; or, the After-Death Experiences on the Bardo Plane* (New York: Oxford University Press, 1957).

15. See, for example, Carol Zaleski, *Otherworld Journeys: Accounts of Near-Death Experiences in Medieval and Modern Times* (New York: Oxford University Press, 1987). Zaleski argues that NDEs vary greatly in different historical periods, being culturally shaped. However, she makes no distinctions among first-person interview accounts, sermons, and literary reworkings (such as comparing Dante's Paradise in *The Divine Comedy* to modern first-person reports from hospital emergency rooms). Contrary to her interpretation, the actual documentation Zaleski provides suggests many transcultural and transchronological patterns.

16. It has long been common for scholars to argue that various kinds of supernatural belief are characteristically western European, and that applying such concepts

cross-culturally is ethnocentric. See, for example, Benson Saler, "Supernatural as a Western Category," *Ethos* 5 (1977): 31–53. Theravada Buddhism has often been cited as an atheistic religion that does not include such beliefs. All such arguments that I have seen rely on extremely complex definitions, which naturally have the effect of limiting applicability to a single setting. For a good discussion of this issue and the classic example of Theravada Buddhism, see Melford E. Spiro, "Religion: Problems of Definition and Explanation," in *Anthropological Approaches to the Study of Religion*, vol. 3, ed. Michael Banton (Edinburgh: Tavistock, 1966), 88–92.

17. The Latter-Day Saints, for example, rejected *supernatural* in favor of *spiritual* in the nineteenth century, anticipating the more recent shift by many other religious discourse communities. For many people *supernatural* lost its intelligibility as the older meanings of *natural* shifted and came to mean "the entire universe" or "normal."

18. Rudolf Bultmann, "A Reply to the Theses of J. Schniewind," in *Kerygma and Myth: A Theological Debate*, ed. Hans Werner Bartsch, trans. Reginald H. Fuller (London: S.P.C.K., 1953), 4–5.

19. Anthony F. C. Wallace, *Religion: An Anthropological View* (New York: Random House, 1966), 264–265.

20. Keith Thomas, *Religion and the Decline of Magic* (New York: Scribner's, 1971), ix.

21. Max Weber, *The Sociology of Religion*, trans. Ephraim Fischoff (Boston: Beacon Press, 1963).

22. Gillian Bennett, *Traditions of Belief: Women and the Supernatural* (Harmondsworth, England: Penguin, 1987), 13.

23. See, for example, G. H. Gallup and F. Newport, "Belief in Paranormal Phenomena among Adult Americans," *Skeptical Inquirer* 15 (1991): 137–146; G. Gallup Jr. with W. Proctor, *Adventures in Immortality* (New York: McGraw-Hill, 1982); Andrew M. Greeley, *Sociology of the Paranormal: A Reconnaissance* (Beverly Hills, CA: Sage Publications, 1975).

24. Gallup with Proctor, *Adventures*, 195.

25. Paul Starr, *The Social Transformation of American Medicine* (New York: Basic Books, 1982), 9.

26. Richard T. DeGeorge, *The Nature and Limits of Authority* (Lawrence: University Press of Kansas, 1985).

27. For a good introduction to the philosophical issues involved in the justification of belief, see Robert Audi, *Belief, Justification, and Knowledge* (Belmont, CA: Wadsworth, 1988).

28. This is what H. Paul Grice calls "conversational implicature" in "Logic and Conversation," in *Syntax and Semantics*, vol. 3, ed. Peter Cole and J. L. Morgan (New York: Academic Press, 1975), 41–58.

29. This fact has been ignored in the publication of lists of "beliefs" with no indication of the strength with which they are held, if at all; for example, Wayland D. Hand, ed, *Popular Beliefs and Superstitions from North Carolina; The Frank C. Brown Collection of North Carolina Folklore*, vols. 6 and 7 (Durham, NC: Duke University Press, 1961 and 1964).

30. Robert Hahn, "Understanding Beliefs: An Essay on the Methodology of the Statement and Analysis of Belief Systems," *Current Anthropology* 14, no. 3 (June 1973): 208.

31. For an excellent discussion and presentation of this debate as it relates to belief and cultural issues, see Ronald C. Simons and Charles C. Hughes, eds., *The Culture-Bound Syndromes: Folk Illnesses of Psychiatric and Anthropological Interest* (Dordrecht: D. Reidel, 1985).

32. David Hume, "An Enquiry Concerning Human Understanding," Section X, Parts I–II. 1748; reprint in *Religious Belief and Philosophical Thought*, ed. William P. Alston (New York: Harcourt, Brace & World, 1963), 408–419.

33. For an excellent discussion of these developments in the history of Christian theology, see J. Kellenberger, *The Cognitivity of Religion: Three Perspectives* (Berkeley and Los Angeles: University of California Press, 1985).

34. Sigmund Freud, *Civilization and Its Discontents,* rev. and ed. James Stachey, trans. Joan Riviere, International Psychoanalytic Library, No. 17 (London: Hogarth Press, 1972); Ludwig Eidelberg, ed., *The Encyclopedia of Psychoanalysis* (New York: Free Press, 1968), 280.

35. See Peter Berger's discussion, "The Alleged Demise of the Supernatural," in his *Rumor of Angels: Modern Society and the Rediscovery of the Supernatural,* (1969; reprint, with a new introduction by the author, New York: Anchor Books, 1990), 1–30.

36. Margaret Poloma, *The Charismatic Movement: Is There a New Pentecost?,* Social Movements Past and Present Series (Boston: Twayne, 1987), 28.

37. Eleanor Munro, "The Religious Hunger," review of *A Far Glory* by Peter Berger, *New York Times Book Review,* November 22, 1992.

38. For a good discussion of the role of politics and journalism in this process, see Stephen L. Carter, *The Culture of Disbelief: How American Law and Politics Trivialize Religious Devotion* (New York: Basic Books, 1993).

39. This is an issue that is constantly debated in the philosophy and psychology of mysticism. See, for example, Steven T. Katz, "Language, Epistemology, and Mysticism," in *Mysticism and Philosophical Analysis,* ed. Steven T. Katz (New York: Oxford University Press, 1978); and Wayne Proudfoot, *Religious Experience* (Berkeley and Los Angeles: University of California Press, 1985) to the effect that "religious experience" can only be ordinary experience interpreted in a religious way, and therefore invalid as evidence for religious belief. Arguments to the contrary are summarized in Caroline Franks Davis, *The Evidential Force of Religious Experience* (Oxford: Clarendon Press, 1989).

40. By this I do not insist that core experiences provide "proof." I mean only that they constitute genuine cognitive reasons and can reasonably be considered a kind of evidence for some belief claims. That is, they cannot be dismissed as *prima facie* invalid reasons.

41. Jeff Todd Titon, "The Life Story," *Journal of American Folklore* 93 (1980): 290.

42. Elaine Lawless, "Rescripting Their Lives and Narratives: Spiritual Life Stories of Pentecostal Women Preachers," *Journal of Feminist Studies in Religion* 7 (1991): 57–58.

43. Ibid., 58.

44. Carol Burke, *Vision Narratives of Women in Prison* (Knoxville: University of Tennessee Press, 1992), 54 and 61. For an excellent rebuttal of that description of my position, see Gillian Bennett's review of Burke's book, in *Folklore* 105 (1994): 110–112.

45. For a discussion of this problem in the cross-cultural topic of psychiatric anthropology, see Hufford, "Inclusionism vs. Reductionism in the Study of the

Culture-Bound Syndromes," *Culture, Medicine, and Psychiatry* 12 (1988): 503–512, a book review of Ronald Simons and Charles Hughes, eds., *Culture-Bound Syndromes.*

46. For example, W. Scott MacDonald and Chester W. Oden Jr., "Case Report: Aumakua—Behavioral Direction Visions in Hawaiians," *Journal of Abnormal Psychology* 86 (1977): 189–194; William Foster Matchett, "Repeated Hallucinatory Experiences as a Part of the Mourning Process among Hopi Women," *Psychiatry* 35 (May 1972): 185–194; W. Dewi Rees, "The Hallucinations of Widowhood," *British Medical Journal* (October 1971): 37–41.

47. Rees; Gallup with Proctor; Greeley; all previously cited.

48. Leea Virtanen, *"That Must Have Been ESP!"* (Bloomington: Indiana University Press, 1990).

49. Karlis Osis and Erlendur Haraldsson, *At the Hour of Death* (New York: Avon Books, 1977); Melvin Morse, with Paul Perry, *Closer to the Light: Learning from Children's Near-Death Experiences* (New York: Villard Books, 1990); and Melvin Morse, *Transformed by the Light: The Powerful Effect of Near-Death Experiences on People's Lives* (New York: Villard Books, 1992).

50. Genevieve Foster, *The World Was Flooded with Light: A Mystical Experience Remembered* (Pittsburgh: University of Pittsburgh Press, 1985), 43.

51. Teresa of Avila, *The Interior Castle, or the Mansions,* introduction and notes Father Benedict Zimmerman, O.C.D. (1577; reprint, Union City, NJ: John J. Crawley, 1980), 180–181.

52. For example, Joan Webster Anderson, *Where Angels Walk: True Stories of Heavenly Visitors* (Sea Cliff, NY: Barton & Brett, 1992); Sophy Burnham, *A Book of Angels* (New York: Ballantine, 1990).

53. Hufford, "Epistemologies of Religious Healing," *Journal of Philosophy and Medicine* 18 (1993): 184.

54. Dolores Krieger, "Therapeutic Touch: Searching for Evidence of Physiological Change," *American Journal of Nursing* 79 (1979): 660–662.

55. Richard Katz, *Boiling Energy: Community Healing among the Kalahari Kung* (Cambridge: Harvard University Press, 1982).

56. Ian Stevenson, *Children Who Remember Previous Lives: A Question of Reincarnation,* (Charlottesville: University of Virginia Press, 1987).

57. Caroline Franks Davis, *The Evidential Force of Religious Experience* (Oxford: Clarendon Press, 1989).

58. See, for example, Keith Thompson, *Angels and Aliens: UFOs and the Mythic Imagination* (New York: Fawcett Columbine, 1991).

59. For example, Thomas E. Bullard, "Folklore Scholarship and UFO Reality," *International UFO Reporter* 13 (July/August 1988): 9–13; Bullard, "UFO Abduction Reports: The Supernatural Kidnap Narrative Returns in Technological Guise," *Journal of American Folklore* 102 (1989): 147–170; Hufford, "Humanoids and Anomalous Lights: Epistemologic and Taxonomic Problems," *Fabula: Journal of Folktale Studies* 18 (1977): 234–241; Hufford, *The Terror;* Hufford, "Awakening Paralyzed in the Presence of a 'Strange Visitor,'" in *Alien Discussions: Proceedings of the Abduction Study Conference, Held at MIT, Cambridge, MA,* ed. Andrea Pritchard et al. (Cambridge, MA: North Cambridge Press, 1994), 348–354; Peter M. Rojcewicz, "The Boundaries of Orthodoxy: A Folkloric Look at the 'UFO Phenomenon,'" (Ph.D. diss., Folklore and Folklife

Program, University of Pennsylvania, 1984); Rojcewicz, "The 'Men in Black' Experience and Tradition," *Journal of American Folklore* 100 (1987): 148–160.

60. Hopkins, previously cited.

61. For an overview of this subject from the perspective of investigators and abductees, see Pritchard, previously cited. The specific connections between abduction experiences and Mara attacks are developed in Hufford, "Awakening Paralyzed," previously cited.

62. Carl Sagan, "What's Really Going On?" *Parade,* March 7, 1993, 4–7.

63. Tobin and Friedman, 445.

64. See J. Z. Santa Cruz, "The Pathology of 'Bangungot,'" *Journal of the Philippine Medical Association* 27 (July 1951): 476–481; J. B. Nolasco, "An Inquiry in 'Bangungot,'" *AMA Archives of Internal Medicine* 99 (1957): 905–912.

65. Koh Gotoh, "A Histopathological Study on the Conduction System of the So-Called 'Pokkuri Disease' (Sudden Unexpected Death of Unknown Origin in Japan)," *Japanese Circulation Journal* 40 (1976): 753–768.

66. Ronald G. Munger, "Sudden Death in Sleep of Laotian–Hmong Refugees in Thailand: A Case-Control Study," *American Journal of Public Health* 77 (1987): 1187–1190.

67. For an excellent and critical overview of the culture-bound syndrome literature, see Simons and Hughes, *Culture-Bound Syndromes.*

68. Robert H. Kirschner, Friedrich A. O. Eckner, and Roy C. Baron, "The Cardiac Pathology of Sudden, Unexplained Nocturnal Death in Southeast Asian Refugees," *JAMA* 256 (1986): 2700–2705.

69. Shelley R. Adler, "Ethnomedical Pathogenesis and Hmong Immigrants' Sudden Nocturnal Deaths," *Culture, Medicine, and Psychiatry* 18 (1994): 23–59.

70. Glen O. Gabbard, Stuart W. Twemlow, and Fowler C. Jones, "Differential Diagnosis of Altered Mind–Body Perception," *Psychiatry* 45 (November 1982): 361–369.

2

The Moccasin Telegraph and Other Improbabilities: A Personal Essay

Barre Toelken

IN 1956, I TOOK MY PARENTS ON A SUDDEN UNPLANNED TRIP TO MEET THE Navajos I had been living with for the previous two years. I had borrowed a friend's car, and we had driven all night long from Salt Lake City to Blanding, a tiny town in Utah's southeast corner. We arrived just after dawn in the Navajo settlement called Westwater, just on the opposite side of a small canyon that marks Blanding's western edge, and as we drove up to the hogan of my friend, Grandma Johnson, we could see and smell the juniper smoke from her fire. Relieved that the elderly woman was already up and around, I dispensed with the usual fifteen- to twenty-minute wait outside and just went up to her hogan, knocked, pushed the door open, and walked in. We found her sitting alone by the open fire with a large pot of coffee beside her, a stack of Navajo bread already made, and a skillet with eight eggs in it sizzling on a raked-out bed of hot coals. I shook hands with her, careful not to look her in the eye, and explained that these strangers were my parents. "Of course," she said, "that's why I cooked up all this food!"

I had left the area about a month earlier, telling my Navajo friends that I was going back to the university and would not be back for a long time. I had had no contact with anyone in this family in the meantime. Grandma Johnson spoke no English, had no electricity or phone, and no windows in her hogan through which she could have seen a car approaching in time to throw eight eggs in the pan (the Navajo bread would have been started while we were still forty-five minutes away from her vicinity, anyhow). No one else arrived who might have accounted for Grandma Johnson being up early preparing a large meal. To make things even more complex and interesting, we had a sudden visit later that day from Little Wagon, an old man who had adopted me into his family a couple years previously; he had come all the way from Montezuma Creek (about thirty miles south) by burro and had left there the previous day—about the same time we were leaving Salt Lake City. "I came over to meet your parents," he announced.

Anecdotes like this abound in the conversations and reminiscences of those who have spent any considerable time in "Indian country," and the events they depict are usually attributed to a network of Native premonition or supernatural communication called "the moccasin telegraph" by non-Natives (and by many Native people as well). From a non-Native perspective, the Native peoples seem to know what's going to happen—or at least they participate in what happens without surprise and with considerable awareness of the details. For non-Indians this certainly falls into the category of supernatural or mysteriously-out-of-the-ordinary experience. Indian people are aware of it but seldom have an intellectualized way of explaining it to anyone else: for them it represents a field of assumptions, a range of normal possibilities the only logical response to which is well-articulated by the phrase, "Of course."

When Joseph Epes Brown was working on his doctorate in religious studies, he wanted to seek out and interview Black Elk, the subject of John Neihardt's well-known *Black Elk Speaks*.[1] But when Brown asked Neihardt for Black Elk's whereabouts, he was rebuffed and was told the old man didn't receive visitors, that he was old and ill, and that young students would do well just to leave him alone. Brown was persistent, however, and kept searching and inquiring; he eventually found Black Elk living with his son's family near Manderson, South Dakota. There in a canvas tent Brown introduced himself and took out the red stone pipe he had brought along as a traditional means of petitioning the old man for insight. Black Elk's response was, "I'm glad you're finally here! I've been expecting you for quite a while, and I hope you're prepared to stay the winter, because I have a lot of sacred things to tell you."[2]

On many occasions when I was living with my adopted Navajo family in the 1950s, people would begin acting as though they had received some information from afar. For example, after a month or so of herding sheep and carrying water to our corn plants day after day, some family members would suddenly prepare for a trip, packing bedrolls, cooking utensils, firewood, and food supplies in the wagon while others went to search for horses. I would hear offhand comments like, "Perhaps there's a sing [curing ceremony] down by Red Mesa," and others would respond, "Mmm, maybe." On our way toward the Red Mesa area, which could take a couple of days because we had to cross the San Juan River, we would encounter other Navajos heading more or less in our direction and stop to chat with them. Someone would say, "Maybe there's a sing over by Red Mesa," and the others would nod in agreement and say, "Mmm." A day later we would pull our wagon over the crest of a hill and find a gathering of perhaps a hundred people near someone's hogan, either waiting for a sing to start or resting up from the previous day's session of the sing which was already in progress. No phone calls, no maps, no addresses, no written invitations, no messengers running or galloping out from Red Mesa to spread the word. Yet every time this kind of behavior took place, we would arrive at a place where there was indeed a sing going on. Of course, there are always sings in progress *somewhere* on the Navajo Reservation, but the reservation itself is the size of Belgium, and families often live miles from the next family group; just stumbling upon a sing by heading off on a blind hunch across the desert in the direction of Red Mesa would not be entirely impossible, but could hardly be expected to yield such consistent results.

While on these long trips we often would camp out overnight. On one such occasion, I remember saying that perhaps our friend Yazzie had had her baby by now (her family lived about thirty-five miles from us, and we had not been in touch for several weeks). Helen, my adopted sister, and her husband, Yellowman, stared up intently at the moon for a few minutes (like a doctor consulting his watch while taking someone's pulse, I thought), then announced almost in unison, "No, not yet; maybe five more days," with that kind of detached finality one normally associates with the obvious. When we reached Blanding on another trip about a week later, Yazzie had just had her child, and I was the only one who expressed surprise that the Yellowmans' estimate had been so close.

There is no doubt in my mind that these events, and those to be discussed below, actually "happen," for they are witnessed by everyone who is involved. *How* these happenings are categorized and understood, however, is another matter, for the empirical, experiential "data" the Navajos and I observed were of course routed through our culturally learned notions of what is normal, obvious, logical. For me, many of these experiences were explainable only through the idea of coincidence, for I could see no logical connections between the principal parts. For the Navajos, however, and for many other Native tribes whose logic is not linear in nature, normal events are not necessarily caused by that which immediately precedes them. Thus, there is no question that such an event happened; the question is how to understand its meaning. When people from two (or more) different cultures actually see and experience the same event, then we can probably say that the occurrence is not imaginary;

but which culture is experiencing the event the way it really *is?* (Or is there such a thing as "really is"?)

Roger Welsch, a Nebraska folklorist, tells of being summoned to an Omaha Indian dance in which he was to be head dancer. He was given the date, but not the time and place. He drove all over town to find out where the ceremony was to be held, but even his Omaha friends didn't know. He finally located one of the other principal people in the dance watching a baseball game, and Welsch went into the stands to sit with him and to find out where they were supposed to go. After the game was over, the man said, "Well, it looks like everyone came here. We might as well have the dance here."[3] Unnoticed by Welsch, all the other Omahas (who were also trying to find out where the ceremony would take place) had started to arrive, because they had been cruising around town looking for the cars of central participants. The dance then occurred at a time and at a place which were *unknown* less than an hour previously, yet everyone was there and the event *took place* (a very apt term for this kind of phenomenon!).

Recently, as my Navajo family worked to arrange a Blessing Way ceremony for me, we had to change the dates several times because of complications in my schedule or that of the singer. On one trip to southern Utah I encountered some of my Navajo nieces who said, "I think your *hozhoji* is going to be this next week." Had they been in touch with the singer? No, but they thought there would be a Blessing Way, and they saw other people preparing for one, so it must be coming up. Although I had not heard anything from the family members directly involved, or from the singer, I nonetheless thought I was hearing something on the moccasin telegraph, so I went home and made preparations for going back there the following week (the trip is about 400 miles). I arrived back in Blanding and asked around for where the Blessing Way might be, but almost everyone I knew was not at home. Finally, one of my family members drove me some seventy miles further into the reservation to Sweetwater so we could visit the singer himself; but when we arrived there, we found that he had just left a few hours earlier for Blanding where he was going to perform a Blessing Way ceremony. We turned around and sped back to Blanding, knowing, of course, that he couldn't start without the patient. This time, we knew from the singer's wife where the ceremony was going to be, so we headed for a Navajo family who lives just east of Blanding. There, indeed, a Blessing Way *was* to have occurred, and a great crowd of people had gathered (including all my friends who had not been at home), but it had turned out that the young woman who was supposed to have been the patient was having her menstrual period, and the ceremony had been postponed. The singer had gone back home to Sweetwater. So it turned out that it was not my Blessing

Way that was in progress; in Anglo terms, I had been mistaken. I had interpreted the "rumors" in the wrong way. Yet, from the Navajo point of view, I
had indeed behaved in a natural way by being there for a Blessing Way for
someone in my adopted family—as they will all be present when it comes time
for mine. They were already gathered there, in the right spot, and they had
come from all over the northern reservation without specific information; I
had raced all over southern Utah and northern Arizona, seeking "facts," and
was the last person to arrive. Which of us had the most correct "fix" on what
was happening?

An even more striking episode occurred in 1968, some twelve years after I
had lived with the Navajos. I had been invited to teach summer session folklore
courses at UCLA, and just before leaving Eugene, Oregon, for Los Angeles I
had had a conversation with Tom Yellowman, who told me he thought his
older sister Joanne "maybe" was living in Los Angeles going to hairdresser
school. He asked me to look her up and see how she was doing. After I got settled in an old Japanese hotel near Western Avenue, I got Joanne's phone number from information, called her up, and found she was living in a small
apartment house on exactly the opposite side of the same block. At the end of
the summer, as I prepared to drive back to Eugene, she asked if she could ride
along as far as Oakland, because she had heard that her sister Helen, newly
married to Eugene Yazzie, had moved to Oakland. I pulled off the freeway at
the second Oakland exit, stopped at a gas station, got a map, and asked for the
name of the street we were to find. Joanne didn't know. In fact, she hadn't
heard directly from her sister, so she only thought "maybe" Helen was there.
She had never been to Oakland before, and neither had I. My Anglo logic told
me to call information and find out if there was a phone listing; no luck. I
called all the Navajo names in the phone book (Yazzie, Begay, Benally, Nez);
no one had heard of new arrivals named Helen and Eugene. What to do? At
this point, Joanne said, "Maybe they've got my younger sister Ursula with
them, and if they do, they would want to be near a playground. Are there any
playgrounds around here?" None showed on the map, but there were several
lakes and parks which might have playgrounds; I decided to humor Joanne for
awhile and drive around, then simply invite her to travel on to Eugene with
me. However, at the fourth or fifth small park we passed (by now it was dark),
she thought we might be near her sister, and suggested I drive up a nearby
street. "Stop! See the pickup? It's got an eagle feather hanging from the mirror." "Aha," I said, "do you recognize Eugene's pickup?" No, in fact she didn't
think he owned one, but "maybe" he had used one to move with. We parked,
and she chose a small apartment house across the street from the pickup, and
we read the names on the hallway directory; when we pushed the button next

to E. Yazzie, the electronic lock buzzed, we went down the hall and were warmly greeted by Eugene and Helen, who had been in bed but had the feeling that "maybe" family members were coming. They already had gotten up, dressed, and had made a pot of coffee and a stack of fried bread. Ursula was asleep on the couch. They had moved in yesterday. It had taken us less than an hour to find them from the time we were at the gas station. "How do you guys know how to do this?" I asked, and Eugene countered, "How do *you* guys know how to get water out of a faucet?"

This sense of self-evident logic is shared best, of course, among those who recognize all the coordinates. Once when I was scheduled to fly to Salt Lake City for some lectures, I called some Navajo friends who were living there and told them of my arrival time and the locations of all my presentations. They did not meet my plane; they did not show up at any of the lectures; they did not make it to the airport for my departure. I assumed that other responsibilities had intervened—perhaps a sing that required them to be in southern Utah—and thought no more about it until a year or so later when I ran into one of those friends, who demanded to know what had happened to me. "We waited around for you all four days, and you never showed up," he complained. Then it was that I discovered they had been waiting around at the bus depot, the place where most Native people intersected with folks from out of town. I knew that, of course, but since I had told them explicitly I was coming by plane, I had canceled other possibilities out of conscious thought (*my* set of assumptions); since they normally met people at the bus station, and they knew I was aware of this, they canceled other possibilities out of consideration (*their* set of assumptions). Such a misfire is not itself unusual, and I do not include it as an example of the moccasin telegraph gone awry. Rather, I suggest it might be one of several possibilities for explaining the deep structure of the telegraph—the cultural set of assumptions within which some signal or event may be said to attain such an obvious validity that "of course" is the natural response.

Quite the most remarkable, complex experience of my life, with regard to supernatural logic, occurred in bits and pieces over a span of two years. While I will recount the fragments in lineal time, the reader will see as we go onward that the apparently unconnected events in fact coincide in striking ways. The immediate sequence apparently started in the summer of 1979, when I visited Joseph Epes Brown on his ranch in Montana, accompanied by my Coos Indian friend, George Wasson. But maybe the whole constellation started back in the 1950s, when I first became acquainted with—and deeply interested in—the Navajo Coyote stories. The stories and my discussion of them had eventually brought me into contact with Joseph Brown, who was teaching religious studies at the University of Montana. Brown had invited me there several times for lectures, and to teach summer school classes in Native religious and traditional topics. During those classes I had met a number of Native people in the area around Missoula, some of whom—the Flatheads—play roles in the rest of this account. But in the summer of 1979, our visit was a social one, just prior to my departure for a year's Fulbright professorship in Germany. Wanting to send something along with me for "spiritual protection," and knowing of my interest in Coyote stories, Joseph Brown gave me a rolled-up photographic poster of a coyote. Inside the roll were some pieces of sage, a sprig of juniper, and a hank of buffalo hair (from his own buffalo: "They lend a much greater sense of spirit power to a ranch than mere cows do," Brown had said).

I took this talisman to Germany with me that fall, kept it on a shelf near my desk, and then brought it back to Oregon and stowed it away in a closet in my study. In the fall of 1980, I was contacted by a group of Native people at Carroll College in Montana; they were organizing a symposium on Native storytelling and had asked Native elders and a few others to participate. On the advice of Joseph Brown, who would also participate, they were inviting me. However, since the conference was to be held in April 1981, and since the Navajo Coyote tales can't be told except during winter months, I said I would have to talk about the stories of some other tribe. After accepting the invitation, I immediately called George Wasson to see if he would give me permission to use a Coos story as an example for my lecture. He had to think about it and would let me know later. As the time came closer to April, George finally said, "Well, there are some restrictions on these stories, as you know, but after all, you'll be telling the tale in English, and to an audience that doesn't know the Coos material, so why don't you go ahead. But one proviso: Tom Yellowtail [a Crow elder and leader of the Crow sundance] will be there, and I want you to clear it with him first. Maybe there'll be folks from other tribes with similar problems about proprieties of time and place, and he'll want to mention all this in his opening prayer." I promised to check with Tom Yellowtail on my arrival and started getting my talk ready.

When my daughter arrived to give me a ride to the airport, however, I bent over to get my luggage and passed out so suddenly that my head snapped back, and I struck my chin against the edge of my study closet door. I was awake again in seconds, and we headed for the airport with me holding a plastic bag of ice cubes and paper towels against my chin to stanch the bleeding from a 1.5" split. The airline let me on my flight only after a lot of persuasion, and the bleeding slowly lessened. In Portland I had to explain it all again, and in doing so I started bleeding once more. And again in Spokane, and again in

Missoula; every time I started to talk, I would start to bleed (the reason for this self-indulgent detail will become more apparent below). I arrived in Helena and was taken to the Carroll College campus, where Tom Yellowtail said he thought I had already "paid my fine" for telling stories out of season and told me I might as well tell the one I had prepared. His wife Suzie chimed in, "Yeah, go ahead; we need the rain anyway" (reflecting the widespread belief that some stories are so powerful they can change the weather). My Flathead friend Willie Wright repaired the cut with a "hair stitch" (normally used for scalp wounds, it draws the sides of a gash together by tying hairs in a row), and I went on to participate in the symposium.

However, most of the traditional people at the conference declined to tell stories because it was now spring. Agnes Vanderburg, a venerable Flathead elder, came to the podium and said simply, "The signs have been seen over our way, so I'm not going to tell any Coyote stories," and then went and sat down. Much to her disgust, I followed her at the podium and made my presentation on Coyote stories, using the Coos example taught to me by George Wasson. Even though it was from another tribe, even though I had permission from the teller and from Tom Yellowtail, I should have known better than to act counter to my elders, she lectured me later; small wonder that I had injured myself in the offending region of my body, my mouth.

Smarting from her disapproval, I finished the conference and then went to attend the wedding of my friend Roger Welsch in Dannebrog, Nebraska. Since I was a surprise guest, I had nowhere to sleep but the cramped attic of Roger's rebuilt log cabin, where I spent most of the night being serenaded by wandering coyotes—a fitting conclusion, as Thoreau might have said, to an ill-spent week. When I awoke in the morning, I was looking straight into the eyes of a full-grown coyote who seemed intensely curious about my presence in his domain. Realizing that a coyote was very unlikely to be floating around the rafters of a log cabin, I closed my eyes and attributed the image to the previous night's indulgences and to the effects of the nocturnal coyote choir. But every time I opened my eyes, the coyote was still there, staring hypnotically at me. As I became more alert and concerned about the state of my mind, I sat up, immediately bumping my head against the roof. Actually, I had bumped my head against the photographic poster of a coyote which Welsch had tacked to the roof; apparently, it was so close to my face that I had not seen the edges and had had only the sensation of seeing a coyote. As I lay back on the bed and got my thoughts together, I suddenly realized that this poster was identical to the one Joseph Brown had given me two years earlier. Now, it seemed to me that the whole series of events formed a network of some kind, connected by Joseph Brown and a coyote poster.

When I returned to Eugene, I phoned George Wasson and told him everything that had happened; the long silence on his end, and the strain in his voice
when he began to speak, told me that he was emotionally moved by the
details. "I didn't want to mention it," he said, "because I didn't really know if it
pertained to situations like this. But some people say that when you tell stories
out of season, you'll be punished in an appropriate part of your body by having
something happen to you, like what a white person might call an accident." Of
course, now that this poster had become so central in my affairs, I searched the
house for it, and found it still rolled up with buffalo hair, sage, and juniper, in
the closet whose doorway I had fallen against before leaving home; in fact, it
was in the corner just inside the door frame on the same side I had collided
with.

But I had had the "accident" *before* telling the story out of season: how
could the injury be seen as any kind of "punishment" for that which had not
yet happened? Indeed, in this story, how can anyone make a causal sequence
out of the principal parts without seeming to blame Joseph Brown or George
Wasson? Out of all the important things that must have happened in the
world that week, why is it in any way meaningful for me to dwell on my own
injury (I still don't know why I passed out) and to insist that it had some connection with other activities? Seen from an Anglo perspective on logic, this
anecdote simply glorifies an odd set of coincidences; from a common Native
American viewpoint (not to argue, however, that all Native American cultures
would agree on all details), these events coincide and interrelate because they
are seen to connect a group of widely separated friends and colleagues through
a common image (coyotes, Coyote stories, a coyote poster) and a common
concern (proprieties about the telling of stories). Rather than privileging any
kind of sequential logic, the anecdote uses what I would call "cluster logic," in
which all things that are seen to be functionally related are recognized for their
reflexivity and intertextuality—regardless of the sequence of particulars. One
could say that as I became more and more interested in Coyote stories, a constellation of possibilities began to grow in which both proper usage and misuse
were possible, certain friendships would naturally develop, certain images and
meanings would become more recognizable and functional.

One could also say that when I decided to tell *any* Coyote story out of season (and by the way, why was it, after all, that the Native American people
planning that conference insisted on having it in the month of April anyhow?), I was making an injudicious move toward the articulation of powerful
material out of ritual control. The injury to my chin and the consequent
bleeding every time I opened my mouth to speak might thus be seen, in
Native terms, as the dramatic enactment of personal responsibility for which

the rest of the anecdote simply provides context. In any case, I believe that the kind of cluster logic discussed here, which assumes that relationships are more important than sequence and lineal causation, represents the thought process out of which the moccasin telegraph and other similar ways of knowing may grow. This way of thinking looks more like a spider web than like a calendar, and its coordinates are not usually taken seriously by "Western" culture—while the calendar grid pattern is viewed with more reverence than it probably deserves, which is why we feel we are operating in the Unnatural when we start talking about Native thought.

But there are other ways of tribal knowing which use cluster logic to interpret a realm which is clearly supernatural. For the Navajos, this can be illustrated by the beliefs and stories associated with the so-called "skinwalkers" (*yenaaldlooshi:* lit. "by means of trotting like a canine"), but every tribe has its own dramatic examples. Navajo legends and anecdotes about the skinwalker range from first-person accounts by credible people to friend-of-a-friend narratives told with equal conviction by Navajos who see them as confirmation of their own beliefs and experiences. The young children of the Yellowman family, with whom I used to live, assure me that they all saw a skinwalker in their yard in Blanding, Utah; when a teenaged brother tried to shoot it with the family varmint rifle, he was paralyzed and could not pull the trigger (after the intruder left, the rifle fired harmlessly into the air). Ray Hunt, longtime trader to the Navajos, told me that while he was at Chilchinbito he was asked by local Navajos to come and shoot a skinwalker they had found in their fields. Hunt found a very strange animal which appeared to be part dog and part cat (a cheetah-like animal, but what would it be doing on the Navajo Reservation?), and although he had no special beliefs about skinwalkers, he did aid the Navajos by destroying the animal.

A Navajo friend of mine remembers driving along in his pickup near Red Mesa when he noticed a dog-like animal running along parallel to him about fifty yards away from the highway. No matter how fast he went, the dog not only kept up, but kept looking at him intently. Finally, the dog disappeared, but later in the day my friend drove off the road for no apparent reason, wrecking his car and coming close to being killed.

Another friend who once worked for the Navajo Nation Police told me that he pulled over a speeding pickup west of Dinnehotso just after dark. He walked up to the driver's window and shined his flashlight inside; there he saw four human figures, each with the head of a dog. Almost in unison, they turned and looked at him. He turned off his flashlight, returned to his car, drove directly to Kayenta, and tendered his resignation from the force. More recently, a non-Native colleague of mine was camping on the Navajo Reservation while doing research on the effects of radiation on Navajo uranium miners. As she set up her tent one evening in late twilight a human figure with the head and shoulders of an animal ran past the spot a few yards away and disappeared into the darkness.

A young man in Tuba City, Arizona, was repairing his motorcycle outside his home one day when suddenly the gasoline he was using as a cleaner exploded in his face. He was taken to the nearby Public Health Service Hospital, where the doctors quickly treated him and stabilized his condition. The boy insisted that the explosion had been caused somehow by a certain older woman whom he believed to be a skinwalker, and he begged the doctors not to let that woman into the hospital. The doctors, of course, assured him that he was fine and on the mend, and that his burns had nothing to do with witchcraft. Nonetheless, that particular woman was found roaming the halls of the hospital on several occasions and had to be forcibly removed. And although the boy's burns were starting to heal properly, he died suddenly in the hospital for no apparent reason, according to a former student of mine who was his doctor.

The skinwalker is a kind of Navajo "witch" who can be of either sex and who is believed either to change into canine form by using a certain ritual or to "put on" canine hides and wear them as outer clothing. They are thought to dig up graves and use the powdered remains of corpses for their magical rituals; they are believed to copulate with the dead and with their own relatives (the taboo against incest, as well as a dedicated avoidance of contact with dead bodies, are among the strongest of Navajo mores); they are supposed to gain their powers by ruining those of others—that is to say, by using means which we would call competitive and aggressive, they seek to become strong by making others weak, become healthy by making others sick, become wealthy by making others poor, and so on. The dog/coyote/wolf imagery is so closely associated with these shamans that the very appearance of a strange dog, or the unexplained odd behavior of any canine, or persistent appearance of coyotes in close proximity to a human are interpreted as signs of impending trouble.[4]

Recently, I have had a surprising number of close encounters with coyotes: last summer, one walked across the road in front of my car while staring at me; last fall, while I was walking toward an Anasazi ruin, one ran past me from behind, not more than twelve feet away; a month later, as I was driving back to Utah from Montana, three coyotes in single file paralleled the highway for a time; I recently did some narration on a PBS film about coyotes and came into contact with coyote pelts; just last week, a coyote ran across the sidewalk in front of me here on the campus where I work. Except for the fact that I normally don't see so many coyotes, these encounters do not form a particularly meaningful frame of reference for me. But my Navajo family and friends are deeply concerned: One asked, "Why are you subjecting yourself and your family to this kind of treatment?" And I am expected to be the patient in a Blessing Way ceremony which will include a special segment for making offerings to the coyote. It is an employment of "cluster logic" on a religious level.[5]

Clearly, any understanding of these events is shaped *both* by our own experiences and by cultural factors which encourage us either to *assume* certain events have occurred in connection with each other or to assume that they were entirely coincidental. This means that either interpretation is based on assumptions about relationships and on our need to see, register, and interpret meaningful codes among these assumptions. Admittedly, I now "process" these codes far differently than I would have had I not had several years' experience living with—and forty years' experience studying—the Navajo. Does this mean, however that I have simply become more gullible or soft-headed when it comes to being objective about the events described? I think not. I also do not believe that I have "become" in any way Navajo (for example, my encounters with coyotes interest but do not panic me, while my Navajo friends are visibly shaken by them). What I have learned through personal experience is that my own culture—however fond or critical of it I may be—does not provide *all* the possible ways of processing and understanding the events of everyday life, much less to define and understand events which lie outside the domain of physical data.

To the Navajo, skinwalkers are not supernatural, for they are believed to be constituents of everyday life—perhaps even our neighbors. To Anglo Americans, they seem supernatural because their rituals and activities seem magical, out of the norm, out of the realm of everyday possibility. "Who is correct in this?" is a question which is impossible to resolve, however, for each culture looks at the phenomena described with its own very natural, very common, very normal "eyeglasses." One of the reasons we have difficulty discussing the supernatural is that we have almost no serious vocabulary for it, and that probably stems from our unwillingness to acknowledge its validity unless it has been codified for us in language which suggests that someone (the clerics, the theologians) has the issues under *control*. In short, we see pretty much what we are encouraged to see; or, as a student of mine once reshaped an old phrase, "If I hadn't believed it, I never would have seen it." Intercultural explorations into such unlikely but widely used concepts as the moccasin telegraph or cluster logic have the value of at least exposing us to other quite valid ways of organizing, and thus understanding, what happens in the often confusing world around us.

Endnotes

1.   John G. Neihardt, *Black Elk Speaks: Being the Life Story of a Holy Man of the Ogalala Sioux* (Lincoln: University of Nebraska Press, 1961).

2.   Joseph Epes Brown, private correspondence and conversation with the author; see also his account of his first meeting with Black Elk in the Preface to *The Sacred Pipe* (New York: Penguin Books, 1971), xiii–xiv.

3.   Roger Welsch, *It's Not the End of the Earth, But You Can See It from Here* (New York: Villard Books, 1990), 51–56.

4.   For more about skinwalkers and stories recounting their activities, see Margaret K. Brady, *"Some Kind of Power": Navajo Children's Skinwalker Narratives* (Salt Lake City: University of Utah Press, 1984); and Barre Toelken, "Ma'ii Jold-looshi lá Eeyáa: The Several Lives of a Navajo Coyote," *The World and I* 5, no. 4 (April 1, 1990): 651–660.

5.   Terry Tempest Williams, who once taught school on the Navajo Reservation, gives an interesting personal account of an encounter with a coyote in Williams, *Pieces of White Shell: A Journey to Navajoland* (New York: Scribner's, 1984), 75–84 (and an equally fascinating meeting with rattlesnakes and accidents, 143–145).

3

Folklore, Foodways, and the Supernatural

Timothy C. Lloyd

I CONCEIVE OF FOLKLORE AS THE INTERSECTION OF ARTFULNESS AND EVERYDAY life. I say *artfulness,* rather than *art,* for a reason: folklore does not depend on the creation of works of art comparable to those of "high" art. Very often this artfulness is exercised in the making of everyday things. These things don't have to be objects, such as baskets, quilts, or fishnets. They can also be practices or occasions: storytelling, games, meals, and so on. Saying *artfulness* instead of *art* also, appropriately, directs our attention to the process of creation as well as to the things created. When this artful process occurs many times over time—in other words, when it recurs, regularly, in everyday life—what it makes is patterns. Recurrent artfulness in everyday life makes patterns in space and time, patterns which we use to make, recognize, and judge objects, or practices, or occasions.

Several years ago William A. Wilson, speaking of folklore and the humanities, wrote, "Art, music, literature, and dance come into being . . . when we move to a deeper necessity, to the deeper human need to create order, beauty, and meaning out of chaos"; he cites the "human need to combine words, sounds, colors, shapes, and movements into aesthetically satisfying patterns."[1] In what appears to be a fundamental human process, we continually create, respond to, and look for patterns. Other scholars agree, in the language of their own fields: Gustav Jahoda wrote in his book *The Psychology of Superstition* that

> [A] fundamental characteristic of human thinking, and indeed of human cognitive processes in general . . . is the tendency to organize the environment into coherent patterns, to find meaning in the most diverse grouping of phenomena, and to

derive satisfaction from such an achievement; conversely, an environment or events which fail to make sense are felt to be threatening and disturbing.[2]

A fair amount of the research on folklore and the supernatural has focused on the ways in which the supernatural and many of its denizens—ghosts, spirits, and "things that go bump in the night," all of whom are separate from us—unexpectedly cross the border to visit us in the everyday world. These visitations are often portrayed as random, unexpected, exotic experiences that happen only to a very few of us. Even visitations by benevolent or helpful beings are portrayed and reported this way.

New scholarship, however, is challenging this view as too narrow. For instance, take Gillian Bennett's 1987 book *Traditions of Belief: Women and the Supernatural.* For the great majority of the elderly English women who told Bennett narratives of their encounters, the supernatural is not only a friendly but a domestic realm, populated by departed family members, friends, and anonymous helpers who visit here to provide useful advice, timely predictions, and kindly solace to the living. Bennett also suggests that this homely variety of the supernatural is anything but separate from these women's lives, and that it is a part of the lives of a great many more people than we commonly suppose.[3]

Following from Bennett, I want to propose that "the supernatural" is more than just the eerie or mysterious, more than the realm of spirits or of the departed, whether friendly or menacing. I suggest we reconceive the supernatural as the realm of the fundamental patterns and rhythms—of time, space, growth, and decline, for example—which, connecting, give purpose and governance to life. These are what Gregory Bateson has called "patterns which connect": higher-level patterns which relate and, in relating, give meaning to simpler ones.[4] These patterns and rhythms are expressed in the natural world in the life cycles of the individual and family (as in the narratives Bennett presents), in the annual round of the seasons, in the division of space into directions and dimensions, and the like. The precise figuring of these patterns and rhythms is a central matter of cultural identification, priority, and difference; in this light, these sets of figurings are most often referred to nowadays as *worldviews.*

Seen this way, the supernatural is not a separate, exotic, largely closed realm; rather, it is connected to, or underlies, all life. It is supernatural not in the sense of being unnatural or in being separate from the natural, but in the literal sense of being the largest version of the pattern of the natural. Bennett reached a similar conclusion:

For these women, it would seem, academic distinctions between the natural and supernatural, the normal and the paranormal, are virtually meaningless . . . [for them] the boundary between the mundane and spiritual worlds is a flexible one.[5]

Everyday folklore of all sorts—narratives, customs, beliefs, and events—can provide the means for regular connection between our "natural," everyday world and the "supernatural" realm, and folklore of all sorts can also artfully express this connection. This process works in a different direction, however, than the one usually assumed in discussions of the supernatural, in which its inhabitants contact us whenever and however they like. I believe that folk belief and practice can make it possible for us to connect with the supernatural. More correctly, folklore can be a vehicle for our active engagement in our everyday lives with these major patterns and rhythms.

The engagements with the supernatural I will discuss have to do with foodways: not simple recipes, but different aspects of the entire cycle of food generation, production, preparation, and consumption. Foodways are important in our connections with the supernatural because the food cycle itself—from seed to table and onward—is one of the very most fundamental sets of natural and social patterns, and is interlaced with others like it. In fact, neither of the examples here is focused on cooking technique—which is usually conceived as the "centerpiece" of food activity—precisely because I want to show how significant the supposedly "peripheral" aspects of the food cycle are.

Lloyd and Emma Farley live on a small hillside landholding in the eastern part of southeastern Ohio's Jackson County. At the time folklorist Sandy Rikoon and I first met them in 1980, they were both in their early sixties. We had been directed to their place by farmers in the area who, responding to our inquiries about older farm methods, suggested we should talk to the Farleys about water-witching.

Like a great many people in their part of the state, the Farleys are not regularly employed, although they are hardly unskilled or idle. To get by, they have both become jacks-of-all-trades: they know many skills needed in a poor, rural area, and they are able to get by through their own self-sufficiency, supplemented by an informal combination of carpentry, blocklaying, plumbing, gardening, gathering ginseng and other medicinal plants, and veterinary and farm work done for others.

A great many of their skills involve what we commonly call the supernatural. Although both can find water, Lloyd is the more accomplished dowser of the couple. Unlike many people who have the water-witching gift, he can find water without a forked branch or bent pieces of wire. He walks over the area where he thinks water may be, holding his arms straight out at shoulder height, and figures the water's exact location, extent, and depth by the tingling or tensing feelings in his arms and hands. Emma has the ability to recite one's past and predict one's future through palm reading and the feeling of forces in one's arm. She claims, though, that she received the best part of this ability through her association with Lloyd and his family, all of whom, she says, "know things."

Most notably, however, both Lloyd and Emma have detailed and expert knowledge of the system of conducting agricultural and livestock practices— planting, harvesting, castrating, and butchering, to name just a few—according to the signs of the moon. *The Old Farmer's Almanac* gives a bare-bones annual summary of this system of signs, but the real body of it is to be found in practice and in oral tradition. This is, or at least was, one of the most widely known and followed techniques of traditional agricultural practice in this country. Many people still believe in and practice it to some extent. In addition to everyday word-of-mouth communication, farmers' almanacs and calendars— often distributed by seed, feed, or implement companies—have made this information available in this country for almost two centuries.

This system is based on the moon's astrological position in the zodiac. When the moon is said to be in a particular sign on a particular day, this means that it will be in the astrological part of the heavens occupied by one of the twelve constellations of the zodiac, such as Gemini or Virgo. (It is important to note that astrological and astronomical positions are not identical.) In a lunar month of around twenty-nine days, the moon passes through all twelve astrological signs. As Figure 1 shows, each sign of the zodiac also stands for a part of the body—Gemini for the arms, for instance, and Virgo for the belly. In fact, most people who are familiar with or use this system for farm work use the humanly scaled body names, not the names of the constellations, to refer to the signs. For instance, they say "the sign's in the arms," not "the moon's in Gemini." Each sign is said to govern or affect its part of the body, including certain farm tasks that involve that body part. Signs indicate good or bad days for doing those tasks.

Knowing the system first involves knowing which signs are good and bad for particular tasks. If you know this, you can look on the *Almanac* pages for each month of the year (see Figure 2) and, reading down the "Moon's Place" column near the far right-hand side, you will find the best days for your job by matching the lunar constellation in that column with your knowledge. For instance, one of the good butchering signs is the thighs (Sagittarius). The three days in January 1993 when the moon was in Sagittarius were the 20th, 21st, and 22nd; those were the days on which you should have butchered.

Figure 1

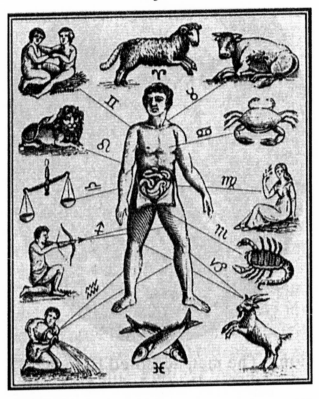

The signs also indicate bad days for doing particular tasks. One of the bad signs for butchering is the heart (Leo) since, according to the Farleys and to the larger tradition, meat butchered during this time will become dark. So it would not have been wise to have butchered on January 11, 12, or 13 in 1993. I didn't choose January by chance; the winter months are the ones for home butchering, because the colder temperatures help keep the meat from spoiling. Even June has Sagittarius days, but no one would butcher then. The system of moon signs does have its limits.

Now we begin to see one of the patterns that connects all of this information. In livestock work at least, there is a physical and symbolic correspondence made between the astrological place of the moon in the sky—the pattern of the heavens, we might say, as an indication of the way things are to work—and the nature of the work to be done. Darkened beef or pork is actually bad-

Figure 2

1993 **JANUARY, THE FIRST MONTH**

Mars reaches opposition on the night of January 7th-8th, with the full Moon passing south of it as both set at night's end. The ruddy planet greatly outshines Castor and Pollux, near it in Gemini, and is closest to Earth, about 58 million miles away, on the 3rd. Only Sirius (in the southeast at mid evening) slightly outshines Mars. Venus reaches greatest elongation (47 degrees east) on January 19th. To the right of Mars and Sirius, Orion forms the most splendid of all star patterns. Jupiter rises in late evening. Just before dawn on the 3rd and 4th, watch for Quadrantid meteors from the northeast. Earth is at perihelion on the night of the 3rd.

ASTRONOMICAL CALCULATIONS

○ Full Moon	8th day	4th hour	38th min.
☾ Last Quarter	14th day	20th hour	2nd min.
● New Moon	22nd day	10th hour	28th min.
☽ First Quarter	30th day	15th hour	20th min.

FOR POINTS OUTSIDE SAN FRANCISCO SEE KEY LETTER CORRECTIONS — PAGES 198-202

Day of Year	Day of Month	Day of Week	☉ Rises h. m.	Key	☉ Sets h. m.	Key	Length of Days h. m.	Sun Fast m.	Full Sea San Francisco Light – A.M.	Bold – P.M.	☽ Rises h. m.	Key	☽ Sets h. m.	Key	Declination of Sun ° '	☽ Place	☽ Age
1	1	Fr.	7 25	E	5 02	A	9 37	*14	5¼	**6¼**	11Å50	B	12Å34	E	22s.56	PSC	9
2	2	Sa.	7 25	E	5 02	A	9 37	*14	6	**8**	12P22	B	1 36	E	22 51	PSC	10
3	3	**C**	7 26	E	5 03	A	9 37	*15	6½	**9**	12 58	B	2 36	E	22 45	ARI	11
4	4	M.	7 26	E	5 04	A	9 38	*15	7½	**10**	1 41	A	3 38	E	22 38	ARI	12
5	5	Tu.	7 26	E	5 05	A	9 39	*15	8¼	**10¾**	2 32	A	4 40	E	22 32	TAU	13
6	6	W.	7 26	E	5 06	A	9 40	*16	9	**11½**	3 31	A	5 39	E	22 25	TAU	14
7	7	Th.	7 26	E	5 07	A	9 41	*16	9¾	—	4 38	B	6 35	E	22 17	GEM	15
8	8	Fr.	7 26	E	5 08	A	9 42	*17	12	**10½**	5 49	B	7 24	E	22 09	GEM	16
9	9	Sa.	7 25	E	5 09	A	9 44	*17	12¼	**11¼**	7 02	B	8 08	E	22 00	CAN	17
10	10	**C**	7 25	E	5 10	A	9 45	*18	1¼	**12¼**	8 15	C	8 46	D	21 51	CAN	18
11	11	M.	7 25	E	5 11	A	9 46	*18	2	**1**	9 27	C	9 21	D	21 42	LEO	19
12	12	Tu.	7 25	E	5 12	A	9 47	*18	2½	**2**	10 37	D	9 54	C	21 32	LEO	20
13	13	W.	7 25	E	5 13	A	9 48	*19	3¼	**3¼**	11P47	D	10 26	C	21 21	LEO	21
14	14	Th.	7 24	E	5 14	A	9 50	*19	4	**4½**	— —	–	11 00	B	21 11	VIR	22
15	15	Fr.	7 24	E	5 15	A	9 51	*19	5	**6¼**	12Å55	E	11Å37	B	21 00	VIR	23
16	16	Sa.	7 24	E	5 16	A	9 52	*20	5¼	**7¾**	2 02	E	12P17	B	20 48	LIB	24
17	17	**C**	7 23	E	5 17	A	9 54	*20	6½	**9**	3 06	E	1 02	A	20 37	LIB	25
18	18	M.	7 23	E	5 18	A	9 55	*20	7¼	**10**	4 06	E	1 52	A	20 24	SCO	26
19	19	Tu.	7 23	E	5 19	A	9 56	*21	8¼	**10¾**	5 00	E	2 47	A	20 12	OPH	27
20	20	W.	7 22	E	5 20	A	9 58	*21	9¼	**11½**	5 48	E	3 44	A	19 59	SAG	28
21	21	Th.	7 22	E	5 21	A	9 59	*21	10	—	6 30	E	4 43	B	19 45	SAG	29
22	22	Fr.	7 21	D	5 22	A	10 01	*22	12	**10¾**	7 06	E	5 42	B	19 31	SAG	0
23	23	Sa.	7 20	D	5 23	A	10 03	*22	12¼	**11¼**	7 38	D	6 41	B	19 17	CAP	1
24	24	**C**	7 20	D	5 24	A	10 04	*22	1	**12**	8 06	D	7 38	C	19 03	CAP	2
25	25	M.	7 19	D	5 26	A	10 07	*22	1¼	**12½**	8 33	D	8 34	C	18 50	AQU	3
26	26	Tu.	7 19	D	5 27	A	10 08	*23	2	**1¼**	8 59	C	9 30	D	18 33	PSC	4
27	27	W.	7 18	D	5 28	A	10 10	*23	2½	**2**	9 24	C	10 27	D	18 17	PSC	5
28	28	Th.	7 17	D	5 29	A	10 12	*23	3	**2¾**	9 52	C	11P24	D	18 01	PSC	6
29	29	Fr.	7 16	D	5 30	A	10 14	*23	3½	**4**	10 21	B	— —	–	17 45	PSC	7
30	30	Sa.	7 16	D	5 31	A	10 15	*23	4½	**5¼**	10 55	B	12Å23	E	17 28	ARI	8
31	31	**C**	7 15	D	5 32	A	10 17	*23	5	**7¼**	11Å34	B	1Å22	E	17s.11	ARI	9

60 OLD FARMER'S ALMANAC 1993

tasting and indicates an unsuccessful butchering and probably spoiled meat. Butchering on a heart day symbolically brings the heart and its blood, which will darken meat, into a sort of contagious connection with the butchered meat, which can turn dark as though blood had contaminated it. So you butcher when the moon is in one of the signs as far away from the heart as possible: the thighs (Sagittarius), the legs (Aquarius), the feet (Pisces). Most veterinary work is best done when the sign is in the affected part. A very important and notable exception is castration, which should never be done when the signs are in the secrets (Scorpio).

Similar patterns apply in agricultural work. Crops that develop above ground (say, corn or cabbage) should be planted when the signs are in high parts of the body (the head is best). Climbing crops, such as beans or cucumbers, should be planted when the signs are in the arms. Crops planted when the signs are in the secrets or bowels develop blooms but no fruit.

This set of patterns is paralleled by another, simpler one having to do with the moon's other monthly cycle: from new to full moon and back. Vance Randolph describes this system in his book *Ozark Superstitions:*

> What the [Arkansas] hillman calls the "dark" of the moon is the period from the full moon to the new, the decrease or waning of the moon; the other half of the lunar season, from the new moon to the full, when the moon is waxing or increasing in size, is known as the "light" of the moon. In general, it is said that vegetables which are desired to grow chiefly underground, such as potatoes, onions, beets, turnips, radishes, and peanuts are best planted in the dark of the moon. Garden crops which bear the edible part above ground, such as beans, peas, tomatoes, and so on, are usually planted in the light of the moon.[6]

This second system—of the moon's waxing and waning—applies to livestock work as well. Randolph writes that butchering, for example, should be done in the light of the moon: butchering done in the dark of the moon apparently also produces tough, bad-tasting meat.[7] Other classic published collections of folk belief and practice—including Newbell Niles Puckett's *Folk Beliefs of the Southern Negro,* to name just one[8]—as well as unpublished material in folklore archives contain many examples of both systems in other parts of the country.

Following are transcriptions of two excerpts from an interview with the Farleys, done by Sandy Rikoon in 1980, each of which contains a personal experience narrative, told by Lloyd Farley, about livestock work.

> *Lloyd Farley:* A fellow [named Boone] wanted me to butcher a big sow for him down here and I said, "Boone, you don't want to butcher that sow." [Boone said], "Why?" I said, "Signs is in the secrets. You don't want to butcher her." "Oh," he said, "they ain't nothing to them signs. I want her killed." He's working up to Columbus and . . . I said, "Well, now I can kill her, but now your meat ain't going to be no good." And he said, "That don't make any difference. Signs ain't got nothing to do with butchering." I said, "All right, you'll see." I went down, shot her,

brought her up here and then, so, I butchered her, rendered the lard, and made sausage. That stuff pretty near run you out of the house. Just smelled like when you'd wet [urinated] on a hot iron. Now that's the way it smelled. The signs was in the secrets.

And so, his wife come up here and got it, took her down there, and she said, "I couldn't use that meat." Said she give it to people over in Kentucky where she's from. She said, "I couldn't use it. That stink just run me out of the house." And she come up here, and I had some big cakes of sausage left over from breakfast, you know, and she just jumped into 'em, warmed 'em up by herself, and I had them big hillbilly biscuits, you know, and them and milk gravy, and she sat down and eat her some of that sausage and she said, "Lloyd, how does it come that your sausage tastes different from mine?" And I said, "Well, I told you, Betty, not to kill that hog. Signs wasn't right. I killed that one when the signs was right." And she said, "There surely is a difference in it."[9]

The second excerpt is not about doing livestock work by the signs of the moon, but rather about the value of practical experience in veterinary work, in contrast to the more formal experience of the licensed vet. I include this narrative because it will help us understand the combination of supernatural and practical considerations that shape Farley's work.

Lloyd Farley: A fellow had three big sows there, weighed about four hundred pound apiece, and he was gonna get a pig from the government. They bring you a bred sow, and she'll have so many pigs, and if I get her I'd have to give two of them pigs to somebody else; they can get a start of 'em. So he [a government man] went over there and checked, and he said, "Well, I can't let you have any [hogs] because them other hogs is there and that vet, he went in and checked them, and he [the veterinarian] said, 'They've got an incurable disease. All you can do is just kill 'em, and burn the barn here, put three ton of lime on this lot here for the next three years, and don't have another hog around here. They got an incurable disease.'" Well, he knowed I'd fooled with hogs a lot, you know, and I raised 'em here, and what I know, *I experienced it.* So, he called me, and I went over there, and I said, "Tom, I can have them big sows up on their feet eating, within, in two shots."

He said, "I'll buy the medicine, and pay you good if you'll bring them out of it." And I said, "I will." So I went to Jackson the next day, and he called my wife and he said, "Tell Lloyd he won't need to come up. Every one of them hogs is out down there in the cornfield, broke out of the barn." Well, here comes the vet and that government man back out there, you know, and [the veterinarian says], "Where them hogs at?" Tom said, "Down there's one of them big sows in the cornfield, them other pigs's around in there too." "Why," he [the veterinarian] said, "what'd you do to 'em?" [Tom] said, "I got a man knowed something about hogs." And that vet said, "Who was he?" And [Tom] said, "What would you do if I'd tell you?" "Well, if he didn't charge you," [the veterinarian] said, "I can't do anything, but if he charged you, we can fine him, 'cause he's not licensed." [Tom] said, "Well, Lloyd Farley over there come over here and give them hogs a shot." The vet said, "What'd he do?" [Tom] said, "I don't know. He don't never tell nothing. You know, he's a part Indian and he won't talk. And I don't know what he done." "Well," he [the veterinarian] said, "I'll give him twenty-five dollars if he'll tell me what he done." Well, he comes over here and stops. "Mister Farley," he said, "I'll give you twenty-five dollars if you'll tell me what you done for them hogs." I said, "Well, now, Steve, it's just like this: you're an educated, licensed vet; I'm an experienced dummy. Now *you* find out." I won't tell him nothing. I ain't told him yet to this day. There's different times he's seen me in town there and he's offered me twenty-five dollars if I'll tell him. I said, "Yeah, you take twenty-five dollars off of my idea and you'll make ten or fifteen thousand dollars, and I sit back with your twenty-five dollars, a dummy." And I said, "I ain't telling you nothing; now you find out like I did." Now I won't tell him nothing.[10]

In this story, you'll notice that Farley leaves out a very important episode—the part where he gives the hogs injections. Farley says to the farmer Tom that he can cure his hogs with two shots. What he doesn't tell you is that he gives them the first of the two that same day. Then on the second day, when Farley is in town before going to give the hogs the second shot, Tom calls to tell him that he doesn't need to come again: the hogs are recovered enough after just one shot to have broken out of the barn.

Are these narratives about the supernatural? I'd argue so, even though on their surface they seem to be about farming—that is, foodways—practice. They say that despite developments in farming technology, business, and economics, the everyday world of farming has always been, is still, and will always be part of the annual (and longer) rhythms of birth, growth, maturation, and decline, and the interlocking rhythms of the production, preparation, and consumption of food—both patterns of the sort I'd call supernatural, in the sense of being fundamental. They are, among other things, personal experience narratives of supernatural belief. They unite practical action with this belief by connecting day-to-day farming with its fundamentals, first showing what happens when that connection is not honored in farm work, and then showing what happens when it is.

As he tells us, Lloyd Farley lives in a world of unbelievers; in fact, we could also look at this as a personal experience narrative of supernatural unbelief. Boone, for instance, says "ain't nothing to them signs." When you come down to it, though, Boone isn't simply an unbeliever. He does believe in something: he believes in another way of doing livestock work, one in which timing for such things as butchering is not important, and this is in turn based in another way of looking at the world. His world is patterned, too, but differently than Farley's. Boone's practice is also supernatural, as I am using the word: it is based in his beliefs about the way the world works.

Farley's narratives show his ways of belief and of action victorious over those of Boone. The results are plain, simple, and entirely practical—ones that anyone can understand. In another story, a farmer with pigs made sick by castrating in the wrong sign tells Farley, "Ain't nothing to them signs." Farley replies, "You see your pigs, don't you?" And Farley's butchering narrative ends with an epilogue, in which the former disbelievers—we might say—convert.

What are the sources of Farley's belief and knowledge? To hear him tell about them, they are both supernatural and natural. He learned the signs from his father. He claims to be the "seventh son of a seventh son": the classic pedigree for a man of special powers. In other interviews with Sandy Rikoon and with me, he goes into more detail about his father's work and teaching. As Emma Farley told us, Lloyd Farley's knowledge and practice are part of a family process: it runs, as people often say, "in the blood."

This blood is also partly "Indian" blood, and as Farley said elsewhere, working by signs is "an Indian type of thing." People call him "Indian" in many of his narratives, and Farley claims, as do many people in his part of the country, a partly American Indian inheritance. At least where Farley lives, this is taken to indicate a greater ability for communion with nature and a special awareness of or attunement to the "mysterious side of life," to the conventionally defined supernatural. As Farley says later in his interview with Sandy Rikoon, "Indian blood makes me smart." And as Barre Toelken has pointed out, American Indian time (to the extent that there is a single time system for all Indians), like moon-sign time, tends to the cyclical. In this sort of time there is a sense, as Toelken puts it, of a round of "natural fruition," which develops, wanes, disappears, and then returns in its own time or, as we say, "when the time is ripe."[11]

But Farley's work also has practical sources: as he said elsewhere in what amounts to his working motto, "What I know, I experienced it." He has spent years in day-to-day farm work. His narratives favorably compare his knowledge to farmers' lack of knowledge; what usually separates him from them is both his practical skills and his incorporation of the supernatural into his work. In other stories of his, his workingman's knowledge is compared to veterinarians' and bureaucrats' professional knowledge—which seems to blind them to truths he finds easy to recognize. In one such story, he says, "You're an educated, licensed vet; I'm an experienced dummy."

More important, his supernatural and practical knowledge are integrated in his work. While knowledge of the signs is critical to certain kinds of work, the value of practical experience holds true whether or not the work is governed by the signs. Farley told us several stories of his success due to superior practical experience in the healing of sick hogs. These are emergencies—potential or actual disruptions in the cycle of life—rather than an expected part of the cycle, as are birthing, weaning, castrating, or butchering. (We do have to remember here, too, that castrating and butchering are among the human interventions into the life cycle of another species that have led to a more complex "natural" system.) This suggests that we can divide Farley's farm work into two large parts: life-cycle work, which balances supernatural knowledge with practical action, and emergency healing work, which draws more upon practical experience alone. What he told Sandy Rikoon and me in other interviews confirms this, and it stands to common sense as well: sick hogs must be made well immediately or they might die; within limits, hogs can wait to be butchered until the time is ripe.

In life-cycle work, where the signs are important, just what do they tell Farley? They don't tell him what to do or how to do it; in other words, they don't have much to do with matters of technique. What the signs tell him is when to do what he does. Doing life-cycle work at the right time is absolutely crucial: as the butchering story indicates, even someone with Farley's butchering experience cannot avoid making bad sausage if the work is done when the signs are in the secrets. All he can do is butcher away and wait for a later chance to bring his point home.

Workers of all sorts share this pragmatic disposition toward success in their work. Folklorist Patrick Mullen and I have summarized it as "If it works, use it." Lake Erie fishermen, for example, use lucky coins and St. Christopher medals, as well as National Weather Service reports, to protect themselves from the bad weather that can quickly stir up their shallow lake.[12] We can see this same approach in the way Farley describes how he reads what the signs are and say. Twice in other stories he tells a farmer, in movie-Indian dialect, "Me look at-um big moon," but when he gets home, does he follow some tradition-honored Indian ritual practice? No; he looks at the calendar thumbtacked to his kitchen door. What he reads there, combined with his belief that signs influence farming practices and with his knowledge of which signs influence which practices, leads to his divination.

Unlike those who are only visited by the "mysterious side of life," Farley has an active, intricate, and—we might even say—professional relationship with the supernatural. This relationship depends on a repeating rhythm in nature above and below (a cyclical pattern which orients earthly processes and their development to heavenly processes and their movements); it is evidenced in work which combines practical and supernatural concerns and in narratives which dramatize that intertwining, in this case through foodways.

Food behavior is at one and the same time an everyday and a profound human activity, and so it is not surprising that it can be a vehicle for approaching and communicating regularly with the supernatural. Seeing the connections between these two realms is sometimes difficult from the midst of everyday life. This may be because we haven't been taught to; in fact, the western European worldview (to speak of a very large thing too simply) embodies and expresses a linear organization of the world.

In the circular view, however, there is both a general correspondence and a whole system of interlacing relationships between the cosmic and the particular—for instance, between the cycle of all life and the cycle of my life. This is an old, old worldview, long maintained by many systems of traditional wisdom and practice, and it continues here today. The fundamental rhythms of time are often very slow, and the basic patterns of space are often very large; perhaps so slow and large that they are difficult to comprehend whole. However, by making them miniature through a narrative, an object, or a practice, especially those that we can repeat, we can become able to enact the whole process, and see the relation of its parts at once. In this way and in others, foodways—and much of folklore—can make possible our active engagement with the supernatural.

Acknowledgments

Figures 1 and 2 in this chapter are reprinted with permission of *The Old Farmer's Almanac*, © 1993, Yankee Publishing Inc., Dublin, New Hampshire. All rights reserved.

Endnotes

1. William A. Wilson, "The Deeper Necessity: Folklore and the Humanities," *Journal of American Folklore* 101 (1988): 158–159.
2. Gustav Jahoda, *The Psychology of Superstition* (Harmondsworth, England: Penguin, 1970), 120.
3. Gillian Bennett, *Traditions of Belief: Women and the Supernatural* (Harmondsworth, England: Penguin, 1987), 29–32, 51–55. See also Bennett's essay in this volume.
4. Gregory Bateson, *Mind and Nature: A Necessary Unity* (New York: Dutton, 1979), 8.
5. Bennett, 33.
6. Vance Randolph, *Ozark Superstitions* (New York: Dover, 1964), 34.
7. Randolph, 47.
8. Newbell Niles Puckett, *Folk Beliefs of the Southern Negro* (Chapel Hill: University of North Carolina Press, 1926).
9. Lloyd and Emma Farley, interviewed by Sandy Rikoon, July 10, 1980.
10. Lloyd and Emma Farley, interviewed by Sandy Rikoon, July 10, 1980.

11. Barre Toelken, "Folklore, Worldview, and Communication," in *Folklore, Performance, and Communication,* ed. Dan Ben-Amos and Kenneth Goldstein (The Hague: Mouton, 1975), 272. See also Toelken's essay in this volume.
12. Timothy C. Lloyd and Patrick Mullen, *Lake Erie Fishermen: Work, Identity, and Tradition* (Urbana: University of Illinois Press, 1990), 72–75.

II

Supernatural Power and Other Worlds: Making Contact

Throughout the world, it is not unusual to find cultures where people believe in an afterlife or in spiritual healing or in premonition. But often, when individuals are attempting to contact someone who has died, or they are seeking supernatural healing or trying to divine the future, people will contact an intermediary—a person to act as a guide or interpreter, someone who will somehow interface between this world and the afterlife or with supernatural powers or forces. This person may be considered a shaman, a witch doctor, a fortune teller, a healer, a sensitive, a psychic, or somehow especially gifted. Regardless of the bestowed title or the attributed capacities, the individual having this ability is generally thought of as either being "chosen" for this calling, or "blessed," or as having special training or disposition for this purpose.

The essays in this section examine the nature and function of those who purport to have various supernatural powers. The first chapter, by Kenneth Pimple, is a critical evaluation of the history of Modern Spiritualism in the United States, and its implications and ramifications. Although eventually, though equivocally, proven to be a hoax, vestiges of the initial movement in Modern Spiritualism continue with us today. Pimple not only provides an account of the history of the movement but also considers why it became so popular, and he takes a broader look at belief in general.

In Chapter 5, Maxine Miska presents research findings from her work with traditional seances in Taiwan, where mediums are employed to make contact with dead loved ones. Within the Taiwanese culture, the seance is a powerful female-oriented event and functions in part as a balance to the predominantly male social structure. Significantly, Miska analyzes not only the dynamics of belief but also the function of skepticism as an integral part of the seance experience.

Sociologist James McClenon continues the discussion of shamans with his analysis of spiritual healing. McClenon not only addresses the general topic of shamanic healing and how belief in the supernatural relates to healing, but also provides a specific look into the lives of a few individual healers. Drawing from a diverse population of informants, McClenon asserts that certain kinds of supernatural experience provide a foundation for belief, including belief in spiritual healing, and specifically form a basis for beliefs in the occult (paralleling the position of David Hufford).

Gillian Bennett, who has worked extensively and thoughtfully in the field of belief, presents an article based on her research with a group of women in England who are considered to have powers of foreknowledge. Bennett gives an account of how the women themselves regard their abilities, and also discusses how those abilities function for them socially as members of their community, providing certain kinds of status or power without detracting from their more traditional roles.

4

Ghosts, Spirits, and Scholars: The Origins of Modern Spiritualism

Kenneth D. Pimple

STARTING IN 1850, THROUGH MOST OF THE NINETEENTH CENTURY, THOUSANDS of Americans of every class were enraptured, entertained, and mesmerized by drawing-room seances in which the spirits of the dead were reputedly conjured up to answer, primarily through audible raps, any question put to them. As R. Laurence Moore puts it, "Scarcely another cultural phenomenon affected as many people or stimulated as much interest as did spiritualism in the ten years before the Civil War and, for that matter, through the subsequent decades of the nineteenth century."[1] There are not nearly as many believers in Modern Spiritualism[2] today as there were at its peak in the 1850s, but the Spiritualist seance has entered the vernacular. The intent seekers holding hands around a table in a darkened room, the exotic medium summoning the spirit, and the only half-expected response are by now all quite familiar.

The history and development of Modern Spiritualism have been well documented and thoroughly analyzed. The movement had its origin in traditional ghost beliefs, but evolved within the first few months into quite a different set of beliefs. This evolution is reported in virtually every history of Spiritualism, but I have found none that take the analytical step of commenting on this evolution; that is to say, they all *describe* the transformation, but none identify it *as* a transformation, thus leaving an interesting gap in the scholarship on Modern Spiritualism. I hope to shed light on two traditions, then: Spiritualism and scholarship on Spiritualism.

The First Raps

One remarkable aspect of Modern Spiritualism is the fact that its precise date of origin is well known and the events of that fateful night were thoroughly documented. The first communicative raps were heard in the farmhouse of one John D. Fox in the town of Hydesville, New York, on March 31, 1848. Shortly after the events, no later than April 12, 1848, one E. E. Lewis, Esq., took depositions from Mr. Fox, Mrs. Fox, and several of their neighbors. While no copies of this pamphlet[3] seem to have survived, in 1850 D. M. Dewey drew heavily on it for his own *History of the Strange Sounds,*[4] and several other Spiritualists quote from Lewis's pamphlet as well.[5] I have collected the data below from the earliest sources available; in every case, these data are reported in more than one source.

Unfortunately, the transition between the first manifestations in the spring of 1848 and the eventual first public demonstration of John Fox's daughters' new-found paranormal abilities, which took place on November 14, 1849,[6] does not seem to have been described so exhaustively. From the evidence that I have been able to amass, it seems that a fundamental change had taken place by the time of this demonstration.[7]

"In December of 1847, one John D. Fox, a farmer by occupation and a Methodist by religious conviction, moved with his family into a small, crude farmhouse in Hydesville," a small hamlet on the outskirts of Newark, in the township of Arcadia, about thirty miles from Rochester, New York.[8] The Foxes had had seven children, six of whom were living in 1848; however, only the youngest two, Margaretta (Margaret) and Catherine (Katie) were living with their parents at the time. An older married sister, Leah Fish, was living in Rochester. Leah was probably born in 1814, making her about thirty-four at the time of the first rappings.[9] The ages of Margaret and Katie are variously reported, but Mrs. Fox's sworn deposition, dated April 11, 1848, puts Katie's age at "about twelve years old" and Margaret's at fifteen.[10]

According to Mrs. Fox's statement, which was countersigned and affirmed by Mr. Fox, the noises were first heard about a fortnight before her deposition, or sometime in the last week of March. Since these events are central to my point, Mrs. Fox's deposition deserves extensive quotation:

> It sounded like some one knocking in the east bedroom, on the floor. Some-times it sounded as if a chair moved on the floor; we could hardly tell where it was. This was in the evening, just after we had gone to bed. The whole family slept in the room together, and all heard the noise. There were four of our family, and some-times five.[11] The first night we heard the rapping we all got up, lit a candle, and searched all over the house. The noise continued while we were hunting, and was

heard near the same place all the time. It was not very loud, yet it produced a jar of the bedsteads and chairs, that could be felt by placing our hands on the chairs, or while we were in bed. It was a feeling of tremulous motion, more than a sudden jar. It seemed if we could hear it jar while we were standing on the floor. It continued this night until we went to sleep. I did not go to sleep until nearly twelve o'clock. The noise continued to be heard every night.[12]

Up to this point there is nothing particularly remarkable about the event; while mysterious knocks are unusual enough in any one family's household, poltergeists have been reported through history from all over the world.[13] However, on March 31, things got more interesting. I continue with Mrs. Fox's deposition:

> On Friday night, we concluded to go to bed early, and not let it disturb us; if it came we though [sic], we would not mind it, but try and get a good night's rest. My husband was here on all these occasions, heard the noise and helped search. It was very early when we went to bed on this night; hardly dark. We went to bed so early, because we had been broken so much of our rest that I was almost sick.
>
> My husband had not gone to bed when we first heard the noise on this evening. I had just laid down. It commenced as usual. I knew it from all other noises I had ever heard in the house. The girls, who slept in the other bed in the room, heard the noise, and tried to make a similar noise by snapping their fingers. The youngest girl is about twelve years old; she is the one who made her hand go. As fast as she made the noise with her hands or fingers, the sound was followed up in the room. It did not sound any different at that time, only it made the same number of noises that the girl did. When she stopped, the sound itself stopped for a short time.
>
> The other girl, who is in her 15th year, then spoke in sport and said, "Now do just as I do. Count one, two, three, four," &c., striking one hand in the other at the same time. The blows which she made were repeated as before. It appeared to answer her by repeating every blow that she made. She only did so once. She then began to be startled; and then I spoke and said to the noise, "count ten," and it made ten strokes or noises. Then I asked the ages of my different children successively, and it gave a number of raps, corresponding to the ages of my children.
>
> I then asked if it was a human being that was making the noise? and if it was, to manifest it by the same noise. There was no noise. I then asked if it was a spirit? and if it was, to manifest it by two sounds. I heard two sounds as soon as the words were spoken. I then asked, if it was an injured spirit? to give me the sound, and I heard the rapping distinctly. I then asked if it was injured in this house? and it manifested it by the noise. If the person was living that injured it? and got the same answer. I then ascertained, by the same method that its remains were buried under the dwelling, and how old it was. When I asked how many years old it was? it rapped 31 times; that it was a male; that it had left a family of five children; that it had two sons and three daughters, all living. I asked if it left a wife? and it rapped. If its wife was then living? no rapping; if she was dead? and the rapping was distinctly heard; how long she had been dead? and it rapped twice.[14]

By all accounts, the Foxes then sent for several of their neighbors, who quizzed the ghost in like manner. They determined that it

> was murdered in the bedroom about five years ago, and that the murder was com-
> mitted by Mr. _____ [sic], on one Tuesday night, at twelve o'clock; that it was
> murdered by having its throat cut with a butcher knife; that the body did not
> remain in the room next day, but was taken down cellar, and that it was not buried
> until the next night; that it was not taken down through an outside door, but
> through the buttery, down the stairway; that it was buried ten feet below the surface
> of the ground.[15]

It was further discerned that the spirit was that of a peddler who had been murdered and robbed of five hundred dollars. Sometime during the investigation someone thought of asking the spirit to spell out its name. "A neighbor began to call off the letters of the alphabet, pausing after each letter for the intelligence initiating the raps to signify the correct ones by knocking. In this manner, the victim of the murder disclosed his name as Charles B. Rosma."[16]

Although various attempts were made to dig up the corpse, none had clear success. The digging in 1848 was stopped at three feet when the hole filled with water. Later that summer, when things had dried out a bit, David Fox (a married son) and some neighbors found some teeth and bones at five feet deep. There was alleged to be a skeleton found in the *walls* of the crumbling house in 1904, but there is no conclusive evidence that the bones found in either 1848 or 1904 were those of a human being. As Burton Gates Brown Jr. points out, "The facts [concerning whether evidence of the murder has been found] . . . leave room for serious doubt."[17]

Although communication with murdered persons is by no means an ordinary experience, every bit of this account fits into a traditional pattern widely reported in Western European and North American folklore. From a poltergeist (motif number F473.5) the rapper has developed into a ghost; the ghost is that of a murdered man haunting the spot where he was killed.[18]

From Ghost to Spirit

At this point the history is that of a haunted house, not unlike the sort found in virtually every neighborhood in the United States; if things had not developed further, the episode in the Fox household would have been just another curiosity. House hauntings do not commonly lead to worldwide religious movements, but this one did. It was not simply because Rosma's ghost provided proof of life after death; after all, Rosma only demonstrated that murdered people live on after death (E410, "The unquiet grave. Dead unable to rest in peace"); this is small consolation to those of us who hope not to be murdered, especially when we consider that the unquiet dead are probably also unhappy. Further, even if Rosma had provided inspiring and optimistic news of the Other Side, Spiritualism could scarcely thrive if communication with the dead could only be undertaken at the spot of Rosma's (or anyone else's) murder and burial. Before Spiritualism could burst upon the world, the ghost had to be freed from tradition. If a ghost is the revenant of a person who met an unhappy end and haunts a certain spot for that reason, ghosts would not do; the ghost had to become a mobile spirit, free of earthly bonds, including the tragedy of its own death.

The evidence from Mrs. Fox's deposition is clear about the characteristics of the first manifestations. The evidence gets a bit more speculative hereafter, having been pieced together at various times by various people and lacking, for the most part, firsthand accounts. It is not possible to follow the further developments in the detail given above in regard to the first rappings; however, the general outlines seem to be well established and adequate to my purpose.

According to Dewey, "when the sounds first began to attract attention, and during the investigation at Hydesville, they were heard in the presence of any member of the Fox family. They were also distinctly and repeatedly heard by persons who were examining the house *when every member of that family was absent*" [emphasis added].[19] That Rosma's ghost would be willing to communicate with anyone, regardless of who was or was not in the house, fits with traditional notions about ghosts.

But then the next phase of the transformation took place: "It was not long, however, before the noises were made more freely in the presence of the two youngest girls."[20] This was the first sign that Katie and Margaret were "mediums," and that mediums were needed to communicate with ghosts. A Spiritualist medium is particularly sensitive to the presence of spirits and serves as a conduit for communication between this world and the other side. Sometimes mediums also provide the physical channel for the messages, through trance-talking or through automatic writing, but the most spectacular mediums merely have to be present for the spirits to make noises of their own, much as a catalyst allows a chemical reaction to take place between two substances without actually entering into the reaction itself.[21] Of course, the idea of communicating with the supernatural world through a human medium was not originated in 1848; Siberian shamans and ancient Hebrew prophets, among others, can both be considered mediums. However, the specific characteristics of a medium in the context of Modern Spiritualism were unique and original, as far as I have been able to determine, and as Spiritualism developed, this particular form of mediumship became formalized and spread rapidly.

Before long, the uproar in their house became too much for the Foxes—between the ghost's noise, which had already been costing them sleep, and the number of curious people invading their home, estimated to be as many as five hundred at times,[22] they were driven out, hoping to leave the ghost behind. The family left the Hydesville farmhouse to move in with David Fox, two miles away. To their surprise, the noises were not confined to the burial spot; the raps followed them. Katie was sent to Rochester with Leah Fish, who had come to investigate the matter.[23] "In Rochester there was such a performance on the first night that no one in the house was able to get to sleep until three or four A.M. Mrs. Fish, deciding that the house was haunted, moved into a new one never before occupied. It made no difference to the spirits and the disturbances continued as before."[24] Mrs. Fish's removal to a previously unoccupied house as a means of escaping the noises indicates that she was still operating under traditional concepts.

By the time of the move to Rochester, the ghost had become a number of nameless spirits; it might have seemed that the Fox sisters themselves were haunted, or plagued by communicative poltergeists. Soon, however, the final revelation came. About a month after Katie Fox and Leah Fish arrived in Rochester, another attempt was made at reciting the alphabet so that the spirit could spell out a message.[25] It told them, "'We are all your dear friends and relatives, Jacob Smith.' Jacob Smith was Mrs. Fish's grandfather."[26]

Now the essential transformation was complete; some elaboration remained to be done, but the framework of Spiritualism was in place. The dead could communicate with the living through a medium, and having died a tragic death was not a prerequisite. *Any* spirit could be summoned from *any* sitting room. These were the qualities essential to making Spiritualism both comforting and compelling, for now people could be assured that their beloved departed were still "alive" and happy, and that the living had solid hope of eternal life. The assurance of a dead stranger is hardly reassuring, but when a spirit claims to be your infant son and correctly answers every test-question you put to it, and when the answers cannot possibly be known by the medium (as happened to the Rev. C. Hammond[27] and in dozens of other similar instances)—when this is the case, belief in the afterlife seems to have been proven empirically.

It took some time for the Spiritualists to begin to interrogate the spirits systematically about the nature of life after death. A great deal of energy was spent trying to prove or disprove that the mediums were frauds, and many questions posed were only designed to confirm the identity of the particular spirit contacted—questions to which the questioner already knew the answer, such as, "How old were you when you died?"

In short, by the time of the Fox sisters' first public demonstration, the traditional qualities which had informed the first manifestations had given way to a set of characteristics that lent themselves to empirical, "scientific" testing; the mediums and the spirits could be tested, results could be compared, data could be verified, and hypotheses proved or disproved.

Within months, Spiritualism was spreading rapidly across the United States, and within years it had spread around the globe. Like Handsome Lake for the Seneca[28] and Ellen Harmon White for the Seventh-Day Adventists,[29] the Fox sisters were in the right place, with the right message, at the right time; they introduced spirit rappings to a world that was hungry for spirit rappings.

The Scholarly Response

I suspect that I have stated the obvious in describing the transformation from traditional ghost beliefs to the now-familiar Spiritualist seance. The question remains why no one has seen fit, as far as I have been able to tell, to make this obvious statement before now. It seems to me that the answer lies in a different understanding of the notion of *origin*. I have argued that Spiritualism originated in traditional ghost beliefs and evolved into something else. But the overwhelming number of commentators on Modern Spiritualism—believers, disbelievers, and objective scholars—have tended to see the origin of Spiritualism *in the raps themselves*. Believers, of course, contend that the raps were evidence of communication with spirits; detractors see the raps as evidence of human fraud (conscious or unconscious).

For almost a hundred years, virtually everything written on Spiritualism was a part of this debate. Commentators on Spiritualism from 1850 to about 1950 fall into two major camps and one minor camp: scoffers, believers, and "scientists." Interestingly, even the scientists tend to focus on the question of whether "the spirit phenomena are genuine or they are perpetrated by fraud."[30]

One of the best-known scoffers was Harry Houdini, who spent a good part of his career medium-bashing.[31] P. T. Barnum included Spiritualism as one of his "humbugs of the world."[32] Likewise, it is clear that the response of much of the general public and of many writers was to wonder how Spiritualists could be so easily duped.

Even scholars with less interest in showmanship than Houdini and Barnum seem eager to dismiss Spiritualism as a mere fraud. The tendency is to demonstrate that the Fox sisters were frauds and, on the basis of this, to conclude that Spiritualism itself is a fraud.[33] Of course, this ignores the salient fact that there were scores, perhaps hundreds, of other mediums in practice by the time the Foxes were discredited.[34] Modern Spiritualism can only be fraudulent if hundreds or thousands of mediums have perpetrated a tremendous, unbroken series of frauds over the last 150 years. Of course this is possible, but it is hardly proved by the assertion that the first two mediums were frauds.[35]

The largest body of literature on Spiritualism is, naturally, by Spiritualists. Some of this literature[36] is overtly concerned only with the beliefs of Spiritualism, but the beliefs are presented in a doctrinal manner, rather than an interpretive one. Most literature by Spiritualists, however, consists largely of anecdotes about the amazing events in the lives of particularly gifted mediums.[37]

There is also a small group who have representatives in both of the major camps, namely those who style themselves scientists. These scholars have tried to discuss the history of Spiritualism even-handedly, but they, too, focus on the question of where the knocks come from.[38] In this respect the scientists enter the Spiritualists' project—the empirical proof of the existence of life after death. Of course, the Spiritualists prove that there *is* life after death and most of the scientists, using the same evidence, conclude that sufficient proof has yet to come forth. There are a few scientists who have been converted to Spiritualism, notably Professor Robert Hare.[39]

Writings on Spiritualism with a primary concern other than the ontological status of the raps did not appear in numbers until recently. In 1958, Katherine H. Porter published the first substantial analytical study of the culture of Spiritualism. Her work "examine[s] the little-known but significant impact of spiritualism on a few men and women of genius [including the Brownings, the Tennysons, Thackeray, and Dickens] in the heyday of the movement. . . . It does not attempt to appraise the belief in spiritualism itself but rather to get at the basis of its hold on these people, to discover by what roads they came to it, and what satisfaction they found in it."[40] Other works that look at Spiritualism as a cultural phenomenon include Howard Kerr's 1972 *Mediums, and Spirit-Rappers, and Roaring Radicals* and Russell M. Goldfarb and Clare R. Goldfarb's 1978 *Spiritualism and Nineteenth-Century Letters*,[41] which discuss the influence of Spiritualism on nineteenth-century American literature; Mary Farrell Bednarowski's 1973 Ph.D. thesis, *Nineteenth-Century American Spiritualism: An Attempt at a Scientific Religion*, Burton Gates Brown Jr.'s 1973 Ph.D. thesis, *Spiritualism in Nineteenth-Century America*, and Geoffrey K. Nelson's 1969 book, *Spiritualism and Society*, which approach Spiritualism as a religion to be understood in its cultural context;[42] Ann Braude's 1989 *Radical Spirits: Spiritualism and Women's Rights in Nineteenth-Century America*[43] and Alex Owen's 1990 *The Darkened Room: Women, Power, and Spiritualism in Late Victorian England*,[44] which look at the place of women in the Spiritualist movement (Braude in the United States, Owen in England); and Logie Barrow's 1986 *Independent*

Spirits: Spiritualism and English Plebians, 1850–1910,[45] which takes up the class issue.

One good explanation for the popularity of Modern Spiritualism is the modernist crisis in religion. As Mary Bednarowski demonstrates, the increasing influence of science in the United States in the nineteenth century was coupled with an increased anxiety about the status of religion. "The result of all this scholarship was a religious skepticism in nineteenth-century man [sic], a gradual inability to believe in either the divine origins of the universe or in the efficacy of adhering to an organized religion."[46] She also argues that:

> Spiritualism represents a concerted, perhaps even a desperate, effort to reconcile science with religion, to supply those suffering from religious skepticism [with] scientific data, [namely] the spirit manifestations, upon which to base their beliefs in an afterlife.[47]

In a similar vein, R. Laurence Moore argues that "over the past 175 years spiritualism and then psychical research have offered Americans a 'reasonable' solution to the problem of how to accommodate religious and scientific interests."[48] As Moore contends, a critical aspect of Spiritualism's popularity in the United States stemmed from its obsession with empiricism.[49]

Empiricism and the Scientific Impulse

Believers in Spiritualism might have been credulous and gullible, but from the very start they were also skeptical. The first time that Mrs. Fox spoke with Rosma's ghost she not only asked it about itself, but she also demanded information from it to test its standing, to try to discover if indeed this were a ghost, and if so what the limits of its knowledge were. All of the other communicants with this ghost did likewise. The tests were not exhaustive, to be sure, and they were not performed in a rigorous fashion, with independent variables held constant and a single dependent variable tested, but the lack of scientific expertise does not belie the presence of a scientific intent.

There have been plenty of reports of communication with the dead through history. What seems unique in the phenomenology of Modern Spiritualism is that the source of the communication, the channel, is obscure. Possessed mystics who speak for gods or spirits still use their own mouths and tongues, if not exactly their own voices; automatic writing requires perfectly mundane paper; the Ouija board depends on the planchette in contact with fleshly hands. But the Spiritualist raps seemed to come from nowhere, and both believers and scoffers agreed that this was the true source of their interest. Spiritualism did not become an occasion for a significant debate over the status of life after death; the afterlife was largely accepted both by Spiritualists and their most vehement detractors. The issue was whether the spirit rappings constituted proof. Empiricism is such a central part of the American worldview that for a hundred years many interesting questions about Spiritualism as a cultural and social phenomenon could not be asked; the searchlight of empiricism left all other issues, such as the relationship between Spiritualism and women or class, and others mentioned above, in the shadows.

The empirical quality of Modern Spiritualism seems to have been the one aspect most focused on by everyone—its believers, its detractors, even its historians. Virtually all arguments about Spiritualism concerned the ontological status of the raps. Where did they come from? Were they the result of fraud, of disembodied spirits, or of psychic abilities of living mediums? Interestingly, both the traditions of belief and the "traditions of disbelief"[50] clustered around Spiritualism agreed on the centrality of empirical evidence. While some Christians ground their religion in unadorned faith and others are converted by a profound but ultimately subjective experience, to the Spiritualists *and* to their detractors the one great truth was empirical evidence; religious authority did not reside in a charismatic leader or in a book or in a church, but in the continued proofs offered at seances. It seems clear that partially due to this shared interest in empiricism, scholarship on Spiritualism, up to the last few years, has basically been a debate about fraud. The traditional belief in place-bound ghosts lent credence to the new idea of mobile spirits who willingly communicated with the living through mediums, with knocks or raps functioning as empirical evidence; in other words, because of the knockings, "belief" moved from possible to probable to provable, and thus to "truth."

It is common to think of "folk beliefs" as beliefs that are wrong, that are not supported by scientific evidence, or that are held by the unlearned.[51] What I have tried to point out is that there is a subtler sense to the notion of folk belief: the sense in which the importance of empiricism in the American worldview is itself a folk belief. Belief in empiricism—experimental method relying upon human observation—is the application of a cultural assumption that is grounded in Western civilization and that is generally part of American worldview (which is not to argue, by the way, that other worldviews are not found in the United States); but empiricism, sounding "scientific," implies veracity. Credulous and incredulous, learned and unlearned, believer and detractor, scholar, historian, scientist—every kind of American has taken for granted that what is most important about Spiritualism is, first and foremost, the source of the "mysterious noises." Both Spiritualist enthusiasts and their detractors seem to have shared this folk belief, that empiricism provides irrefutable evidence of what *is*, and the evidence of our senses constitutes the ultimate authority. It seems that in this regard both believers and unbelievers—at first glance, irreconcilable and fundamentally opposed camps—were engaged in the same enterprise.

Acknowledgments

This is a substantially revised version of a paper originally written for Roger L. Janelli's course, "Folklore and Religion" at Indiana University in December 1987; other versions were presented for the American Studies Program at Indiana University in March 1988 and for the national meeting of the American Folklore Society in Cambridge, Massachusetts, in October 1988. I am indebted to Professor Janelli for his encouragement through several classes and for his insights into folk religion. I would also like to thank Polly Adema, William Hansen, Charles Johannigsmeier, Gail Matthews, David Nordloh, and John Wolford for comments and encouragement. William F. Guinee and Patricia E. Sawin were particularly helpful during the first drafts; Jennifer E. Livesay's advice and patience were invaluable for the latest. I also benefitted from a conversation with Ann Braude. Editorial help from Barbara Walker and John Alley helped the flow of my argument considerably. I am grateful to David H. Smith, Director of the Poynter Center at Indiana University, for supporting the writing of this version through released time.

Endnotes

1. R. Laurence Moore, *In Search of White Crows: Spiritualism, Parapsychology, and American Culture* (New York: Oxford University Press, 1977), 4.

2. Throughout this paper, except in direct quotations, I capitalize the word Spiritualism and occasionally use the phrase Modern Spiritualism to make it clear that I am concerned specifically with one cultural movement, and not with *spiritualism* broadly construed.

3. E. E. Lewis, *A Report of the Mysterious Noises Heard in the House of Mr. John D. Fox* (Canandaigua, New York, 1848).

4. D. M. Dewey, *History of the Strange Sounds or Rappings, Heard in Rochester and Western New-York,* authorized edition (Rochester: D. M. Dewey, 1850).

5. Eliab Wilkinson Capron, *Modern Spiritualism: Its Facts and Fanaticisms, Its Consistencies and Contradictions* (1855; reprint, New York: Arno Press, 1976); Robert Dale Owen, *Footfalls on the Boundary of Another World* (Philadelphia: Lippincott, 1860); Emma Hardinge Britten, *Modern American Spiritualism: A Twenty Years' Record of the Communion between Earth and the World of Spirits* (London: J. Burns, 1869); A. Leah Underhill, *The Missing Link in Modern Spiritualism* (1885; reprint, New York: Arno Press, 1976).

6. Burton Gates Brown Jr., "Spiritualism in Nineteenth-Century America' (Ph.D. diss., Boston University, 1973), 48.

7.   My close scrutiny of the early days of Spiritualism was inspired by Robert P. Weller's distinction between "ideologized" and "pragmatic" beliefs in *Unities and Diversities in Chinese Religion* (Seattle: University of Washington Press, 1987), 7ff. An ideologized system of beliefs is systematized and elaborated, and some attempt has been made to make it exhaustive and logically coherent. Pragmatic beliefs, on the other hand, deal with immediate and practical concerns; they are directed toward solving real and specific problems which are palpable at the moment when the belief or practice is exercised. Established churches create and maintain ideologized beliefs; individuals tend to deal more with pragmatic beliefs. I first sought to find how Spiritualism moved from being "pragmatic" to being "ideologized"; what I found was that Spiritualism has remained pragmatic all along, even as it has been elaborated. However, I would not have noticed Spiritualism's debt to tradition if I had not had this theory in mind.

8.   Brown, 35–36.

9.   Brown, 36–37.

10. Dewey, 15. The youth of the Fox sisters has not gone unremarked; for example, Charles A. Huguenin observes that "it was nine-year-old Elizabeth Parris, eleven-year-old Abigail Williams, twelve-year-old Ann Putnam, and their playmates who pointed accusing fingers at innocent souls in Salem Village as tools of Satan during the witchcraft mania in 1691–2" (Huguenin, "The Amazing Fox Sisters," *New York Folklore Quarterly* 13, no. 4 [1957]: 275).

11. The fifth member might either be Mr. and Mrs. Fox's son, David, who normally lived with his wife and children about two miles away, or Leah Fox Fish's fifteen-year-old daughter Elizabeth Fish (Brown, 37).

12. Capron, 39. Dewey does not quote this part of the deposition, so I am forced to rely on Capron. The parts of the deposition which both Dewey and Capron quote match exactly, except in some small punctuation changes and the statement, "My husband had gone to bed" (Capron, 40) vs. "My husband had *not* gone to bed" (Dewey, 15, emphasis added).

13. Motif F473.5, "Poltergeist makes noises." The motif numbers cited in this chapter are drawn from Stith Thompson's *Motif-Index of Folk Literature* (5 vols., rev. and enl. ed., Bloomington: Indiana University Press, 1966), an index of the narrative units of an astounding number of the folktales, legends, and myths of the world. Thompson sought to index the smallest narrative units capable of surviving in tradition; the motifs are unusual characters or striking incidents that occur in a number of different narratives. As far as this paper is concerned, the important thing about the motif index is that it provides evidence that a given concept or belief is traditional rather than innovative.

14. Dewey, 15–16.

15. Capron, 42.

16. Huguenin, 242.

17. Brown, 40.

18. Some of the motifs which were played out in 1848 were E402.1.5, "Invisible ghost makes rapping or knocking noise"; E334, "Non-malevolent ghost haunts scene of former misfortune, crime, or tragedy"; E334.2.1, "Ghost of murdered person haunts burial spot"; E411.10, "Persons who die violent or accidental deaths cannot rest in grave"; E231, "Return from dead to reveal murder"; and E231.1, "Ghost tells name of murderer." All of these motifs also appear in

Ernest W. Baughman's *Type and Motif-Index of the Folktales of England and North America* (The Hague: Mouton, 1966), along with these interesting additions: E334.2.1(e), "Ghost of murdered peddler seen near burial spot" and E402.1.8(k), "Scraping noise is made by ghost of murdered peddler." Peddlers have often been seen as suspicious characters; see Lewis E. Atherton, "Itinerant Merchandising in the Ante-bellum South," *Bulletin of the Business Historical Society* 19 (1945): 35–59 (my thanks to John Wolford for this reference).

19. Dewey, 19–20.

20. Dewey, 20.

21. This passive participation of the medium inevitably led to linking Spiritualism with Mesmerism; many later mediums had to be "magnetized" before the spirits would communicate through them (see Dewey, p. 21, for one example).

22. Brown, 41.

23. It has often been speculated that the original rappings were merely a prank pulled by Katie and Margaret, and that it was Leah—older, wiser, and more ambitious—who capitalized on the phenomena.

24. Brown, 43.

25. The telegraph was patented in 1840, and the first message was sent using Samuel F. B. Morse's code in 1844. The possibility of long-range communication via a series of taps was obviously of interest to Spiritualists, for "the most widely circulated spiritualist newspaper of the [1850s] was the *Spiritual Telegraph*" (Moore, 13). Perhaps Mrs. Fox's understanding of the telegraph inspired her to make the leap from hearing those first raps as mere noise to hearing them as a potential means of communication. But it is interesting that, as far as I have seen, mediums stuck to the cumbersome method of reciting the alphabet and waiting for the spirit to rap at the proper letter, rather than trying to use Morse code. One explanation is that Morse code is extremely difficult for living people to master (the dead seem to have been assumed to know everything). A skeptic's explanation might be that when the questioner recites the alphabet, at least halfway expecting a specific message to be spelled out (such as the name of her departed infant son), she gives subtle nonverbal cues when the expected letter is reached, thereby tipping the medium off on when to rap. This is known as the Clever Hans phenomenon—see Oskar Pfungst, *Clever Hans: The Horse of Mr. Von Osten*, ed. Robert Rosenthal, trans. Carl L. Rahn (1911; reprint, New York: Holt, Rinehart and Winston, 1965).

26. Brown, 44.

27. Dewey, 29.

28. Anthony F. C. Wallace, *The Death and Rebirth of the Seneca* (New York: Vintage Books, 1969).

29. Jonathan M. Butler, "Prophecy, Gender, and Culture: Ellen Gould Harmon [White] and the Roots of Seventh-Day Adventism," *Religion and American Culture: A Journal of Interpretation* 1 (1991): 3–29.

30. Mary Farrell Bednarowski, "Nineteenth-Century American Spiritualism: An Attempt at a Scientific Religion" (Ph.D. diss., University of Minnesota, 1973), 6.

31. Harry Houdini, *A Magician among the Spirits* (New York: Harper and Brothers, 1924).

32. P. T. Barnum, *The Humbugs of the World* (New York: Carleton Publishers, 1866). I should also note that devoted Spiritualists readily admit to fraud when

it is demonstrated, but they also consistently point to seances and phenomena which have not been shown to have a materialistic explanation as proof for their beliefs.

33. See, for example, Huguenin, 1957; and Rossell Hope Robbins, "The Rochester Rappings," *Dalhousie Review* 45 (1965): 153–164.

34. The Fox sisters were discredited, with varying degrees of success, at least three times. In February 1851, three medical doctors claimed that the sisters produced the raps by cracking their knees (Brown, 57–59); in April of the same year, Mrs. Norman Culver, a relative by marriage to the Foxes, signed a sworn affidavit claiming that the sisters had attempted to enlist her aid in producing spirit phenomena (Brown, 62–63); and in 1888, Reuben Briggs Davenport published *The Death-Blow to Spiritualism* (1888; reprint, New York: Arno Press, 1976), which contains the confessions of both Katie and Margaret that they, and not spirits, had created the first phenomena. The first two discreditings only served to publicize Spiritualism; by the time of the last one, Spiritualism was past its prime and there were enough mediums other than the Fox sisters by then that it could not kill the movement. Even the last confession is open to question; by that time both Margaret and Katie were poor and alcoholic, and Margaret later recanted—see Earl Wesley Fornell, *The Unhappy Medium: Spiritualism and the Life of Margaret Fox* (Austin: University of Texas Press, 1964).

35. For the latest example of the Spiritualism-as-fraud approach, see Ruth Brandon, *The Spiritualists: The Passion for the Occult in the Nineteeth and Twentieth Centuries* (New York: Knopf, 1983). Compared to many scoffers, Brandon is not scalding in her critique; she handles her subject with a good sense of humor, though at the expense of Spiritualists. Earlier and more vituperative scoffers include Davenport 1976 [1888]; and John Bovee Dods, *Spirit Manifestations Examined and Explained: Judge Edmonds Refuted* (New York: DeWitt and Davenport, 1854).

36. See, for example, Peggy Barnes, *The Fundamentals of Spiritualism* (Chesterfield, IN: Psychic Observer Book Shop, n.d.).

37. See, for example, Maurice Barbanell, *This Is Spiritualism* (London: Spiritualist Press, 1959); Britten, *Nineteenth Century Miracles: Spirits and Their Work in Every Country of the Earth* (1884; reprint, New York: Arno Press, 1976); Capron, *Modern Spiritualism*; Arthur Conan Doyle, *The History of Spiritualism*, 2 vols. (New York: George H. Doran, 1926); and Underhill, *The Missing Link.*

38. See particularly Frank Podmore, *Modern Spiritualism: A History and a Criticism*, 2 vols. (London: Methuen, 1902), cited as the "best available history of spiritualism in general and of the early American years in particular" by Howard Kerr in *Mediums, and Spirit-Rappers, and Roaring Radicals: Spiritualism in American Literature, 1850–1900* (Urbana, IL: University of Chicago Press, 1972), 3.

39. Robert Hare, *Experimental Investigation of the Spirit Manifestations* (New York: Partridge and Brittan, 1855).

40. Katherine H. Porter, *Through a Glass Darkly: Spiritualism in the Browning Circle* (Lawrence: University Press of Kansas, 1958), vii.

41. Russell M. Goldfarb and Clare R. Goldfarb, *Spiritualism and Nineteenth-Century Letters* (London: Associated University Presses, 1978).

42. Geoffrey K. Nelson, *Spiritualism and Society* (New York: Schocken Books, 1969). Bednarowski and Brown (each cited earlier) limit their consideration to

America, but Nelson also considers the spiritualist movement after it was imported to England. Nelson makes the point that in the middle of the nineteenth century, the United States in general and upstate New York in particular were characterized by rapid and massive social and geographic mobility. Nelson argues that this fluidity and instability brought about the rise of Modern Spiritualism, as well as the other new religions of the "burned over district." As Barre Toelken pointed out to me, this same mobility no doubt made the idea of mobile, transportable spirits appealing; we might have to leave our graveyards behind, but we can take our ancestors with us.

43. Ann Braude, *Radical Spirits: Spiritualism and Women's Rights in Nineteenth-Century America* (Boston: Beacon Press, 1989).

44. Alex Owen, *The Darkened Room: Women, Power, and Spiritualism in Late Victorian England* (Philadelphia: University of Pennsylvania Press, 1990).

45. Logie Barrow, *Independent Spirits: Spiritualism and English Plebians, 1850–1910* (London: Routledge and Kegan Paul, 1986).

46. Bednarowski, 27.

47. Bednarowski, 20.

48. Moore, xii. See also Janet Oppenheim, *The Other World: Spiritualism and Psychical Research in England, 1850–1914* (Cambridge: Cambridge University Press, 1985), for the interrelationship between Spiritualism and psychical research.

49. Of course, Modern Spiritualism was not the only popular fad in the nineteenth century to fill this need; consider Christian Science, Mesmerism, and Seventh-Day Adventism.

50. David J. Hufford, "Traditions of Disbelief," *New York Folklore* 8 (1982): 47–55. See also Hufford's essay in this volume.

51. Kenneth D. Pimple, "Folk Beliefs," in *The Emergence of Folklore in Everyday Life: A Fieldguide and Sourcebook*, ed. George H. Schoemaker (Bloomington, IN: Trickster Press, 1990).

5

Aftermath of a Failed Seance: The Functions of Skepticism in a Traditional Society

Maxine Miska

I REMEMBER HEARING A STORY ONCE ABOUT AN ATHEIST RIDING ON A BUS WHO said, "God, if you really exist, make a rainbow appear in the sky right now." Suddenly, a rainbow appeared. The atheist remarked, "What a coincidence! A rainbow!"

Belief in the supernatural or the transcendent is clearly not simply the result of one's experiences. Belief systems provide the *a priori* interpretations for experience. The belief system persists, as though carried along by its own inertia, even if events occur which appear to subvert it.

I had the opportunity to witness the vitality and durability of a supernatural belief system under duress when I observed a seance ritual that ended in failure. Why study a failure? The investigation of an unsuccessful ritual—unsuccessful in the participants' own terms—allows us to look beyond a generalized description of ritual as a preprogrammed series of events and to approach it as an essentially unpredictable performance contingent upon the actions and competencies of all the participants.[1] The deceptively close fit between performance of a ritual, belief in the religious system associated with the ritual, and the coherence of individual motivations are broken apart when that ritual fails. The participants give voice to their disappointed expectations and make explicit the criteria by which the ritual and the ritual practitioner are evaluated.[2] They also articulate the disparate motivations—not all of which include belief in the ritual—that brought them to the ritual setting. Finally, in the situation of failure we can examine the belief system under attack and observe what sort of defenses might be marshalled to bolster it. In fact, it is precisely in the evaluation of the ritual performance that the resilience of a belief system is found: the failure of a ritual does not directly implicate the belief system. The responsibility may rest with the competence of the performers and the circumstances of the performance.

Hakka Seances

In Taiwan I observed several seances held in a rural Chinese family in the Hakka-speaking area of the island.[3] The Hakka people originated in north central China and over the centuries migrated gradually to southeastern China and over to Taiwan. They have formed a distinct language group wherever they have lived, and they are very conscious of their cultural distinctiveness. The Hakka people are enthusiastic students of their own history and traditions. They have a Hakka historical society and a magazine of Hakka culture and history. They welcomed my interest and saw it as a means of acquainting more Westerners with their history. While I had intended to study some of the genres they had recorded in their publications, such as folk songs and proverbs, I found myself concentrating on learning about the rituals of death. I frankly was overwhelmed by the importance accorded the dead by the Hakka and the place reserved for them in everyday life.

The seance I will be discussing was held for a woman I will call Tshia Mui-moi, the eighty-six-year-old family matriarch who had died forty-nine days earlier. The seance did not succeed in the participants' eyes, because the spirit medium was not possessed by the dead woman and the dead woman's spirit did not return to speak to her relatives. At the time of the seance, I had been living with the Tshia family for one year and had taken on the role and title of adopted daughter. I had participated in all the funeral rituals and was expected to be present at the seances (where I participated by lighting incense and calling for the spirit to return).

To understand the significance of a seance in traditional Chinese culture, it is necessary first to be familiar with the principles of the family system. A traditional Chinese family is multigenerational and patrilineal. Men and their sons continue to live in the same family compound, while daughters move out and are buried with their husband's families. The matriarch for whom our seance was performed was the last remaining representative of her generation. She was the head of the family consisting of her sons and their wives, her grandsons and their wives, and her great-grandchildren. At the time of her death, she lived with her third son, Tshia Yen-hong, and the seance took place in his living room.

In a traditional Chinese family, death is not a dissolution of the bonds between living and dead, but rather a transformation. Living and dead continue as one interdependent system, where the living provide the dead with prayers and sacrifices to ensure their comfort in the afterlife. After death, family members become ancestors who continue their nurturing function as protective spirits. In this system, it is the obligation of the living to produce descendants to honor and worship the dead, and the duty of the dead to protect and ensure the prosperity of the family. If the dead are unhappy or uncomfortable, the good fortune of the family may suffer. It is therefore important for the family to keep in contact with the dead; the seance is one of the most explicit and elaborate forms of communicating with departed family members. Seances are performed for both men and women as an expected part of the mourning rituals, though they may also be performed at other times if there are unexplained misfortunes in the family. The first opportunity to perform a seance is forty-nine days after death, when the departed soul has passed through the seven gates of the underworld. (The next prescribed opportunities are 100 days after the death and at the first anniversary of the death.)

Hakka seances always employ a female medium who is either totally or partially blind. The medium is not personally known by the family and is (allegedly) unfamiliar with the history of the family. She usually comes from a settlement ten to twenty miles away. There are significant reasons for these conditions: the medium must have no way of knowing about the family except through her supernatural powers. The precautions of finding a stranger and preventing her from gaining any information about the family before the seance are deemed essential. The Hakka seance does not involve manifestations of supernatural power familiar in Western popular culture, such as levitating tables or ectoplasm. The supernatural aspect of the seance derives from the medium's ability to be convincingly possessed by the spirit of the deceased person and to speak with that person's memory and experience.

The efficacy, or *lin,* of the spirit medium is measured by her knowledge of personal, private affairs and her ability to realistically present them in the voice of the deceased relative. The family is wary of mundane sources of information reaching the medium. They try to restrict her access to information about the family, in order to ensure that her knowledge can come only through her supernatural abilities—that she cannot fake her spirit possession by accruing gossip about their family and pretending that the information came from the spirit world. The participants themselves are acutely aware of the possibility of being duped. The family hopes that they will be involved in a ritual to contact their departed ancestor, yet they realize that the medium, while appearing to participate in the same actions, may give them a performance that is theatrical rather than supernatural—a "fabrication," in Erving Goffman's terms, in which it is "the intentional effort of one or more individuals to manage activity so that a party of one or more others will be induced to have a false belief about what is going on."[4] Family members therefore maintain a critical stance and closely scrutinize the medium's performance.

A corollary of this circumspection is that the invocation of the ritual frame does not automatically provide access to the supernatural domain for the participants: they need to be convinced. At the beginning of the seance, the belief of the participants is stratified into varying degrees of skepticism. There are some who may believe in the existence of life after death but who doubt the capacity of the living to reach the dead. There are those who believe in the traditional system of sacrifices, but who doubt the abilities of mediums to be possessed by the dead. And there are those who believe that the dead can be reached by some mediums, but not necessarily the medium in front of them. Finally, there are those who believe in the medium they have invited, and who trust that she will bring their ancestor home to speak. Thus, in looking at a ritual we cannot take for granted that the participants all believe in what they are doing or that they have the same degree of belief, nor that in participating in the ritual they have suspended their critical viewpoints. A spectrum of beliefs is present at this ritual, and whatever social meaning can be extracted from the concerted actions of ritual, individual orientations remain quite disparate.

The Seance That Failed

The medium came by taxi at the appointed time, accompanied by a young girl who acted as her eyes, and a ceremonial lunch was served. The medium then retired to rest and meditate. A card table and stool were set up for the medium in the center of the room, with chairs and couches arranged around it. About thirty people were present. In addition to relatives from the city, there were several of host Tshia Yen-hong's social and political friends, including the mayor of the town. The medium, a rather fierce and unpleasant woman who responded gruffly to the family's polite overtures, sat down at the card table and set up an altar. The altar consisted of three bowls of tea, a bowl of rice wine, a can of raw rice with an egg in it, two candles, a bag of cookies, and a pyramid of oranges. These were used as offerings to the various intermediary spirits involved in the seance. There were also divination sticks (used in fortune-telling) in a cylindrical container, which the medium placed on the table and took back with her when she departed.[5]

The seance began with some Sanskrit chants unintelligible to the audience. Then the medium inquired informally about the name of the person the family wished to reach, the date and time of death, and which member of the household was hosting the seance. This promoted some discussion because it is traditional for the eldest living son, as the head of his generation, to be the host of the seance. But the host in this case was Tshia Yen-hong, the third son, who was probably richer and certainly more aggressive and well-connected than his brothers. After these facts had been established, the medium asked for the name of a daughter-in-law and a daughter. The medium then requested that the family light incense sticks and place them in the doorway, while she herself faced the direction of the matriarch's grave in order to invite the spirit to come.

A more formal interrogation then began, with the medium presenting information and asking whether it corresponded to the situation of the dead person they were seeking to contact. This began with a repetition of the information gathered just before, but went on to establish which relatives were alive and which were dead—in other words, to make a representation of the entire family, spanning the domain of the living and the domain of the dead. The medium also introduced a specialized fortune-telling vocabulary to elucidate the living and dead relatives, referring to males as white flowers and females as red flowers. (In order to ascertain whether she had found the proper soul, the medium checked the number of flowers on a plant in a garden in a supernatural plane of existence. The correct soul had been located if the plant had the correct number of white and red flowers, corresponding to the information about the number of family members she had received from the audience.)

The medium then asked members of the family to invite the dead person home by going out and lighting incense as they called her name. The medium sat at the table with her head on her folded arms, whispering to intermediary spirits and addressing the family, sometimes almost sobbing with the intensity of her concentration. At the end of this procedure, the medium said that the dead person was not willing to come. After some argument, the family persuaded the medium to try again, in case there had been some error in the elucidation of living and dead relatives. The entire interrogation sequence was then repeated. During this process the family became more and more tense and anxious. Members of the family went out to light incense and invite the dead person to come. Divination blocks were thrown by a family member to determine that the matriarch's spirit was on her way home.[6] But the medium told the family to wait until the matriarch had been dead for 100 days. The medium said she was unable to find the soul and resisted further entreaties from the family. When the family was unwilling to concede that the ritual had failed, the medium gathered up her things and stomped out into the road.

The Aftermath of the Seance

After the medium's precipitous departure, the men and women gathered in the living room and relaxed into informal discussion. Tshia Khiuk-fa, granddaughter of Tshia Mui-moi and eldest daughter of Tshia Yen-hong, sat in the front room of the house with the men, while the rest of the women retired to the back kitchen, which is really an enclosed back yard where the chicken coops are.[7] The men and women in different ways discussed the seance that had just occurred. The men exchanged personal experience narratives arguing about their encounters with spirits; the women, from a much less skeptical stance, gossiped about the medium and discussed other affairs.

The men were served coffee, rather than tea. Coffee is an imported, expensive-status, Western drink given to worldly guests—a gesture of both hospitality and generosity on that day; it also constituted a meta-statement distancing the male guests, such as the mayor and other officials, from the traditional event they had just taken part in. In the front room, the mayor gave his opinion of seances and fortune-tellers:

> *Mayor:* I have never believed in this spirit medium stuff. When she divines, she always brings an extra person to find out about the host family's names.
> *Khiuk-fa* [Yen-hong's daughter]: I tried to keep you [everyone] from speaking [the names], but you still did.
> *Tshia Yen-hong:* You should arrange it so that when she comes, say there is no place for her to sit and that no one should talk to her.
> *Mayor:* She [ambiguous] had no way. Perhaps it had something to do with my official position.
> *Khiuk-fa:* The mayor's position is quite high! [laughing]
> *Tshia Yen-hong:* Every time the mayor came, he went to the bed to help her [the matriarch, Tshia Mui-moi, prior to her death] get up. She welcomed him very much. And you can't say she did not recognize him [i.e., she would not have been shy to appear in front of the mayor].[8]

The mayor said that the spirit medium worked her deception by overhearing the normal kinship terms used in conversation and incorporating them into her monologue. The matriarch's granddaughter said that she tried to keep everyone from mentioning these names. Tshia Yen-hong added that they should have kept the medium isolated. The mayor then suggested that the failure had something to do with his official rank. His ambiguous *she* was referring to the spirit medium's fear of performing in front of official authorities, but Tshia Yen-hong took his comment differently, suggesting that the spirit, the matriarch, knew the mayor and would not have been afraid of appearing in his presence.

The ambiguity of interpretation in this exchange is significant. First of all, it relates to the ambiguity of voice, two spirits inhabiting the same body: the spirit medium's own spirit and that of the matriarch. Second, it highlights two different strata of belief. The mayor's statement is: "The spirit medium was afraid because of his official position." Tshia Yen-hong's interpretation is: "Mother couldn't be afraid because she was familiar with the mayor." The mayor does not believe in the veracity of any aspect of the seance event. Tshia Yen-hong is merely disputing the mayor's presence as a cause for the spirit's unwillingness to return; Tshia Yen-hong is not disputing the possibility of the spirit's returning. Tshia Yen-hong's rationale turned on a public/private distinction: although the mayor is a public figure, the spirit knew him in an intimate home setting and would have recognized him.

The mayor then described why he thought the seance was a fake:

My mother had a seance [performed for her]. I did not attend. That was a fake. I did not attend. Today I attended. I wanted to hear and see [for myself] if it was nonsense. I wanted to see whether she spoke or not.

When the medium arrives she has to sleep. Your surroundings are excellent. That little girl, when she hears the names [of the family], she tells her immediately. . . .

Now as for that person from Hok-e-kong [the spirit medium's village], my sister married into Hok-e-kong, and she has observed this medium when she did fortune-telling. Inevitably, as soon as she arrived, she had to sleep. But she did not sleep. Her ears were pricked up listening. Afterwards she calls a name, she calls you uncle. You have to analyze it. She waits until he has to talk and then she can call out the names. But whether or not old people have souls, I don't know, but I do not believe in this. Why? This afternoon when she had her head resting on the table, when you mentioned something she might use, you immediately stopped [yourself], so she had no way [to gain the information she needed].[9]

The mayor stated outright that he did not believe in spirit mediums. He felt that during the section of the ritual event when the spirit medium is supposed to rest and meditate, she actually gains the information she needs by overhearing conversations among the family. He based his opinion on his sister's observations of this particular medium. He felt that the seance failed because the family was sufficiently vigilant in preventing the leakage of the information the medium required to proceed with her charade. In other words, the family was successful in segregating the channels of communication, so that any information the medium obtained would have to have come from the spirit world rather than from incidental conversation. The mayor was careful to qualify his statement in one regard: he could not say whether or not old people have souls, but he said the spirit mediums were not a way to prove that they do.

Tshia Yen-hong countered with a story concerning why he believed that spirits could return. He did not respond directly to whether seances were fakes, but talked about how the spirit of his mother had returned. He began the story, "Now I'll tell you the truth. My daughter that day. Two days ago?" His daughter took up the narrative, since it happened to her:

> Three days ago. I returned here and slept in my grandmother's room. My mother had gone up to Taipei, and no one else was sleeping there, just myself. She was dead one-and-a-half months. Until today, on the seventh of the sevens [the forty-ninth day of mourning], we haven't heard a sound from her once. Oh, yes, I forgot. The third day after she died, I heard the sound of slippers. My sister and my mother slept [in the matriarch's bed], mother on the outside and I in the middle. My mother heard it and nudged me. I heard it and nudged my sister. The three of us. My sister said, "I heard it." The sound went up into the bed. When grandfather died I didn't hear anything at all. Three days ago, ah-oh, my body was uncomfortable. When I finished washing the rice I went to bed to lay down a while. My bed has white sheets—pure white. If I had sand in it, I could see it. I lay down. I thought, "At 11:00 I must go and cook." My head felt dizzy as I was working. When the food was just done, the children hadn't returned [from school], so I thought I would put it over there. I covered it up. I thought I would go in [to the bedroom] and then, as soon as I entered, how could there be sand—how could there be two rows of sand. I thought that it was strange. I cooked lunch, and the children were not there. The littler ones would not dare enter. When I am staying at home, the children would not enter grandmother's room, because I am sleeping there and they are afraid that I would yell at them. They will not dare enter and play. I thought it strange. I asked A-mimi [a small child], "Did you bring any children into auntie's room? Did you play in great-grandmother's room?" She said, "No, no!" It was really not the children. I was there cooking. I was sitting. I saw it clearly. No child entered. My aunt said, "It surely was some children entering." I did not eat. I went in and slept to dawn. At 5:50 in the morning my mother arose to cook. My father got up to write a letter. How did I sleep on? Just awakening, I extended my foot and touched sand. I quickly turned over and called mother—"See, my bed is so sandy. Last night I bathed quite clean."[10]

Her father took up the story, to corroborate and to continue to rule out any possibilities other than the return of the matriarch's spirit:

> *Tshia Yen-hong:* I got up at 5:30 to write a letter, and was called by her. I could not finish my letter.
> *Daughter:* My father and mother entered to see it. I said, "Look, how can there be sand here?" My father said, "Is it your pants leg?" I said, "Yesterday I washed my feet clean. I change my clothing every day. How can there be sand?"
> *Tshia Yen-hong:* She called me to see. The sand wasn't powdery. It was really sand. [It was not just dirt from the courtyard, but sand brought by the spirit walking home.]

Daughter: The children get up at 5:00 or 6:00, but how can there be children [in the room] at midnight?
Guest: Impossible.
Daughter: That's what I say. I saw sand. I just awoke and stretched out my foot. My bed was sandy. I thought, strange. I got up and turned back the cover, and I saw the sand. I quickly ran and said, "Look how grandmother is playing tricks on me." That month or so there were not events like this, she didn't frighten me.[11]

The event described in this passage is the discovery by the eldest daughter of Tshia Yen-hong of sand on the sheets at the foot of the bed. She and her father examined and eliminated normal explanations of the sand deposit, such as children climbing on the bed and sand left in a cuff of her pants, and decided that the sand could only have been left by the matriarch, walking in disembodied form back to her bed, and perhaps, though it was never stated, leaving some residue of the grave.

The perambulation of the spirit through its former abode is an expected occurrence.[12] Sometimes ashes are deliberately left on the floor to capture the footprints of the invisible revenant. The story embedded in the daughter's recounting of the incident is a version of this, where the sound of slippers worn about the household was heard at night. The embedding of this story in her narrative was not merely a thematic variation on the return of the dead. It was a reminder to the audience that walking of the dead through the home is an expected occurrence and thus a reasonable way to explain the sand. Signs or artifacts of the spirit's return are anticipated. This explanation that the dead will walk through the household was combined with the principle that uses the elimination of channels or explanations to pinpoint supernatural occurrences.

The mayor replied with this story:

My wife is very sensitive. One evening she wanted to go downstairs because my mother had died. [She thought she heard something.] She went down and there wasn't anything. I lit incense and said [to my mother], "If you return, you should speak with me. I will wait for you here. Don't scare the children." The first time I said, "Don't scare Curly [a small child's nickname]. I'll come down to meet you." One night I was waiting. I didn't feel like sleeping so I went downstairs to sleep. I said, "If you return speak with me, don't scare Curly." Because my mother loved Curly the best. Afterwards I fell asleep on the couch, but I never saw anything.[13]

The mayor's strategy, as in so many stories of encounters between living and dead, was to channel or manage the interaction; in this case, to divert the encounter from a child to himself. These stories show that encounters with the dead are frightening, even though they are anticipated and officially one should not be afraid of one's ancestor. The mayor viewed his request as a sort of test, and his mother's failure to respond implied his skepticism about departed spirits returning to the family circle. There is a sort of irony here: the mayor, who by his own testimony was skeptical about fortune-telling and the return of the dead, nevertheless went through all the traditional actions such as lighting incense, talking to his dead mother at her altar, and requesting her aid. We see here an instance of the complex relationship between tradition and belief, and the capacity of traditional systems to accommodate a wide range of motives and stances.[14]

Tshia Yen-hong countered with another story about the dead returning to their home:

> I went to a meeting in Taizhung [a city about two hours away]. I lit incense and said, "Mother, I have to go to Taizhung for a meeting; perhaps I won't return until tomorrow morning." After lighting incense, I left. That night, I stayed in Taizhung. The second night I returned. All my grandchildren were calling, "Grandpa . . ." All were calling me, [so I forgot] and didn't light incense to say I had returned. I went upstairs to sleep. As soon as I went upstairs and lay down, an odor came. I thought it strange. I returned and did not light incense. [He imagines his mother saying,] "You didn't tell me [that you returned]. You left and were gone two days." I thought in my heart, "Mother, when I returned I forgot to light incense. Tomorrow I'll light incense." The odor then left.[15]

This story was a direct counter to the mayor's story. Tshia Yen-hong lit incense, the signal marker for communication with the dead, and left his message. He forgot to mark his return by lighting incense, and the spirit returned to seek him out—probably to see if he had returned, and perhaps as a rebuke. The nature of the odor was not specified, but possibly it had to do with the smell of death or the grave.[16] Had the odor been incense, he certainly would have said so. The mayor's response was a joking rejoinder, "Tonight I must creep home [in fear]." Tshia Yen-hong then told another story similar to the one above:

> At twilight, about 5:00 or 6:00 o'clock, I used to sit here. She sat there [his mother, while alive]. In this way we used to chat. As I sat there [after her death], what happened? A smell came. A smell came. No sound. Usually she sat there, and I sat here. So I got up and said, "Mother, sit down. Please sit here." Immediately the odor left. And then somebody came in and plopped himself down, and that odor— whoosh—returned again. I wanted to make him get up, to say that my mother is sitting there. I was embarrassed, so I got up and went to the back of the house.[17]

This story was similar to the preceding story in that it chronicled the continuing relations between living and dead, and the gradual shift of the recently dead to remote ancestorhood. But there was an important difference. In the first, an odor is present, and Tshia Yen-hong identified it as the presence of his dead mother and treated her as he would have when she was alive. In the second story, he again was aware of his mother's presence through the unusual odor, and he invited her to sit in her usual seat. The important difference is that she was perceptible only to him; other people did not know she was present. In fact, the other person entering the room sat on his mother, and Tshia Yen-hong was too embarrassed to explain. Thus, in the second story, he subtly pointed out that failure to appear to one person is not proof of the spirit's inability to return—again countering the mayor's narrative.

The stories told by Tshia Yen-hong and the mayor differed not only in their attitude toward encounters with the dead, but in the type of encounter as well. In the mayor's stories, contact with the dead was initiated and controlled by the living; in Tshia Yen-hong's stories the dead chose the circumstances and nature of contact. The two men were approaching the issue from different viewpoints regarding the boundary between the domain of the living and the domain of the dead.

Another noteworthy and perhaps related characteristic of the men's conversation was its unresolved quality. Neither side was convinced by the other's arguments. Each had related stories about personal encounters or non-encounters with the dead, but while the stories were used as arguments, they retained their personal, local jurisdiction and did not impose their conclusions on other stories.

While the mayor introduced an element of skepticism into the front-room conversation, the women's conversation in the kitchen yard was shaped by a greater degree of belief. In contrast to the men, the women did not question the validity of the seance, but focused instead on why the seance was a failure. They offered the following explanation for the outcome of the seance: The number of strange men present—armed with sharp objects such as rulers and pens in their pockets—scared off the spirit, and it was threatened with the possibility of being snagged upon a pen protruding from someone's pocket. This explanation was a condensed, symbolic description of what the women felt happened. The seance was supposed to be private. It was a family affair involving matters known only to the family and should have been attended only by family members. The host had invited the town mayor and friends of his who were prominent in local politics. The audience, then, transformed a private event into a public one, and thus undermined the event itself.

In addition, seances are not part of local orthodox religion. The seances are run by women, working independently of any official religious structure or hierarchy. The spirit mediums are the only females employed in this mourning process. The other, more orthodox ritual specialists are male Buddhist monks and Taoist shamans. Therefore, the seances are anti-structural, not only in the sense that normal boundaries of everyday life are breached, but also in the sense that they are in contrast to the orthodox funeral rites of the male-dominated religious structure.[18]

These non-kin males present at the seance had breached the appropriate boundaries for participation in the seance. They made a public event out of a private one, and they brought their structural, official capacities into an anti-structural event.[19] This rending of boundaries was identified symbolically by the women, who said that these men had frightened the spirit from approaching. In this explanation, several distinctions were condensed into one symbol: the pen. The writing brush is an implement of disclosure of information, and in Chinese culture it is associated with scholar–officials. Male/female, official/unofficial (what is more official than a pen?), and public/private were clearly juxtaposed.[20]

From the women's perspective, the male host had used the seance as a social occasion to invite some of his prominent friends to a banquet and spectacle, but in doing so, he undermined the seance. The spirit medium did not dare perform in front of the local government. In addition, the skepticism and wariness that are normally a part of the seance confrontation were magnified by the inclusion of non-relatives who had no emotional stake in finding the soul.

The women interpreted the medium's pronouncement that it was too early to call the spirit to mean that the matriarch was still undergoing her judgment in the underworld. Without anyone explicitly stating that they have heeded the spirit medium's advice, the women began to make plans to engage at a later date another medium, one they felt would do a better job.

Tshia Yen-hong's eldest daughter joined the women and retold her story about the sand in her bed, but this time she added an important evaluative comment to her rendition: She had wanted to see if the medium would mention the occurrence, but the medium did not—a further instance of the medium's lack of efficacy. Like the men, the women evaluated the medium and pronounced her performance inadequate, but rather than having their belief shaken, the women agreed upon remedial steps: a different spirit medium, a less precipitous date, a setting more amenable to the spirit's return—one without a large audience of men.[21]

It might seem that the skepticism of the men and the persistence of the women reflect a traditional belief system in transition, eroding under the pressure of Westernization. The skepticism expressed by some of the men might appear to result from the rapid influx of Western culture in Taiwan, to which men have more access than older, rural women. In fact, this dichotomy between the skepticism of men and the belief by women is historically present in traditional Chinese society. In part, the men's position derives from the traditional orthodox Confucian distaste for spiritualism, but it is also related to the fact that the seance is a heterodox ceremony, during which a woman's point of view is foregrounded. In the nineteenth century, de Groot described the same male skepticism toward the women spirit mediums of Amoy. (Amoy, a Hokkien-speaking area, shares the same culture as the majority population of Taiwan and has many similarities with Hakka ritual practice.) De Groot notes that sometimes the seance is held in private female chambers, "should the presence of the stronger sex not be desired. Scepticism exercises an obstructive effect on spiritualism and of scepticism menfolk are the only representatives; indeed, *li teh khan bong,* 'you are bringing up the dead,' is among them a common expression almost equivalent to 'you are telling either idle tales or falsehoods.'"[22]

The Functions of Skepticism

If skepticism seems to be an ongoing part of the traditional system, rather than an attack upon it or an erosion of it, is it possible to speculate upon the function of skepticism? Two related notions are evident: the evaluation of the spirit medium's performance, that is, her *lin* or efficacy, and skepticism about the ability of spirit mediums to contact departed relatives.

The ideas are related in terms of the criteria employed in making both assessments. The participants tried to eliminate all other possible explanations or channels of communication to ensure that the medium could not have gained information from outside sources; they took care through their own circumspect behavior to avoid unintentionally leaking information; and they based their evaluation of the spirit medium's efficacy on the fact that only the dead person (and not the medium) could have known the information. In a similar fashion, when recounting personal experience narratives, they sought explanations in the domain of the living for alleged contacts with the dead. For example, they tried to eliminate a supernatural explanation for the sand in the bed by considering a natural reason, such as sand in cuffs, or children playing in the bed. Even when natural reasons were discounted, there were many who were not convinced of a visitation. It is a short step from the evaluative stance that the family took regarding the performance of the medium to the skepticism that is necessary to ensure that they are receiving the genuine article, skepticism that eliminates non-supernatural explanations for possible supernatural events.

In this religious tradition, skepticism has a long history as an evaluative technique. At the most general level, skepticism and divergence of opinion are characteristic of a complex society like China, where varieties of religion and religious interpretation arise from the same philosophical substratum. Historically, the Chinese have not found the need for a monolithic system of belief or religion. Filial piety can be interpreted in the Confucian sense as respect for one's parents, elders, and ruler without close attention to the intricacies of the afterlife, but it also can be extended to include the complicated clan-based worship, elaborate geomancy, and double burial, characteristic of southeastern China.

In addition to its evaluative function, skepticism serves as a check on the power of mediums vis-à-vis the array of other techniques used to communicate with the dead (such as divination), which are less explicitly articulated than the seance, require more interpretation by the participants, and thus grant the participants more control over what is said. In throwing divining blocks (a popular form of home-based divination), a family asks questions and receives negative or positive answers; the content of the interaction is selected by the family. In contrast, the communication of a medium with the dead is more elaborated and explicit: the questions are asked by the spirit medium and the topics for discussion are decided by the spirit when she returns. The relative completeness of this form of conversation with the dead—as opposed to open-ended, vague, oracular phrases, which are amenable to extensive interpretation—gives the medium tremendous power over the family, since it is difficult not to do what she explicitly commands. The skeptical stance serves as a check upon this power; it reinserts the possibility of interpretation by the family, allowing them to reframe the ritual as a possible deception.

The existence of skepticism is not an indication of the decay of tradition, nor is the function of skepticism to destroy the seance ritual or belief in the supernatural; rather, its function is to keep the ritual and the belief in check. In a belief system where the living and the dead are significantly interdependent, the mediators of a ritualized relationship between them can be extremely powerful. In addition, male skepticism about seances counters the woman-controlled nature of the seance ritual, especially given that the seance is the only funeral ritual where a predominantly female perspective is expressed.

In spite of the men's skepticism in the particular seance discussed here, events proceeded as planned by the women after the unsuccessful attempt. One year after the matriarch's death, a different spirit medium performed a successful seance. This second ritual was held in the matriarch's bedroom with only close family present, and no outsiders other than myself. Tshia Yen-hong, the son of the matriarch, refused to participate in the early phases of the ritual. Not until the medium was possessed by the spirit of his mother did he consent to enter the bedroom. Whether he was more skeptical after the first seance or only more circumspect after his embarrassment at the first seance is difficult to decide. The seance was a dramatic and emotionally fulfilling experience for the family, who were able once again to hear the words of their beloved ancestor, listen to her advice, and be grateful for her satisfaction with them. Tshia Yen-hong was not entirely won over by the efficacy of this medium.[23] He remembered other seances that were even more convincing.

In *Tristes Tropiques,* Claude Lèvi-Strauss places societies on a continuum according to how they treat the dead. At one extreme are those societies that have almost no relation with the dead. They let the dead rest in peace, and the dead in turn rarely trouble the living. He locates Western societies at this pole. At the other end of the continuum are those societies that manipulate and exploit the powers of the dead for the profit of the living. Lèvi-Strauss places Chinese society at the midpoint between these extremes.[24] From this comparative perspective, one can discern a problem that all societies must attempt to resolve: the salience of the dead in the everyday world, the ongoing dynamic of their effect upon the living. Western societies may internalize or psychologize the effect the dead have upon us, but we still face the same existential dilemma: the web of life is both rent by death and yet cannot be rent, since we are formed through our relationships and must continue on, shaped by the imprint of people who have died. Their deaths may limit or preclude future communications, but the dynamic established during their lifetime persists. I may ask of the Tshia family in Taiwan, "How is it that you live so closely with the dead and see their actions everywhere?" But they may ask of me, "How can you ignore what is so clearly present? How can you internalize as mere memory the momentum imparted by the dead which carries you forward?"

Endnotes

1. Richard Bauman writes in *Story, Performance, and Event: Contextual Studies of Oral Narrative* (Cambridge: Cambridge University Press, 1986), 4: "The ethnographic construction of the structured, conventionalized performance even standardizes and homogenizes description, but all performances are not the same, and one wants to be able to comprehend and appreciate the individuality of each as well as the general structures common to all. Every performance will have a unique and emergent aspect, depending on the distinctive circumstances at play within it. Events in these terms are not frozen, predetermined molds for performance but are themselves situated social accomplishments in which structures and conventions may provide precedents and guidelines for the range of alternatives possible, but the possibility of alternatives, the competencies and goals of the participants, and the emergent unfolding of the event make for variability."

2. Dell Hymes notes that the full performance of a genre of folklore involves "the acceptance of responsibility to perform, to do the thing with acceptance of being evaluated." From "Ways of Speaking," in *Explorations in the Ethnography of Speaking,* ed. Richard Bauman and Joel Sherzer (Cambridge: Cambridge University Press, 1974), 443.

3. This paper is based on research sponsored by the U.S. Department of Education and the National Institute of Mental Health.

4. Erving Goffman, *Frame Analysis: An Essay on the Organization of Experience* (New York: Harper and Row, 1974), 83.

5. Divination sticks are long, wooden numbered sticks held in a canister. The supplicant pulls a stick at random from the container. The sticks are numbered with the characters used for the cyclical reckoning of years. The number on the stick corresponds to a set mesage which is related in written form at the temples or in oral form by the fortune-teller. Some interpretation of the written formula is provided by the temple staff or by the fortune-teller.

6. Divination blocks are two crescent-shaped wooden blocks about six inches long. They are flat on one side and convex on the other. The supplicant asks a question of the gods or ancestors while holding the blocks together, then throws them on the ground. A strong positive answer results if the blocks fall with one curved side and one flat side down; a weak positive answer consists of two curved sides down; a negative answer consists of two flat sides down. In contrast to fortune-telling sticks (see Note 5), which are found in temples or used by professional fortune-tellers, divination blocks are employed as a home-based method (although they are sometimes used in temples) of divination that requires no intervention or interpretation by ritual specialists.

7. The domain of the men is in the front of the house near the ancestor hall, which is the public area of the house. The domain of the women is in the back where food is prepared, sacrifices to wandering spirits are performed, and the private life of the family is contained. This arrangement is not a strict rule of social conduct or a kind of purdah, but rather an informal arrangement. Had she been alive, the matriarch, being of the eldest generation and head of the household, would have occupied a seat of honor among the men.

8. These discussions were recorded by the author in March 1975 in Miao Li, Taiwan. The author translated the material based on the transcriptions of her assistant Li Mei-chin. Two tape recorders were used to document the simultaneous discussions of the men and women. Such documentation is an ancient Chinese practice. I was not the only person to tape-record the seance: the seances were being preserved on tape by a family member. Tape recordings of seances are considered a valuable record of communication with cherished ancestors.

9. Ibid.

10. Ibid.

11. Ibid.

12. The appearance of the departed beloved one is not a phenomenon limited to particular sociocultural situations, such as the ancestor worshipping societies of East Asia and parts of Africa. Instances of feeling the presence of a recently departed relative or of seeing that relative are recorded in Western societies as well. The perception of a recently dead person by the bereaved survivor is mentioned in Colin Murray Parkes, *Bereavement: Studies of Grief in Adult Life* (New York: International Universities Press, 1972), 77–80; in John Bowlby, *Attachment and Loss*, vol. 3, (New York: Basic Books, 1980), 96–100; and in Michael F. Hoyt, "Clinical Notes Regarding the Experience of 'Presences' in Mourning," *Omega* 11 (1980–81): 105–111. From the psychological perspective taken in these articles, the phenomena are viewed as part of the process of bereavement.

13. Transcriptions from tapes recorded by the author in March 1975 in Miao Li, Taiwan.

14. A high school English teacher also pointed to the complex relationship between tradition and belief in his explanation of the continued flourishing of the folk religion among the younger generation, who had received a Western-style education. He said that young people often go through the motions of ancestor worship merely to please their parents. When their parents die, however, the young people feel obliged to carry on the traditions, because they loved their parents and feel their parents would expect them to continue the rituals. The death of their parents gave the ritual a biographical, personal dimension for them. (Noted in conversation with the informant, autumn 1975.)

15. Transcriptions from tapes recorded by the author in March 1975 in Miao Li, Taiwan.

16. Tshia Mui-moi was buried in a cemetery according to traditional practice. Five to seven years after her burial, her coffin will be opened, the bones cleaned, placed in an urn, and reburied at the family tomb.

17. Transcriptions from tapes recorded by the author in March 1975 in Miao Li, Taiwan.

18. *Anti-structure* is a concept developed by Victor Turner to describe the liminal period in rites of passage, in which the normal structures of society are inverted. In this case the women mediums replace the male hierarchy. See Victor Turner, *The Ritual Process: Structure and Anti-Structure* (Chicago: Aldine Press, 1969) and *Dramas, Fields, and Metaphors: Symbolic Action in Human Society* (Ithaca: Cornell University Press, 1974), 23–59.

19. This male/female, public/private distinction has been noted in many societies. See Michelle Zimbalist Rosaldo, "Woman, Culture, and Society: A Theoretical Overview," in *Woman, Culture, and Society,* ed. Rosaldo and Louise Lamphere (Stanford: Stanford University Press, 1974).

20. Victor Turner describes the multivocality of important symbols: "Certain dominant or focal symbols conspicuously possess this property of multivocality, which allows for the economic representation of key aspects of culture and belief. Each dominant symbol has a 'fan' or 'spectrum' of referents, which are interlinked by what is usually a simple mode of association, its very simplicity enabling it to interconnect a wide variety of significata." From "Ritual, Symbolism, Morality, and Social Structure among the Ndembu," in Victor Turner's *The Forest of Symbols: Aspects of Ndembu Ritual* (Ithaca: Cornell University Press, 1967), 50.

21. See Leon Festinger, Henry W. Riecken, and Stanley Schachter, "Reactions to Disconfirmation," in *When Prophecy Fails: Social and Psychological Study of a Modern Group That Predicted the Destruction of the World* (Minneapolis: University of Minnesota Press, 1956; reprint, New York: Harper and Row, 1964). In that case, when the flying saucers do not arrive on the expected date, belief in the aliens is not extinguished. Belief systems seem to have a sort of inertia which keeps them in motion despite negative or contrary impetus.

22. J. J. M. de Groot, *The Religious System of China,* vol. 6 (Taipei: Ch'eng Wen Publishing, 1972), 1333.

23. This seance, which took place in February 1976, is described in my dissertation, "The Dramatic Structure of a Hakka Seance: On Being Convinced," University of Pennsylvania, 1990.

24. Claude Lèvi-Strauss, *Tristes Tropiques,* trans. John Weightman and Doreen Weightman (New York: Atheneum, 1975), 232–233.

6

Supernatural Experience, Folk Belief, and Spiritual Healing

James McClenon

SUPERNATURAL EXPERIENCES PROVIDE A FOUNDATION FOR SPIRITUAL HEALING. The concept *supernatural* is culturally specific, since some societies regard all perceptions as natural; yet certain events—such as apparitions, out-of-body and near-death experiences, extrasensory perceptions, precognitive dreams, and contact with the dead—promote faith in extraordinary forces. Supernatural experiences can be defined as those sensations directly supporting occult beliefs. Supernatural experiences are important because they provide an impetus for ideologies supporting occult healing practices, the primary means of medical treatment throughout antiquity.

My analysis is based on surveys of random samples of American, Chinese, and Japanese student populations, as well as of American scientists. More than 1,000 supernatural narratives have been collected. I also observed and interviewed over thirty spiritual healers in America, Korea, Taiwan, People's Republic of China, Thailand, Okinawa, Philippines, and Sri Lanka.

The data indicate that certain forms of supernatural experience have universal features, and people reporting frequent experiences have a propensity to engage in spiritual healing. Also, highly successful spiritual healers describe a series of supernatural events contributing to their socialization as practitioners. Although supernatural events have not been established as "real" to the satisfaction of many scientists, they have real effects on all human cultures.

The Supernatural within the Context of Science

The concept of the supernatural has been shaped by the Western notion of nature and causality. Science has evolved in a manner that is restrictive and sometimes dysfunctional when applied to the study of the supernatural.[1] Early scientists sought to exclude non-measurable parameters from scientific discourse. Galileo distinguished between primary qualities, thought to be genuinely inherent within objects, and secondary qualities, which were "no more than mere names . . . [having] their habitation only in the sensorium."[2] This distinction, refined by Descartes, Boyle, Locke, Newton, and others, became a part of the metaphysical foundation of science, and mental constructs were regarded as not amenable to scientific investigation.

Newton's *Principia,* published in 1684, defined a universe of clockwork quality, governed by immutable, physical laws. The ongoing success of the scientific endeavor seemed to verify the correctness of this model, and scientists gave spiritual forces no role in scientific explanation. Mystical or religious experiences stimulated only slight investigation, since scientists assumed that these events were caused by peripheral aspects of brain functioning.

Science focuses on "nature," a domain subject to empirical investigation. It tends to ignore the "supernatural," an area whose existence is uncertain. This strategy, a product of scientific skepticism, is based in part on Occam's Razor,[3] the rule that complex theories should be replaced by equivalent, simpler ones. If a natural explanation is available to explain an anomalous perception, then scientists prefer the natural explanation to the supernatural one.[4] Philosopher David Hume's argument regarding miracles extends this logic.[5] Because a miracle is considered a violation of the laws of nature, no testimony is sufficient to confirm it, unless it would be even more miraculous for that testimony to be false. Supernatural claims are thought to be so exceptional that all existing proofs for them are deemed inadequate. Such argumentation causes supernatural assertions to be categorized as outside the scientific domain.[6]

Because of this philosophical heritage, modern scientists tend to ignore the social reality of supernatural accounts. Yet apparitions, out-of-body experiences, near-death experiences, precognitions, night paralysis, extrasensory perceptions (ESP), and contacts with the dead contain universal features, allowing cross-culturally consistent classification. Such episodes occur frequently enough to have had significant impact on all societies.

Table 1 compares European and American survey results by nation regarding déjà vu, ESP, and contact with the dead. The data show that these incidents are not unique to any particular culture; all surveyed groups contain individuals claiming anomalous experiences. The data in Table 1 are complemented by a 1990 national survey of the United States, which revealed the continued pervasiveness of supernatural experience: 25 percent of the people surveyed claimed to have healed their bodies "using the power of [their minds] without traditional medicine"; 17 percent had felt that they "were in touch with someone who has already died"; and 9 percent claimed to have "seen or been in the presence of a ghost."[7]

Table 2 presents data from targeted cultural groups: council members and selected section committee members of the American Association for the Advancement of Science, random samples of students at the University of Maryland, the University of North Carolina at Greensboro, Elizabeth City State University (a predominantly black college in North Carolina), three colleges in Xi'an in the People's Republic of China, and Tsukuba University in Japan. The surveys reveal a correspondingly high rate of supernatural experience among the American, Japanese, and Chinese student samples. Rates of ESP experience varied from 26 percent reported by the elite American scientists[8] to 71 percent reported by Chinese students. The percentage reporting contact with the dead varied from 10 percent (elite American scientists and Japanese students) to 40 percent (Chinese students). The percentage stating that ESP was a "fact" or a "likely possibility" varied from 20 percent (elite American scientists) to 76 percent (Chinese students). The elite scientists revealed lower rates of belief and experience than virtually all student groups. Although cultural factors, as well as the scientific mindset, affect the percentage reporting these episodes, all sample populations reported each category of event.

Narratives collected from the populations surveyed in Table 2 illustrate some of the natural categories into which experiences fall. Respondents were asked, "If you have had a very unusual experience, would you describe it briefly?" Although interpretations of experiences differed, primary features within each type of episode created clearly distinguishable categories. For example, the following are responses dealing with out-of-body experiences:

African American Student: I was in my bedroom . . . [when] I began to feel my body lift off the bed and begin to float, but my physical body was still on the bed, yet I was up in the air looking at my body on the bed.
Caucasian American Student: I was mentally 'out of it' and saw myself standing with two friends. I felt I was seeing this several feet off the ground—not 'in my body.'
Japanese Student: Once when I was meditating, I had the fleeting feeling that I was seeing myself from outside my body.
Chinese Student: Often I thought as if I were not me. I am another person who is looking at 'me.' I can feel what 'she' or 'he' feels. I don't know what was the reason

Table 1:
Percent Reporting Supernatural Experience Once or More

Surveyed Population	Supernatural Experience, Expressed in Percentages		
	Déjà Vu	ESP	Contact with Dead
American National Samples			
USA, 1973	59	58	27
USA, 1984	67	67	42
USA, 1988	67	65	40
USA, 1989	64	58	36
European National Samples			
Great Britain	*	36	26
Northern Ireland	*	24	12
Republic of Ireland	*	19	16
West Germany	*	35	26
Holland	*	27	11
Belgium	*	18	16
France	*	34	23
Italy	*	38	33
Spain	*	20	16
Malta	*	28	19
Denmark	*	14	9
Sweden	*	23	14
Finland	*	35	15
Norway	*	18	9
Iceland	*	33	41
Western Europe as a Whole	*	32	23

* Data about déjà vu experiences was not computed in the European study.

Sources for American data: A. M. Greeley, *Sociology of the Paranormal: A Reconnaissance* (Beverly Hills, CA: Sage Publications, 1975); A. M. Greeley, "Mysticism Goes Mainstream," *American Health* 6, no. 1, (1987): 47–49; and J. W. Fox, "The Structure, Stability, and Social Antecedents of Reported Paranormal Experiences," *Sociological Analysis* 53 (1992): 417–431.

Source for European data: E. Haraldsson, "Representative National Surveys of Psychic Phenomena: Iceland, Great Britain, Sweden, USA, and Gallup's Multinational Survey," *Journal of the Society for Psychical Research* 53 (1985): 145–158.

Table 2:
Comparison of Sample Surveys

Surveyed Populations	N	% Response	Déjà Vu	Percent Reporting Experience Once or More				Belief in ESP*
				Sleep Paralysis	ESP	Contact with Dead	OBE	
Elite American Scientists	339	71	59	**	26	10	20**	20
University of Maryland	214	42	89	37	44	25	27	66
University of North Carolina, Greensboro	532	98	86	32	42	20	18	60
Elizabeth City State University, North Carolina	391	99	80	50	35	25	18	68
Three Colleges in Xi'an, People's Republic of China	314	40	64	58	71	40	55	76
Tsukuba University, Japan	132	33	88	50	35	10	13	61

* Percent considering ESP "a fact" or "a likely possibility."

** Elite scientists were not polled about sleep paralysis experiences. The OBE (out-of-body experience) question for elite scientists was used by Andrew M. Greeley (*Sociology of the Paranormal: A Reconnaissance*, Beverly Hills, CA: Sage Publications, 1975), differing from that used on the other surveys.

Source for data: J. McClenon, "Surveys of Anomalous Experience in Chinese, Japanese, and American Samples," *Sociology of Religion* 54 (1993): 295–302.

of this sense . . . I don't think it is possible, perhaps, it is better to say that I don't wish it is possible.

Elite American Scientist: A family member was ill and hospitalized. I 'kind of went into a trance' [and] 'traveled' in my mind 400 miles to the hospital where I had never been, looked down into the operating room, saw her there at the beginning of the surgery. As the surgeon prepared to make the incision on the right side, I said to him (in my mind), 'No—it's on the left side.' The surgeon changed over, made the incision. . . . When I received information about the surgery, I asked, 'Which side was involved?' I was told, 'They finally decided it was on the left side.' I understand that this kind of ethereal travel is possible.[9]

If these episodes were totally a product of socialization, we would expect each group to produce distinctive forms of experience since each culture is unique. Because each type of incident contains primary features which allow classification, it is logical to argue that belief proceeds, to a degree, from experience rather than being fully a product of socialization.[10]

Some respondents report that supernatural events have shaped their convictions. Apparitions and out-of-body experiences engender and reinforce belief in spirits and souls. Precognitive dreams and ESP contribute to the belief that reality harbors a hidden spiritual structure with unseen connections among people and events. Sleep paralysis experiences reinforce belief in spiritual forces, particularly demonic ones.[11]

Some people undergoing medical emergencies describe a constellation of events that include leaving their bodies, passing through a transition stage, coming into contact with spiritual entities, meeting a being of light, experiencing a "life review," and then returning to their bodies.[12] These near-death experiences (NDEs) support specific elements within religious ideology, such as belief in a deity, an immediate judgment after death, and the existence of intermediate spiritual entities and planes. NDEs have contributed to parallel features within Buddhist, Christian, and Moslem concepts of the afterlife.[13]

Folk belief is based on the oral transmission of accounts passed down over generations. The persons who have experienced such events, and those listening to their accounts, socially construct occult belief by discussing and interpreting supernatural perceptions. During modern eras, the media participate in this process, selecting accounts that support folk conceptions of the supernatural.

Personality and the Distribution of Supernatural Experience

People vary in their capacity to experience supernatural events.[14] Within all groups surveyed for Table 2, some respondents reported many supernatural episodes, while many people reported none. Those who stated they had one type of experience had a greater probability of reporting an alternate form.

ESP, contact with the dead, and out-of-body experience were significantly intercorrelated in all samples [$p < .05$].

People who report frequent experiences tend to regard psychic events as normal, having adjusted to recurrent encounters. They label some experiences (such as NDEs) as more "real" than "normal reality." Family, friends, and neighbors often label frequent experiencers as having psychic abilities. Some individuals claim a degree of control over their capacity to experience the supernatural.

Even the elite scientists' opinions were influenced by supernatural experience. Those who believed in ESP cited "personal experience" most frequently as grounds for their belief, rather than newspapers, television, books, journals, hearsay, or a priori grounds. Frequency of extrasensory experience correlated significantly with belief in ESP [$R = .27$, $p < .005$].[15]

Previous studies indicate that people reporting frequent supernatural episodes have special psychological traits. Although they reveal no greater pathology than non-experiencers, they appear more "emotionally sensitive," feeling the joys and pains of life more deeply.[16] Frequency of supernatural experience has been linked with fantasy proneness and hypnotic suggestibility.[17] Because these correlations are consistently slight, they appear non-causal.[18] Frequency of anomalous perception has been found to be more highly correlated with commonly occurring dissociation experiences.[19] The capacity to experience wondrous events is similar to hypnotic suggestibility in that researchers have only a limited understanding of these traits. Hereditary and environmental factors probably contribute to both capabilities.

Spiritual Healing and the Shamanic Biography

Respondents providing numerous supernatural narratives described a pattern which I label the "shamanic biography." They often perceive the first incident at an early age, come to believe they have extraordinary capacities, cope with social reactions, and adjust to their special reputations. For example, one informant states:

> [O]ne night I was going to sleep and [saw an image of my grandfather] . . . I told [my mother] what I saw and she said, "You're always seeing things." After my childhood I got used to it, and it didn't bother me.[20]

They often follow culturally prescribed pathways which lead to their becoming spiritual healers. Western experiencers usually encounter obstacles within this process. Non-Western occult practitioners may engage in a wide array of activities beyond spiritual healing. These include placing magical curses and charms, fortune-telling, crime-solving, spiritual counseling, and finding lost people, objects, or animals. Yet among such enterprises, spiritual healing generally attracts the largest number of clients.

The logical basis for spiritual healing differs from that of Western medicine. Modern medical doctrines explain most sicknesses within an internalizing system.[21] The subsequent physiological explanations are indispensable for organizing treatment strategies. Spiritual healers generally use externalizing belief systems. Practitioners diagnose problems as resulting from the activities of spiritual forces or deities, particularly grudges repaid by witchcraft or ritual lapses punished by ancestral spirits. Supernatural experiences often contribute to faith in a particular externalizing system.

The distinction between internalizing and externalizing systems can be illustrated by their divergent interpretations of altered states of consciousness. The externalizing perspective considers a person in trance to be controlled by spiritual forces. Within the internalizing framework, trance behavior is thought to be a result of hypnotic dissociation, a product of the subconscious mind. The internalizing paradigm regards extrasensory perceptions as anomalous or "paranormal." Yet people experiencing frequent ESP events come to regard such events as normal; they tend to accept an externalizing framework.

Spiritual healers report a progression of supernatural incidents that contributed to their socialization into the practitioner's role. Some claimed a resistant, skeptical attitude that was overpowered by their perceptions. For example, one Filipino practitioner described dubiously watching spiritual lights which periodically urged him to heal others. He felt he was levitating during some of these experiences, but was afraid he was deceiving himself. When his wife saw the lights, he became more certain of their authenticity. His newly gained ability to cure illness also increased his faith in the spiritual entities who claimed to help him.

Another pathway to becoming a healer is for the individual to suffer from medical problems that Western doctors might label as psychosomatic. In the process of dealing with the illness, the individual is cured through non-medical or non-scientific means. Such healings often coincide with alternate supernatural perceptions.

Throughout the rest of this chapter, I will provide example cases from the Philippines, Thailand, and Taiwan to illustrate the forms of supernatural episodes within typical shamanic biographies.

Alex Orbito was raised in a Filipino province where many spiritual healers practiced.[22] After dropping out of high school, he had recurrent dreams of healing people with a Bible in one hand. Alternate dreams included a wise old hermit in a white garment who became his spirit guide. The hermit gave him a secret word that allowed him to pass into trance almost at will.

A distant neighbor's mother, who had been paralyzed for ten years, had a vivid dream in which Orbito healed her. The neighbor asked Orbito to visit the woman. When he complied, she was healed, causing his fame to spread throughout the province.

Because psychic healers generally receive little pay, Orbito sought to escape his mission. He worked at a number of menial jobs under an assumed name to avoid his reputation. While a photographer's assistant, his employer accused him of stealing equipment, and Orbito was jailed as a suspect. As he languished in his cell, voices in his head redirected him to become a healer. When the true thief confessed, Orbito was released but still avoided the healer's role.

Orbito became seriously sick and experienced further voices ordering him to heal others. When he followed the voices' directives and began performing psychic healings, his own sickness dissipated. Eventually, his fame spread throughout the world. He became extremely rich, using what appears to be sleight-of-hand techniques to extract tissue from his clients' bodies, a process known as "psychic surgery" (sleight-of-hand magic is common within shamanic performance). He has performed healings in the United States, Europe, Australia, New Zealand, Nigeria, and Saudi Arabia. Orbito is one of various shamanic practitioners who have gained international reputations and attracted clients from all over the world.

Orbito's biography illustrates the forms of private experience that produce shamanic behavior. From his vantage point, his recurring dreams were precognitive. He regarded the voices in his head as exterior in origin. He allowed supernatural experiences, which seemed to him to have exterior origins, to shape his life. It is common for mental events to play a primary role in forming the practitioner's belief system. For example, a Taiwanese shaman states:

> You do not learn how to heal from another person. A master can help you contact your guardian spirit. Then that spirit heals and teaches you. You must make vows to him. Then, if you fulfill those vows, you can heal others. When you come into contact with that spirit, you lose all doubts.[23]

The characteristics correlated with supernatural experience seemingly aid practitioners in performing for audiences. Parapsychologists have found that altered states of consciousness seemingly enhance extrasensory perception.[24] Trance states can also contribute to special normal skills. Orbito's dissociation may contribute to the dexterity required for executing (apparent) sleight-of-hand surgeries.

Folk Logic and Client Experiences

Most contemporary Western physicians limit their help to the cure of disease—a biological disorder. They are generally unprepared to heal illness—the way the ill person experiences his or her disorder, in a given social and cultural context. Alternative healing, by contrast, appears generally to address illness more than disease.[25]

Success within spiritual healing requires that clients perceive an alleviation of their problems. This occurs by encouraging them to change their relationship to illness.

Spiritual healers communicate on an unconscious, emotional, non-rational, and symbolic level with their clients.[26] Spiritual healing often involves latent suggestions embedded within the context of a ceremony. This contributes to changes in patient attitudes which augment healing. Successful supernatural performances resonate with a sufficient number of audience members so that the healer's reputation for effectiveness is maintained. Such psychological treatments can be highly effective, even for organic disorders. A quantitative review of controlled studies of Western psychological interventions, such as hypnosis, demonstrates that these procedures effectively reduce the length of hospital stays for surgery and heart attack patients.[27]

Wilasinee Wisejsumnom, a Thai healer known as the "Miracle Lady," attracts clients from all over Thailand.[28] Originally, she experienced a series of precognitions that led to her experimentation with mediumship. Under the control of her guiding spirit, she inserts needles through her cheeks. As this somewhat gruesome performance unfolds, her guiding spirit jokes with the audience. Later, members of her team wave knives about her clients' bodies, symbolically cutting away disorders. They also exorcise demons when necessary. Wilasinee Wisejsumnom preaches a Buddhist sermon, and afterward, again in trance, she diagnoses medical problems. She treats ailments by touching her bare foot to a red-hot iron grill and placing it on the infirm part of the sick person's body. Her foot remains unharmed.

Believers follow folk logic when evaluating this performance. They reason that if the spirits can grant her immunity from pain and heat, the spirits can heal those she touches. She maintains that her procedure is designed for "those whom doctors cannot help." She does not "prove" her claims scientifically but creates an emotional link between wondrous performance and client illness. Although many disorders seemed unaffected, most clients stated that their treatments were effective (particularly within the psychological arena). In these instances, folk rationality exhibits greater social utility than scientific logic. Externalizing medical methods may succeed when internalizing systems fail.

The biography of the psychic artist Li Ch'i-ts'e illustrates how wondrous events can transform someone with a scientific, internalizing medical orientation into a shamanic healer.[29] Born in 1907, Dr. Li was trained in Western-style medicine. He left mainland China for Taiwan in 1949 and practiced as a doctor until his retirement. When he was thirty-two, he felt an unusual power affect him and found that he was sometimes able to diagnose his patients' medical problems without examining them. He also felt compelled to express himself using brushes and paints, although he had no knowledge or training in Chinese painting. He found he could paint in trance using his left hand, even though he was right-handed. He painted very rapidly with the paper turned sideways, apparently with no effort. He claimed to be helped by the spirits Tsi Gong (Buddha Tsi, a Chinese Buddhist monk of the Sung dynasty) and the Goddess of Mercy (Quan Yin).

Those who seek Dr. Li's help need not tell him their problems, since they believe Buddha Tsi can read people's minds. Every two weeks, hundreds of people pay a fee equivalent to $12.50 so that their names will be added to a list of those seeking a painting. Dr. Li paints picture after picture in trance, his paper turned sideways. He seems impervious to those around him. Each painting consists of a colorful portrayal of objects and a calligraphy presenting a phrase theoretically meaningful to the questioner's problem. Dr. Li is not informed of anyone's problem or question. Two "psychic interpreters" are available, who later explain each painting's symbolism for the benefit of clients.

Although no one claimed that Dr. Li/Buddha Tsi was 100 percent accurate, many stated that his messages had helped them. Virtually every client interviewed supplied a glowing anecdotal story of Dr. Li's wondrous powers. They claimed that Dr. Li supplied information gained through extrasensory means, making many diagnoses of medical problems previous to their discovery by traditional means.

F. S. Yin, for example, reported that he had silently asked that Dr. Li paint a picture of his grandfather, who had died when Yin was ten years old. Neither Yin, nor Li, had ever seen the grandfather, and there were no known photographs of him. In 1978, fifty-two years after the grandfather's death, Dr. Li painted the man's portrait while in trance, though it would be highly unlikely that he could have talked with anyone who had seen the man. Mr. Yin took the picture to some relatives who had known his grandfather. They stated that it was an exact representation of him.

I designed an experiment to test the correspondence between clients' secret questions and Dr. Li's responses. I supervised four clients, verifying that they did not reveal their questions to Dr. Li or his assistants. I photographed Li's paintings and recorded the psychic interpreters' comments. Although three of the four clients were highly satisfied with Dr. Li's answers, outside judges were unable to match clients' questions to Dr. Li's and the interpreters' responses. Analysis revealed no statistically significant correspondence.[30]

The experiment did not verify a paranormal quality within Dr. Li's performance. It appears that part of the supernatural quality attributed to him is created through social interaction and audience expectation. Yet Dr. Li's paintings are not mundane. Supernatural experiences, such as that of F. S. Yin, need not be verified for them to have social effects. Dr. Li's ability to create intricate and seemingly appropriate Chinese paintings in an unusually rapid manner is a rare talent, particularly suited for shamanic performance. The wonder of seeing someone rapidly paint in trance encourages clients to pay particular attention to the advice of skilled "interpreter/counselors." Such guidance apparently has therapeutic effects. Like Alex Orbito, who engages in sleight-of-hand magic while in trance, or Wilasinee Wisejsumnom, who demonstrates pain-and-heat-immunity, Li Ch'i-ts'e and his performances are beneficial for many clients.

Much parapsychological evidence, gained through controlled laboratory experiments, indicates that some spiritual healers can produce anomalous effects beyond what is possible through normal means.[31] Although participant observation cannot evaluate such claims, parapsychological studies reinforce the social impact of folk experience. Various spiritual practitioners cite psychical research as validation for their procedures. Although scientific proponents provide no fully convincing theoretical framework, the wonder associated with supernatural experience grants externalizing belief systems longevity within the folk domain.

Conclusions

Apparitions, precognitive dreams, ESP, sleep paralysis, out-of-body experiences, and near-death episodes contribute to folk belief in spirits, souls, and an afterlife. Those with the highest propensity for supernatural experience are prone to fulfill spiritual healer roles. They tend to follow logical progressions, based on their own supernatural experiences, which seemingly compel them to learn skills required to create wondrous performances.

The latent suggestions embedded within healing ceremonies address a wide spectrum of client problems. The healer's performance connects wondrous experiences with images of health. The need for psychosomatic treatments creates a continuous demand for occult performances. Since psychological factors affect the healing process, spiritual treatments can speed recovery from organic disorders. The universal elements inherent within some forms of supernatural experience, the special constellations of events that contribute to shamanic recruitment, and the reduction of illness within clients who have not responded to other forms of treatment imply that spiritual healing is part of human nature. Universal forms of experience, triggering wonderment, provide an empirical basis for occult beliefs and spiritual healing.

Acknowledgments

An alternate version of this chapter has been published under the title "The Experiential Foundations of Shamanic Healing," in *Journal of Medicine and Philosophy* 18, no. 2 (1993): 107–127. Various narratives and parallel comments appear in James McClenon, *Wondrous Events: Foundations of Religious Belief* (Philadelphia: University of Pennsylvania Press, 1994). I wish to thank Barbara Walker for assisting with the revision of the present version.

Endnotes

1. David J. Hufford, "Traditions of Disbelief," *New York Folklore* 8 (1982): 47–55; Hufford, "The Supernatural and the Sociology of Knowledge: Explaining Academic Belief," *New York Folklore* 9 (1983): 47–56. See also Hufford's essay in this volume.
2. Galileo Galilei (The Assayer), in *The Controversy on the Comets of 1618*, ed. and trans. Stillman Drake and Charles Donald O'Malley (1623; reprint, Philadelphia: University of Pennsylvania Press, 1960), 311.
3. William of Occam (or Ockham), c.1284–c.1349, Dominican theologian and philosopher, set forth the proposition that "multiplicity ought not to be posited without necessity," a doctrine commonly labeled Occam's Razor.
4. Joseph Hanlon, "Uri Geller and Science," *New Scientist* 64, no. 919 (October 17, 1974): 170–185.
5. David Hume, *An Enquiry Concerning Human Understanding*, 2d ed., ed. L. A. Selby-Bigge (1777; reprint, Oxford: Clarendon, 1961).
6. James McClenon, *Deviant Science: The Case of Parapsychology* (Philadelphia: University of Pennsylvania Press, 1984).
7. George H. Gallup and Frank Newport, "Belief in Paranormal Phenomena among Adult Americans," *Skeptical Inquirer* 15 (1991): 137–146, especially 141.
8. The survey population is labeled "elite" since these individuals have administrative roles within the prestigious American Association for the Advancement of Science. Comparison of "elite" survey response with that obtained from a random sample of American college science professors indicates that the "elite" group is far more skeptical regarding paranormal claims than "average" college scientists; McClenon, *Deviant Science.*
9. McClenon, "The Experiential Foundations of Shamanic Healing," *Journal of Medicine and Philosophy* 18, no. 2 (1993): 124.
10. Hufford, *The Terror That Comes in the Night* (Philadelphia: University of Pennsylvania Press, 1982); McClenon, "Chinese and American Anomalous Experiences: The Role of Religiosity," *Sociological Analysis* 51, no. 1 (1990): 53–67.
11. Hufford, *The Terror.*

12.   Kenneth Ring, *Life at Death: A Scientific Investigation of the Near-Death Experience* (New York: Coward, McCann, and Geoghegan, 1980); Ring, *Heading toward Omega: In Search of the Meaning of Near-Death Experience* (New York: W. Morrow, 1984).

13.   McClenon, "Near-Death Folklore in Medieval China and Japan: A Comparative Analysis," *Asian Folklore Studies* 50 (1991): 319–342.

14.   John Palmer, "A Community Mail Survey of Psychic Experiences," *Journal of the American Society for Psychical Research* 73 (1979): 221–251; McClenon, "Chinese and American Anomalous Experiences"; McClenon, "Surveys of Anomalous Experience in Chinese, Japanese, and American Samples," *Sociology of Religion* 54 (1993): 295–302.

15.   McClenon, "A Survey of Elite Scientists: Their Attitudes toward ESP and Parapsychology," *Journal of Parapsychology* 46, no. 2 (1982): 127–152; McClenon, *Deviant Science.*

16.   Andrew M. Greeley, *Sociology of the Paranormal: A Reconnaissance* (Beverly Hills, CA: Sage Publications, 1975); Erlendur Haraldsson and Joop M. Houtkooper, "Psychic Experience in the Multinational Human Values Study: Who Reports Them," *Journal of the American Society for Psychical Research* 85 (1991): 145–165.

17.   Theodore X. Barber and Sheryl C. Wilson, "The 'Fantasy-Prone Personality,' the Psychic, and the Excellent Hypnotic Subject ('Somnambule'): Are They the Same Person?" in *Research in Parapsychology 1981,* ed. William G. Roll, Robert L. Morris, and Rhea A. White (Metuchen, NJ: Scarecrow Press, 1982), 41–42; Sheryl C. Wilson and Theodore X. Barber, "The Fantasy-Prone Personality: Implications for Understanding Imagery, Hypnosis, and Parapsychological Phenomena," in *Imagery: Current Theory, Research, and Application,* ed. Anees A. Sheikh (New York: John Wiley and Sons, 1983), 340–387; Robert Nadon and John F. Kihlstrom, "Hypnosis, Psi, and the Psychology of Anomalous Experience," *Behavioral and Brain Sciences* 10 (1987): 597–599; Mahlon W. Wagner and Fredrick H. Ratzeburg, "Hypnotic Suggestibility and Paranormal Belief," *Psychological Reports* 60 (1987): 1069–1070; Ian E. Wickramasekera, *Clinical Behavioral Medicine, Some Concepts and Procedures* (New York: Plenum Press, 1988).

18.   Douglas G. Richards, "Hypnotic Susceptibility and Subjective Psychic Experiences," *Journal of Parapsychology* 54 (1990): 35–51.

19.   Richards, "A Study of the Correlations between Subjective Psychic Experiences and Dissociative Experience," *Dissociation* 4 (1991): 83–91; Colin A. Ross and Shaun Joshi, "Paranormal Experiences in the General Population," *Journal of Nervous and Mental Disease* 180 (1992): 357–361.

20.   McClenon, unpublished collection; over 1,000 anomalous experience narratives collected in northeastern North Carolina (1987–93).

21.   Allen Young, "An Anthropological Perspective on Medical Knowledge," *The Journal of Medicine and Philosophy* 5 (1980): 102–116.

22.   Orbito's biography was obtained through personal interviews and participant observation by the author in Quezon City (north of Manila), Philippines, December 1982, September–October 1983, and November 1984–March 1985; and from the written accounts of Jaime T. Licauco, *Born to Heal: The Amazing Story of Spiritual Healer Rev. Alex Orbito* (Manila: Jaime T. Licauco,

publisher, 1978); Licauco, *The Magicians of God* (Manila: National Book Store, 1981).

23. McClenon, unpublished field notes, Taipei, Taiwan, December 1985.

24. Charles Honorton, "Psi and Internal Attention States," in *The Handbook of Parapsychology*, ed. Benjamin B. Wolman (New York: Van Nostrand Reinhold, 1977), 79–90; C. Honorton et al., "Psi Communication in the Ganzfeld: Experiments with an Automated Testing System and a Comparison with a Meta-Analysis of Earlier Studies," *Journal of Parapsychology* 54 (1990): 99–139.

25. Meredith McGuire and Debra Kantor, *Ritual Healing in Suburban America* (New Jersey: Rutgers University Press, 1988), 6.

26. Sudhir Kakar, *Shamans, Mystics, and Doctors* (New York: Knopf, 1982).

27. Emily Mumford, H. J. Schlesinger, and G. V. Glass, "The Effects of Psychological Intervention on Recovery from Surgery and Heart Attacks: An Analysis of the Literature," *American Journal of Public Health* 72 (1982): 141–151.

28. Wilasinee Wisejsumnom's biography was obtained through personal interviews and participant observation by the author, conducted in Bangkok, Thailand, December 1984.

29. Participant observation of Li Ch'i-ts'e was conducted by the author, in Taipei, Taiwan, in August and December 1985.

30. The experiment took place in December 1985; McClenon, *Wondrous Events: Foundations of Religious Belief* (Philadelphia: University of Pennsylvania Press, 1994).

31. Michael Murphy, *The Future of the Body, Explorations into the Further Evolution of Human Nature* (Los Angeles: Jeremy P. Tarcher, 1992), 273–282.

7

"If I Knew You Were Coming, I'd Have Baked a Cake": The Folklore of Foreknowledge in a Neighborhood Group

Gillian Bennett

In 1705, the British antiquarian John Beaumont observed that:

> To say absolutely, that all dreams, without distinction, are vain Visions and Sports of Nature . . . and to banish all Divination from the Life of Man . . . is contrary to Experience and the common Consent and Agreement of Mankind.[1]

The focus of this essay is this "common consent and agreement" about knowledge of the future, as it is understood by a group of elderly women in my own hometown, and the ways in which I believe that the women's social situation and moral code shape the folklore that they share. I want to begin rather obliquely, however: first looking at past traditions in order to get a historical perspective on the present, and then, by way of further contextualization, describing my research strategy and the study group members themselves.

Historical Perspective

Perhaps the best place to begin any survey of British traditions is with John Aubrey, that curious and often credulous seventeenth-century antiquarian, whose *Miscellanies* were written in 1696. This work is a collection of current rumors, legends, and personal experience stories on supernatural topics, orally told and jotted down as he heard them. Three chapters are directly concerned with omens, foreknowledge, and divination. A remark in Chapter 3, "Portents," sets the tone of what is to follow:

> How it comes to pass, I know not; but by Ancient and Modern example it is evident, that no great Accident befalls a City or Province, but it is presaged by Divination, or Prodigy, or astrologie, or some way or other.[2]

Chapter 4, "Omens," contains a multitude of such examples. The fall of Charles I, for example, was said to have been presaged by numerous strange happenings: in 1642 a group of partridges attacked a hawk, and this unnatural act was taken to signify that the country would turn on its monarch; at the beginning of the "Long Parliament," a scepter fell off a statue of the king; and it "was commonly known" that the top of the king's staff fell off at his trial.[3] According to Aubrey, the life of James II, another deposed king, was equally presage-filled: at his coronation his crown was knocked from his head by a courtier;[4] when he entered Dublin after his return from France in 1689, his mace-bearer stumbled and the little cross on the top of the mace fell off. ("This is very well known all over Ireland," says Aubrey, "and did much trouble King James himself with many of his Chief Attendants."[5]) In Chapter 5, "Dreams as Omens," the list of significant events continues: Lady Seymour dreamed that she found a nest of nine finches and she subsequently had nine children; the Countess of Cork dreamed of her father's death while he was actually dying; Sir Christopher Wren dreamed (correctly, as it happened) that his fever would be cured by eating dates, and so on.

A hundred years later, people were hardly less influenced by the desire to predict death and foretell the future, despite the supposed enlightenment and rationalism of the eighteenth century. Visions, apparitions, and wraiths continued to hold number-one place as omens of death; mysterious lights, fires in the sky, night birds seen during the day, unaccustomed breakages, and noises of various sorts—especially footsteps and mysterious creaks and bangs around the house—were all intrinsically ominous; and any ordinary thing in an extraordinary context was commonly interpreted as signifying disaster or change. In 1787, the antiquarian Francis Grose was able to compile a three-page inventory of contemporary omens of death, which included items such as hearing screech owls, hearing three knocks at the bed's head, rats gnawing at the bed-hangings, having a bleeding nose, the breaking of a looking glass, coffin-shaped coals in the fire, winding sheets on candles, corpse-candles and phantom fire, and, of course, the tick of the death-watch beetle.[6]

The eighteenth century, however, was a time in which a different emphasis began to develop. This was largely a product of the rational–mechanical worldview brought about by the Scientific Revolution. As far as supernatural beliefs were concerned, the effect was not to abolish traditional concepts altogether, but to restrict their more extravagant expressions. As time went by, accounts of omens, signs, and warnings became less dramatic and their range more restricted. The most striking effect, however, was the gradual internalizing of supernatural experience.[7]

By the mid-nineteenth century, therefore, there were two main strands in British folkloristic writing about foreknowledge: on the one hand, accounts of divinatory practices and the interpretation of signs and tokens; on the other, accounts of visions, dreams, and "presentiments." For example, in 1866 William Henderson, one of the best-known British collectors of regional folklore, compiled a large list of death tokens—deformed lambs, hens laying an all-female brood, the tick of the death-watch beetle, and the noise of a house falling down. On the other hand, in 1848 Catherine Crowe collected seventeen narratives about "Allegorical Dreams, Presentiments" and thirty-one pages of accounts of "Double Dreaming and Trance, Wraiths."[8] Both these strands of tradition continue to be actively transmitted in our own century: the one relying on the interpretation of external stimuli, the other dependent upon a sensitive response to personal events—"internal" events such as dreams, visions, "hunches," and strange perceptions or states of mind.[9]

The first strand is now chiefly represented by astrology, fortune-telling, or visits to psychics or mediums. Surveys in Britain and the United States between 1925 and 1985 show levels of belief in astrology and fortune-telling between 7 percent and 30 percent of the sample population. In 1925 H. K. Nixon surveyed American students' beliefs and found that 29 percent had faith in astrology and 25 percent in fortune-telling; twenty years later a similar questionnaire in the United Kingdom gave rise to figures of 18 percent for astrology and 20 percent for fortune-telling; British sociologist Geoffrey Gorer had very similar results in 1955 with a nationwide survey (20 percent belief in astrology, 30 percent belief in fortune-telling); and more recently, a survey by sociologists of religion at Leeds University in the United Kingdom found 14 percent belief in astrology and 35 percent belief in fortune-telling, also with a large-scale survey by professional interviewers. The lowest figures were obtained in surveys of student populations in the 1950s; an American survey of 1952 showed only 7 percent belief in astrology and 5 percent belief in fortune-telling, and a British survey of students in 1956 showed levels of belief at 6 percent for both fortune-telling and astrology. The variations in the findings are teasing: without more information than can now be retrieved about these studies, it is impossible to decide whether they reflect genuine differences between differing populations or at different times, or whether they are a function of the methodologies employed. Nevertheless, even the surveys that returned the lowest percentages do at least show that the subject is familiar and that divinatory practices have not completely disappeared in our materialistic age.[10]

The second strand finds its principal expression nowadays in the concept of extrasensory perception (ESP), and here, levels of belief are significantly higher. For example, in Britain, the Leeds team found that 54 percent of their respondents believed in clairvoyance and 61 percent in telepathy. These findings fit well with Leea Virtanen's study of ESP in Finland in the 1970s, where she was able to collect no fewer than 1,442 individual reports.[11]

In my own work, it quickly became obvious that both strands of tradition were regularly discussed and were part of a vivid, constantly negotiated folklore. Not only were my informants totally unsurprised by my questions, but they immediately fell into a specialized vocabulary for discussing these matters, which I myself was able to acquire after only a few days' exposure to it.

This vocabulary not only includes neologisms such as "a psychic sense" and "a telepathy with the future," but ancient terms such as "a sixth sense" or "second sight" that the women use totally without embarrassment, one even attributing her psychic abilities to being a "seventh child of a seventh child." Their conversation on the subject is full of vague generalizations and references to what "they" or "people" say—"they do say that . . ." or "you hear people say these things" or "there are people like that . . ." and so on—which all strongly suggest that the topic is often talked over within the family and social circle. There is also the otherwise curious lack of descriptive detail about what the experience of having a premonition actually entails. The emphasis of the story is almost invariably upon the circumstances of the experience, not on its nature. Underlying this strange—to the researcher—neglect is surely the speaker's assumption that the nature of the experience is too familiar to need spelling out. The gaps in the stories indicate the narrator's reliance on shared knowledge: in other words, on a common folklore. And finally, when dissenting women challenge the general belief, they use well-established counter-arguments that strongly recall the reasoning that David Hufford calls "traditions of disbelief"[12] and sound somehow "rehearsed," so that the listener feels that this reasoning has often been employed in similar discussions. Apart from obvious objections—for instance, that such beliefs are superstitious and open to religious objection—the dissenting women assert that omens are "sheer imagination," or they allege that premonitions are "really" due to a variety of natural causes (low spirits, poor health, atmospheric conditions, chance reshapings of the previous day's events), or that they are the working out of observations and impressions unconsciously acquired over the course of time. All the evidence thus points to there being an established folklore about forewarnings in this group, which is subject to the sort of discussion, scrutiny, and debate that keeps the traditions in the forefront of conversation and thereby ensures that they are not only kept alive, but also continuously updated.

However, some changes are apparent. The first, most obvious one, is a preference for the visionary over the divinatory tradition. I shall deal with this in some detail later. At present, however, I want merely to observe that this seems to be a general trend. Ninety percent of the accounts that Virtanen collected, for example, were of subjective experiences, and only 4 percent featured objective signs (omens). Fifty-six percent related "dreams" and "intuitions."[13] The second change—a terminological or classificatory shift—was clearly observable in my own work, but it is impossible to say whether it is a general trend, for, as far as I know, there is no other study that has looked at the language by which traditions of foreknowledge are discussed. In the nineteenth century and earlier—unless the folklorists and antiquarians who tell us of these traditions were mistaken or imposed their own, inappropriate, classification system on the material they collected (which is always possible)—people would have seen omens and tokens as examples of external signs signifying future events. The women of my study group, however, would seem to see the ability to perceive omens as a receptive power like ESP. For example, visionary perceptions, disembodied voices, mysterious noises around the house, all of which consistently appear in folklore collections as "omens" of death or danger, were often cited by my informants as instances of "premonitions." Conversely, the clearest account of what a folklorist would call a "premonition" (i.e., a precognitive intuition or signal) was cited as an example of an "omen" of death. Where clear distinctions are made, omens, premonitions and telepathy seem to be differentiated by virtue of the gravity of the outcome. Forewarnings about really bad things tend to be termed omens; warnings about lesser events are thought of as premonitions; and advance information about happy or trivial or undisturbing things is termed telepathy. If this classificatory shift is a general trend, it can be seen as the result of the continuing process of internalizing and subjectifying traditional supernatural beliefs; if it is special to the group of women I studied, it provides further evidence of the greater value they place on the subjective tradition.

Before going on to look at the folklore which the women of the study group share, however, I would like to discuss the research itself, in order to paint the specific contextual picture.

Research Context

Since the subject of my research might be thought "delicate" or controversial, I had to find a venue conducive to personal conversation, and an intermediary to introduce me to potential informants and put them at their ease. After several false starts, I eventually hit on the idea of asking my father, who after fourteen years at the same podiatrist's clinic was nearing retirement, to let me talk to his patients during clinic hours.

My father's practice was a large and thriving one, situated near the shopping center of a middle-class suburb of a large northern city. His patients used the same doctor, shopped at the same local shops, and were part of the same social network. The majority also attended the local Methodist church, as he did. So his patients formed a fairly homogeneous social and cultural group based on the local neighborhood. With their permission, I simply sat in on their treatment, told them what I was researching and how I was planning to use the material, and recorded everything that was said. In the course of the five months I worked in my father's clinic, I interviewed 120 people of both sexes and of all ages from sixteen to ninety-five. The majority (ninety-six) of these people were elderly women, so this was the group I chose as my primary informants. Nine interviews had to be discarded for technical reasons, so the discussion that follows is based on the responses of eighty-seven women aged sixty to ninety-five years.

My father was able to give me at least a minimum of demographic information about the majority of these women—their approximate age, their marital status, and their domestic circumstances. This information is expressed in Table 1. As far as religion was concerned, my information was a little more impressionistic, drawn in part from my father's personal knowledge and in part from what was let fall during the conversation, or could be deduced from it. On this information, I concluded that all but one woman had some religious faith; one was Roman Catholic and one was Presbyterian, a handful were at least nominally Church of England, and perhaps a dozen were Jewish. The majority, however, were Methodists attending the same local church as my father himself.

These women were knowledgeable about every aspect of traditional beliefs about foreknowledge and, with very few exceptions, were happy to discuss these matters with me and tell me their personal experiences. In all, eighty-one expressed opinions about astrology, sixty-nine spoke about premonitions, sixty about omens, fifty-nine about fortune-telling, and forty-seven about telepathy. In the course of conversation, they told 111 stories, fifty-one of which were memorates about these matters (the remainder concerned death, bereavement, and the spirits of the dead).

Beliefs and Stories about Knowing the Future

It would appear from these interviews, conversations, and stories that these women are familiar with both the divinatory tradition and the visionary one.

Table 1:
Characteristics of 81 Women in the Neighborhood Group Studied*

Marital Status and Domestic Circumstances	Age: 60–70 Years N = 29	Age: 70–80 Years N = 44	Age: 80–90+ Years N = 8
Single			
Living alone	2	7	1
Living with family/friends	3	3	0
Married			
Living alone	0	0	0
Living with family/friends	14	10	2
Widowed			
Living alone	8	20	3
Living with family/friends	2	4	2

* The author interviewed 87 women, but data about marital status and domestic circumstances were unavailable for six of those women.

Most of the women I spoke to had tried the former and experienced the latter; in their own eyes, they were expert witnesses.

The folklore that shaped their experience and was transmitted among them was not simply a descriptive body of information, however; it was judgmental and evaluative. Though they were equally knowledgeable about the divinatory and the visionary routes into knowledge of the future, they did not value them equally. Very large numbers of the women had some interest in astrology and fortune-telling, but they were shamefaced about this behavior and few would admit to believing in these things. Nearly two-thirds of them, for example, were dismissive of astrology, saying "I read it but I don't believe it"; only 2 percent said they believed in it completely and only 25 percent admitted even partial belief. The percentage of disbelievers rose to 75 percent in the case of fortune-telling; only 15 percent of informants were sure that it would work and only 9 percent thought it might do. About seances and mediums, the vast majority were very skeptical and disapproving.

When they discussed the visionary strand of traditional lore, however, their shamefacedness disappeared and they were willing to admit that they had considerable belief. More than half were convinced, for example, that telepathy is possible and that they had experienced it themselves (only 10 percent thought it did not and could not occur). More than half also believed in omens of death, and half of them could cite personal examples. More than three-quarters of them thought it might be possible to be forewarned that "something's going to happen" by premonitions; and 43 percent of them were certain that such things did happen. They interpreted these experiences as evidence that they had some measure of ESP—that, as they expressed it, they were "a little bit psychic."

On the face of it, these differing attitudes, though in line with the findings from Leeds and Finland, seem strange and perhaps contradictory; why should these women so value the visionary tradition and be so wary and skeptical of the divinatory tradition? However, there is a rationale at work here, one that is revealed when looking at their conversation and narratives in more detail.

Stories about "being a little bit psychic" typically feature women who, while engaged in their ordinary routine about the home or the office, suddenly "feel" or "know" that "something" is going to happen, or perhaps see or hear something unusual and unaccountable. After a short time, three days or three weeks, someone dies or has an accident or is admitted to the hospital or gets married, just as was foreseen. The storytellers are invariably precise about places and times and persons, insisting almost dogmatically upon orienting the events with circumstantial details. Storytellers who earnestly espouse the worldview being explored in the story they are telling—whose credibility and self-respect are dependent upon it, like witnesses in a courtroom—pin their hopes of being believed upon demonstrating the wealth, accuracy, and internal consistency of the circumstantial detail they can provide.[14] And so it is here. Almost always the scene is set in "the daily round, the common task," as the narrator walks down the road, does the shopping or the housework, lies in bed or (in one memorable case) uses the bathroom; and the precise date is clearly remembered. The events are said to have happened "in January 1971," or "three years ago last November," or "only yesterday morning." The feeling or knowledge relates to some member of the family, most commonly mothers, sisters, husbands, brothers, and nephews, or to some close friend. Usually its precise meaning cannot be identified immediately; only subsequent events reveal its significance.

Only a few of the stories feature objective tokens of death, but when they do, these signs are very traditional ones—the sound of a brick hitting the wall, bangs in furniture, broken mirrors, the scent of flowers. More commonly, the forewarning comes in the form of strange physical or emotional states. The women say things like:

> I do believe in premonitions, and the feeling I get if it's something not very pleasant is a coldness, a chill. Suddenly, for no reason at all—I can be so happy and

everything seems all right and then suddenly (and it's a horrible feeling) really physically go quite cold and shudder, and then whatever it is, I think about it.[15]

If there's anything going to happen, then my tummy gives a sort of roll and I
say, "Hello! What's going . . . something's going to happen today!"[16]

I think one has a very strange feeling when something very important is going to
happen, that you can't explain. Can't explain it. Almost as if one's on the edge of a
cliff and you *feel* that something *terrible* is going to happen, but you can't put your
finger on it.[17]

I do know that different things have happened and I've seemed to . . . at the
back of my mind, it's as though I've seen something before.[18]

Alternatively, they simply say: "I get such a queer feeling," or "I know
what's coming," or "It has come true just as I dreamt it." Or they may tell an
illustrative story, such as these two from different women, which between
them cover some of the more common themes:

Well, the only personal experience I have had . . . . One day, in the office, I was
going past one of the girls—not a young girl—and I knew nothing about her personal life except she lived with her parents and was very good to them, very devoted.
And as I passed by her, I turned round to her and said, "Rita, someone's going to
ask you to marry him!" I *felt* the . . . .
    And then, the next day, she came in and said the man next door, a widower, had
asked her to marry him. And they got engaged.
    Now that's the only thing I know of personally.[19]

Well, I think I believe in that. One particular occasion was Mrs. Robertson [the
doctor's wife]. Well, you know, she was in hospital, going in to have her hip done.
And when the matron came down the ward, she came to her bed, and Mrs. Robertson turned round and said to her, "You've no need to tell me. It's my husband.
He's died."
    And he was killed, he had a coronary on the road.
    And she did, she turned round and said, "You've no need to tell me. I know it's
my husband and he's died." And he'd just collapsed at the wheel, veered to the side.
    And that's the only one that I've known.[20]

When we look at the women's stories and conversation about fortune-telling and astrology, however, we find that they not only have a quite different
atmosphere, but also a quite different type of detail. Rather than trying hard to
convince their hearers through a wealth of orienting detail, tellers of fortune-
telling stories have a "take-it-or-leave-it" attitude to their narratives. The scene-
setting of their stories is considerably vaguer and more general. Narrators are
content to say that the events happened "ages ago," "when I was younger,"
"once," or "one time I remember." Though the events took place away from
the ordinary environment, the location is seldom described in any sort of detail.

The dramatis personae, too, are only vaguely spelled out—often as not, they are simply described as "we," "this woman," or "she." Almost invariably, the account is very objective, so we do not get to understand the narrator's frame of mind, motivation, or reactions, either. We are simply told about the message which "this woman" delivers. So the total effect is impersonal and distanced.

Another interesting observation is that the predictions featured in these stories are quite different in several ways from the forewarnings afforded by involuntary psychic experiences. In the first place, the message about the future is quite clear and distinct, given the ambiguity common to these occasions. The messages refer primarily to the domestic affairs, health, and finance of the narrator herself, or occasionally of her female relatives. Only time will tell whether there is "anything in it": several narrators say they are still waiting for the husbands, money, or success they were promised! The air of objectivity is enhanced by this slight element of suspense, which narrators exploit by telling the story in strict chronological order without asides or digressions, and by structuring it according to a neatly matched before-and-after pattern. These are all rather good stories technically, but the cumulative effect is of detachment, the narrators perhaps taking most pleasure in simply "telling the tale."

Barbara's story is typical of accounts of visits to fortune-tellers. She does not even date the story; she refers throughout to the fortune-teller as "this woman" and is equally vague about other aspects of the scene, except that the clairvoyant had a "caravan" which suggests that the events took place during a seaside holiday. The dramatis personae are characterized so vaguely that it is often difficult to disentangle who's who. Only the fortune-teller's message is reported, and we are told nothing about how she arrived at her prediction. Again, there is no subjective comment to form a digression, and it moves briskly on in lively and fairly impersonal dialogue.[21] Finally, Barbara blames her friend for the escapade and reports that she found it all "quite amusing."

> We went to a caravan . . . "Oh," my friend [said], "we're going to this palmist!" you see. But anyway, my brother at this time had put his shoulder out and he'd been to the hospital. Anyway! This er—she told me about "someone in your family who's got this shoulder [trouble]." And then she said to me, "Do you know a policeman?"
>
> I said, "No!"
>
> "Well!" she said. "You *are* going to know one."
>
> Well, I thought it was quite amusing.
>
> And when we got home from this holiday—we were staying at Marlborough—I called over to our next-door neighbour to say we were home, you see, and a strange voice answered me, "Oh, do you want Mrs. Warburton?"
>
> And it was this fellow who was [staying] there.

And when Mrs. Warburton came to see me, she said, "That's Perkins. He's a policeman."

Absolutely spot on, wasn't she?[22]

A story—one of only three on the subject of astrology—told by Norah is similarly distanced, vague, and impersonal: it seeks only to entertain for a moment. Whereas Barbara's story is about family and (future) friends, Norah's is about finance; between these two women they cover the topics that occur most frequently as predictions about the future.

I read my horoscope but it's just like water off a duck's back, isn't it? I don't believe in it, really. Because once my horoscope told me that I should buy some Premium Bonds,[23] and I went out and bought them, and they've never won *yet!*

Yes, I remember reading it and it said something about buying some Premium Bonds, and I went out and bought some *like a lunatic!* And I just went *out* and bought this five pounds' worth of *Premium Bonds* but I never won!

So I don't think I'll believe in it *again!*[24]

Overall, then, we find two very different types of experience told in very different ways. In stories about "being a little bit psychic," the women are careful to date the events clearly and to specify both the places and people involved. They try by all means to make the story both real and convincing. They tell of insights that came to them unbidden, as they went about their ordinary lives. In most cases these insights are purely subjective—a mood, a feeling, a sudden knowledge; in the few cases where something more objective is seen or heard, it is only the narrator who perceives the omen and who can interpret its significance. The women to whom these things happen are regarded as being more than usually sensitive, or, at least, in a more than usually sensitive mood or condition. Their premonitions are invariably other-person-centered: their concern is never with their own fate. In most cases, the other person whose distress or need they are responding to is a male member of their immediate family. All the accounts are thus highly subjective and show the narrators as caring, intuitive, sensitive, loving, and responsive to the needs of their family and menfolk.

In contrast, in telling stories about fortune-telling adventures, the women are much more careless and happy-go-lucky, taking little heed, it seems, whether they will be believed or not. They are vague about details, not specifying very precisely who were the characters involved or where the events took place. Rather than telling their listener how they feel about the visit or the predictions, they concentrate on repeating the message they were given and saying whether it has (yet) come true. They construct these stories dramatically, keeping to chronological order and endeavoring to present an entertaining account of their visit. The predictions almost invariably concern their own, not another person's, fate and keep to a range of topics conventionally considered to be feminine preoccupations.

When we list the main characteristics of the two sorts of events and the corresponding stories like this, it becomes plain that they are based on a common evaluative folklore of the "proper" way to handle encounters with the future. We can see, on the one hand, that involuntary ESP experiences, as this group of people see them, are geared toward the concerns of a person other than the self. On the other hand, one goes to a fortune-teller out of concern for one's own fate; it is a deliberately chosen action, and it involves invoking acquired skills rather than passively responding to involuntary feelings, sensations, or perceptions. All this strongly suggests that the women are using their stories as vehicles of moral judgments, accepting elements of the traditional folklore which fit in with their values and rejecting those that run contrary to them.

Traditional Values and Roles

As mentioned earlier, the women I studied were all over sixty years old at the time I talked to them; most were in their late sixties and early seventies, and the oldest was ninety-five. Eighty percent of them were married or widowed, and most had families. Even if they were unmarried, few had led independent lives; most of the single women, for instance, had devoted themselves to caring for their parents. For the entire group of women, the death of parents or husbands had often not substantially changed their situation, however, for half of them now lived with younger members of their family, and they were still deeply enmeshed in family cares and duties.

Like it or not, for reasons of age, class, and religion these women's lives were geared to traditional roles and pursuits: we can assume that they had been taught as children, and had grown up believing, that the ideal member of their sex is an intuitive, caring, unassertive person for whom direct action, independent thought, and concern with self are unbecoming and whose "natural" role is as support, nurse, and helpmate. These traditional views would be specially enhanced for those women whose lives were centered around their church; they would not only be constantly in the company of the like-minded, but their views would be colored by moral considerations, their ideals about the relationship between men and women being modeled on their view of the relationship between humans and God. I believe that, in some ways, their beliefs about involuntary ESP allow these women to square the circle in terms of these traditional ideals and roles.

This becomes clear by examining some of the other narratives I was told during the course of my fieldwork, especially widows' stories about the deaths of their husbands. A very common experience was to have been faced with some difficulty or dilemma in the months following their bereavement. This difficulty was mentally referred to the lost spouse, and the widows received an "answer" to their problems. In distress, for example, the women might speak aloud to the dead man, or even pray to him; their prayers seemed to be answered, and the difficulty resolved, when they physically "heard" a reply or "heard a voice in their heads" or the answer was "put into their heads."[25] Though this experience would seem to be common in bereavement, it is capable of receiving an interpretation in addition to the usual psychological one that dwells on the altered state of consciousness of the newly bereaved person.[26]

The women's glosses to these stories emphasize their helplessness and weakness in the face of their troubles, and firmly attribute their subsequent ability to resolve their problems to the intervention of supernatural forces. "I couldn't have done it under my own steam," they say. "I had help given, and I firmly believe that my husband was beside me telling me what to do." In each case, the insoluble problem involved doing something previously regarded as exclusively a husband's task—filling in income-tax forms, moving to another house, winding up a relative's estate, and so on. In listening to these stories, the overwhelming impression is first of the women's lack of confidence in their own abilities to do these "men's jobs," a lack of confidence so acute that it leads them to attribute even the smallest personal success directly to the man, even though he is dead; and second, perhaps more unkindly, a suspicion that they are disclaiming responsibility for stepping out of role by interpreting their new ability as a more-or-less temporary gift—"You do!" they say. "You get the strength *given* you!"

I want to suggest that narratives about involuntary ESP are structured and presented to others in a broadly similar way. Telling stories like these is one way a woman may claim status and yet not challenge the conventional perception of her proper role. Being capable of having such experiences—being "a little bit psychic," in the women's terminology—confers authority on its possessor, but not improper power.

This is so because being "a little bit psychic" is a "gift" in the sense of an unsought handout, as well as in the sense of a natural talent: indeed, women's discourse often stresses that at times it is an unwelcome gift, a burden—it's a "horrible feeling," a "strange feeling," "something not very pleasant," "I wish I didn't have premonitions, it's like prophesying evil all the time, isn't it." Properly used, the gift confers only passive power—if that is not a contradiction in terms. A woman who has a premonition can *do* very little about it. It is a glimpse into a future where, in their words, "what will be will be, and nothing will alter it." Often, the most that may be done is to prepare oneself psychologically.

I collected very few stories in which women make physical preparations in response to a supernatural warning: a woman who has a premonition that visitors will call bakes some extra cakes; two women agree not to talk to each other because the psychic one has dreamt that they have had a quarrel; a mother waits at home because she is confident that she will hear that her daughter has been involved in an accident. Most often it is psychological preparation that the foreknowledge provides: a sister "sees" her brother with "his leg all shriveled up" before he steps on a land mine; a wife "sees" the accident her husband has been involved in; an aunt has a dream that her nephew has been blinded in the war, and so on. Psychic gifts seem thus specially tailored to the traditional female role, because they demand patience, watchfulness, compliance—not action.

Running like a thread through many of my informants' conversations was the concept of predestination, with its passive–compliant corollary, complete acceptance. As they see it, the future is already ordained and nothing can turn it from its course. It advances on the individual like the infamous "irresistible force." People, however, are by no means "immovable objects"; like trees in a gale, they must bend and submit or be broken. Many of my informants had adopted this philosophy as a coping strategy against the vagaries of chance and fate, the sense of their own powerlessness, and the tragedies of their lives: in submitting to their fate, they said they are "given the strength" to endure it. Psychic gifts, by forewarning the individual of trouble to come yet allowing no remedy by action or interference, increase that passive strength. They also bestow the ability to perceive hidden order in natural chaos. It is easier to say with Milton's Samson that "just are the ways of God and justifiable to Man" if you feel that God does have a purpose. Psychic powers bestow that assurance. If things were not part of God's plan, the reasoning goes, then events would not be predested: if events were not predested, then one could not receive any forewarnings about them. The fact that "sensitive" and gifted people do receive such forewarnings proves that there is a divine plan, and ultimately proves that there is a divinity. It would seem that by increasing the recipient's "passive resistance" to turmoil and sorrow, psychic gifts convey the power to deal with major life events on the terms that these women most approve of.

These alone are considerable benefits, but women with "the gift" have more mundane and worldly advantages over their ungifted sisters. In a very direct way, being "a little bit psychic" guarantees approved feminine virtues, especially those good old standbys of intuition, sensitivity, and tenderness. All the accounts of ESP which I collected are highly subjective and show the narrators as caring, sensitive, loving people who are responsive to the needs of their family and their menfolk. In addition to being handed this informal badge of feminine merit, the possessor of psychic powers has other social advantages, most notably that her abilities confer considerable prestige and authority; as Alma in one of the stories below says, "Whatever I said she took for gospel."

Negative Aspects of Psychic Power

The flattery and attention may be pleasant and may give a welcome sense of power and control, but my informants feel that being "a little bit psychic" places them in moral danger. It is to this danger that I want to turn now, in order to examine the negative aspects of their beliefs in psychic powers. These negative aspects are not only potent and painful, but more than anything else, I think, they help point up the functional picture I have attempted to paint, because they show women stepping out of the traditional feminine role and seeking power, fame, and glory for themselves. They also allow us to disentangle the reasons for the women's negative attitudes to astrology and fortune-telling.

As we have seen, women's ideas about psychic powers center round the concept of *gift*—not only are such powers a gift in the sense of a talent, but they are a gift in the sense of an unsought handout that has been conferred on the woman though she has not asked for it and may not welcome it. This has several implications—most important, that the woman is not responsible for any power or advantage which the gift confers; she cannot be blamed for her success. Though the gift may empower her, that power is excused and she remains uncontaminated by it.

A folktale analogy may be in order here. We may compare the masculine ethos of force and action (as my informants see it) to the eldest sons in a typical "youngest–smartest" story, and the feminine ethos to the youngest son. When the elders fail, and force and action prove counterproductive, the task devolves to the youngest son, unfit and unwilling though he feels that he is. His virtue, deserving modesty, and kindness lead to his being presented with a magic gift, the power of which sees him through the task. The task can therefore be achieved without his being corrupted. He still remains the nice, appealing, helpless young man he was at the start of the story: the only difference is that he now has the princess. He can have the advantages of action without being affected by its corrupting influence. The same is true for women with psychic gifts.

The converse of this is, of course, that to claim the gift as yours and exploit it for personal advantage destroys this delicate balance. My informants called the exploitation of psychic gifts "delving," and delving is the ultimate taboo for this group of women. Significantly perhaps, I collected only six stories about delving (i.e., less than 6 percent), but nevertheless they form a coherent and convincing pattern. These stories feature psychic women reading the cards or the cups for their family or friends. In every case the result is dreadful. Clara has her hand read by a friend and within a year her favorite nephew dies a painful death; Geraldine suffers a distressing domestic upheaval; Berenice foretells—and lives to see—an unsuitable marriage; Alma reads the cups for her mother's friend and the friend dies within three weeks; Rose plays with a Ouija board and has to have an operation; later Rose reads the cards for a relative and almost immediately afterwards their great-nephew visits them, contracts a fatal disease, and dies in their house.

The tenor of the "delving" experience and the moral force of the stories can best be seen by looking at two of the stories told by Rose and Alma. These two women are not just good narrators; they firmly believe that they do have special powers. Their personal experiences therefore deserve serious attention: their cautionary tales can tell us a good deal about the use and abuse of psychic gifts.

Alma
Now, I'll tell you one thing! When I was younger I used to look into teacups. Now, mother had a friend who was terribly superstitious, and whatever I said, she took for gospel. Things did happen that way, but a lot of it didn't. But I know, the last time she asked me, she said, "Oh, you must read my cup!"

And I looked at it and I said, "Oh!" I said. "There's nothing there!"

"Oh!" she said. "There must be!"

I said, "No, there isn't," I said. "Honestly," I said, "there's nothing there at all!" And I couldn't see a . . . .

Well, she was very, very offended about this. And I said, "No, there isn't."

And when I came home, mother . . . "Oh!" she said. "Why didn't you tell her something?"

I said, "Look, mother! There was no future for her. None at all!"

She said, "There must have been!"

I said, "There wasn't," I said. "I couldn't see a thing in that cup," I said, "and I got a queer feeling when I picked it up," I said. There wasn't anything there!

Do you know! That next week, we were out, and we met a friend, and she said, "Ooh! Did you know about so-and-so. . . " She'd been taken ill. She'd had a stroke. And she only lasted three days. The next thing we knew, my mother was going to her funeral.

Well now, that was the last time that ever . . . [27]

Rose
[*Author:* Tell me how you think you're psychic.]

Because I know what's going to happen. I've got a pretty good idea, yeah. How do I know? Inside there (points to her head). And the fact also I've been able to tell fortunes by cards, and I was able to read cups, reading tea-leaves, and this was oh, forty, fifty years ago. I was young. I was in my teens then, you see, and I frightened myself to death. So I said, *"No way!"* So I left the tea-leaf business alone.

When I was married, and we'd been married Lord knows how long—the war interrupted, so of course we never had any children till 1947. Now, in that summer of '47, I used to tell all fortunes by cards.

[*Author*: What's this? Tarot cards?]

No, no. Playing cards. Each card has a meaning and all the cards together spell out a message.

Anyway! I was about six or seven months pregnant and we go down to see my husband's aunt, and she was a great believer in the cards. And they have one son. Now, he was very good in business. He was quite a top notch in Rolls-Royce.

Anyway! We got down there on the Saturday afternoon and there was Auntie Edie, Uncle Bernard, who are my husband's aunt and uncle, myself (complete with lump, of course!), and my husband. And Cousin Charlie met us at Chesney station—with Rolls-Royce, of course, naturally!—and took us to his house.

So, and we had a terrible thunderstorm in the afternoon, so, to pass the time away, Charlie and his wife said, "Let's tell our fortunes, Rose!" So I said, "Oh, OK, then," never thinking anything about it.

And they got the cards out and we started, you know. And all I could tell her was that all I could see and all I could smell—all I could smell was flowers and all I could see was a coffin sitting there in the hall on a bier.

Now, it was a beautiful house, with a great big square hall, you see. There's a lounge at the front, and there's a dining room and there's a morning room, and there's this, that, and the other, you see.

Went to bed at night. Everybody laughed! They thought, "Oh, she's pregnant," you see. So we went to bed at night, like, and I kept crying and my husband said to me, "What the hell's the matter with you?" He says, "I can't understand you!"

I said, "I want to go home! All I can see . . . I can all smell flowers and all I can see is a coffin and it's on a bier in that hall!"

He said, "Oh, don't be silly, Rose! You'll be all right. Get off to sleep!"

No sleep for me!

We went home on the Sunday and Auntie Edie said to me going home on the train, "What was the matter with you yesterday?"

So I told her, so I said, "There's a coffin. There's a funeral in that house, you know."

She says, "Is there?"

I says, "Yes." I says, "I don't know who it is, but it's definitely in that house!"

So anyway, I think it would be July 19th. Now, in the August of '47, the great-nephew, he was fourteen years old, their only son—their only child, everything planned and a brilliant scholar—he came over to see his Auntie Edie and contracted polio, and in three weeks he was dead. Yes. *And his coffin stood on bier in the hall.*

It so affected me, I said, "Never again will I tell a fortune!" *Frightened* me to *death*!

I said, "No!"[28]

As Alma and Rose—and their contemporaries—see it, the proper characteristic of the woman with psychic gifts should be that she reacts to events already ordained, and that she does this by means of a God-given sensibility that is created and consolidated by love of other people. This being the mechanism of the precognitive process, it must be a sinful and graceless distortion to use it to achieve selfish or trivial ends. The women I studied therefore draw a sharp line between unsought precognitive experiences and delving, which is designed to harness these powerful abilities and claim them for one's own. The latter corrupts or backfires, the former does not. Supernatural experience that is not deliberately courted is considered both safe and good because it is an extension of ordinary loving intuition, but any attempt to deliberately seek knowledge of the future is dangerously audacious, and retribution will surely follow. These contrasts, I believe, are born out of the respect that elderly women have for the traditional female role. Their adherence to conventional female virtues leads them to make sharp moral distinctions between the two strands of precognitive traditions outlined earlier, eschewing the active–objective divinatory tradition of which delving is a part, and embracing the receptive–subjective visionary tradition of which psychic gifts are a part. Even consulting horoscopes or fortune-tellers is not without danger and should certainly not be taken seriously, for that could be construed as a willingness to "delve" into what should be kept hidden. Only by treating such activities unseriously can the sting be removed and the potential threat diverted. So the women are careful to stress that they do not "really" believe in these things, and are apt to hedge their stories and experiences with apologies and explanations—"I did it for a laugh," "I did it for a dare," "I've only ever done it once," "I only went with my sister to keep her company," and so on.

Whereas audacious "delving" into the unknown by reading teacups or playing with Ouija boards is morally dangerous, the modest and unselfish acceptance of psychic gifts is both safe and empowering. In terms of sociosexual roles, it allows women to "both have their cake and eat it."

On the one hand, the concept of psychic gifts directly enshrines the conventional feminine virtues of intuition, caring, and sensitivity, and thus glorifies the female character (I choose the word *glorifies* deliberately; psychic powers both glory in the traditional female virtues and make them glorious).

On the other hand, and best of all, while doing this the concept also allows women to act outside the constraints of those characteristic virtues. By concentrating on the notion of psychic powers as "gift"—something unsought and perhaps temporary—women permit themselves, at least for a while, to achieve a personal glory, to play an active role as guide and interpreter of human affairs, to claim status and authority within their group—all without giving up their claim to feminine modesty. In brief, the concept of psychic gifts allows women to act out-of-role while still in-role.

Conclusion

Finally, how far are the beliefs I have described as part of the folklore of a neighborhood group of elderly women common to other social groups?

My work permits only an impressionistic discussion of this question, but some trends are nevertheless discernible and would be worth following up in a subsequent study. During the months I worked in my father's clinic, I also spoke to twenty-one younger women (one sixteen-year-old and twenty women between the ages of forty and sixty) and to thirteen men, nine of whom were husbands of women in the main study group. If the beliefs of these (admittedly small) alternative samples are analyzed, some interesting and suggestive patterns emerge.

Among younger women, belief in fortune-telling, astrology, and other forms of divination is significantly higher than among the older women. Thirty-two percent of them believe in horoscopes, 46 percent think that one's character can be read in one's birth sign, and 53 percent have some measure of faith in fortune-tellers (comparable figures for the older women are 27 percent, 33 percent, and 24 percent, respectively). Elderly men return lower percentages on all topics except omens (where—and I have no explanation for this—they score higher than both groups of women). Among men, scores are particularly low for telepathy (32 percent for men, compared with 67 percent for the older women) and somewhat lower for premonitions (the men score 60 percent, the older women 77 percent).

Though partial and impressionistic, these figures do suggest that the patterns which I have discussed are indeed elderly women's responses to traditional beliefs. On the whole, the younger women are more believing than the older ones. If, for example, one were to average out their level of belief over all six topics that were discussed, one would find that their mean percentage of belief in traditions of foreknowledge is 50.6 percent compared with 47.1 percent among older women. The significant difference, however, is that they are much more accepting of the "active" divinatory traditions. Averaging out the percentage scores over the different aspects of these traditions gives a figure of 29.6 percent for the older women, but 47 percent for the younger women. Conversely, averaging out the percentage scores on the three "subjective" traditions (omens, premonitions, and telepathy) gives a figure of 57.6 percent for the younger women, but 65.3 percent for the older ones. This does suggest that seeking to know one's personal fate for personal advantage is less taboo for the younger women and that, conversely, they lay less stress on the value of involuntary foreknowledge.

Comparisons between the levels of belief among elderly men and elderly women are also suggestive. Averaged out, men's percentage of belief overall is lower than that for either group of women (42 percent). This is despite an inexplicably high level of belief in omens (66 percent). It is virtually impossible, however, to get any figures for belief in the divinatory tradition. Two of the thirteen men said that they read—and believed—their horoscopes: all the rest state or imply that horoscopes are "more for the ladies"—as are interest in birth signs and fortune-telling. One cannot help but guess that this is because men of this age and class feel sufficiently in control of their lives to have no use for these practices.

Not too much should be made of such an impressionistic analysis, of course, but nevertheless it is suggestive. The younger women and the men are directly comparable with the women of the study group, in that they differ only by virtue of age or sex, but not both. This is specially true of the men, the majority of whom were married to women in the study group. It would follow that differences in their patterns of belief are a function of age and sex taken together. In turn this suggests that the operational factor must be age- and sex-related cultural contacts.

More would need to be done to confirm whether these are universal patterns among elderly women, or whether they are perhaps most typical of middle-class churchgoers. I would be most interested to learn of any studies which would serve to confirm or challenge the patterns of belief that I have described here. Meanwhile, I hope that my own work may at least show what a wealth of folklore there is to be explored in even the most prosaic of everyday surroundings.

Endnotes

1. John Beaumont, *An Historical Physiological and Theological Treatise of Spirits, Apparitions, Witchcrafts, and Other Magical Practices* (London: D. Browne, 1705), 220.

2. John Aubrey, *Miscellanies* (London: Edward Castle, 1696), 33–34.

3. Ibid., 39.

4. Ibid., 40.

5. Ibid., 45.

6. Francis Grose, *A Provincial Glossary with a Collection of Local Proverbs and Popular Superstitions* (London: S. Hooper, [1787] 1790), 34–37.

7. See Gillian Bennett, *Traditions of Belief: Women and the Supernatural* (Harmondsworth, England: Penguin, 1987), 175–188.

8. William Henderson, *Notes on the Folk Lore of the Northern Counties of England and the Borders* (1866; reprint, Wakefield: E.P. Publishing, 1973), 30; Catherine Crowe, *The Night-Side of Nature: Or Ghosts and Ghost-seers* (1848; reprint, Wellingborough, Northamptonshire: Aquarian Press, 1986), 48–65, 98–129.

9. Bennett, 110–142.

10. H. K. Nixon, "Popular Answers to Some Psychological Questions," *American Journal of Psychology* 36 (1925): 418–423; Lynn L. Ralya, "Some Surprising

Beliefs Concerning Human Nature among Pre-Medical Psychology Students," *British Journal of Educational Psychology* 15 (1945): 70–75; Geoffrey Gorer, *Exploring English Character* (London: Cresset, 1955); Robert Towler et al., "Conventional Religion and Common Religion in Great Britain," Religious Research Papers, no. 11 (University of Leeds, Department of Sociology, 1981–84); Eugene Levitt, "Superstitions Twenty-Five Years Ago and Today," *American Journal of Psychiatry* 65 (1952): 443–449; F. W. Warburton, "Beliefs Concerning Human Nature among Students in a University Department of Education," *British Journal of Educational Psychology* 26 (1956): 156–162.

11.   Leea Virtanen, *"That Must Have Been ESP!": An Examination of Psychic Experiences* (Bloomington: Indiana University Press, 1990), 24.

12.   David J. Hufford, "Traditions of Disbelief," *New York Folklore* 8 (1982): 49.

13.   Virtanen, 161.

14.   Gillian Bennett, "Narrative as Expository Discourse," *Journal of American Folklore* 99 (1986): 415–484.

15.   Informant 100b, interviewed February 4, 1981.

16.   Informant 76b, interviewed May 4, 1981.

17.   Informant 72b, interviewed March 31, 1981.

18.   Informant 34b, interviewed April 6, 1981.

19.   Informant 56b, interviewed February 24, 1981.

20.   Informant 34b, interviewed April 6, 1981.

21.   Compare the "narrative velocity" of legends "told for laughs," in Gillian Bennett, "Legend: Performance and Truth," in *Monsters with Iron Teeth: Perspectives on Contemporary Legends,* vol. 2, ed. Gillian Bennett and Paul Smith (Sheffield: Sheffield Academic Press, 1988), 13–36.

22.   Informant 3b (pseudonym Barbara), interviewed March 2, 1981.

23.   Premium Bonds are a form of government raffle.

24.   Informant 12b (pseudonym Norah), interviewed January 27, 1981.

25.   See Bennett, *Traditions of Belief,* 63–81.

26.   See Erich Lindemann, "Symptomatology and Management of Acute Grief," *American Journal of Psychiatry* 101 (1944): 141–148; Peter Marris, *Widows and Their Families* (London: Routledge and Kegan Paul, 1958); Colin Murray Parkes, *Bereavement: Studies of Grief in Adult Life* (New York: International Universities Press, 1972); Richard Schulz, *The Psychology of Death, Dying, and Bereavement* (Reading, PA: Addison-Wesley, 1978).

27.   Informant 48b (pseudonym Alma), interviewed February 25, 1981.

28.   Informant 85b (pseudonym Rose), interviewed March 18, 1981.

III

Demons and Gods: Cultural Adaptations and Incorporations

Within a society, elements of the supernatural might be included within a broad spectrum of belief, but how that assimilation takes place or in what form varies from culture to culture. This final section provides three rather diverse accounts of how the supernatural functions among groups in the United States.

In Chapter 8, Erika Brady provides an intriguing look into the world of evil spirits, exorcisms, and Roman Catholic priests. Through her students, Brady collected several accounts in which an individual either was possessed by or somehow encountered a malevolent force, and, accordingly, sought the help of a Catholic priest. Curious about following up on these accounts, Brady undertook field research with Catholic priests in her region, collecting their remarks on these legends. Her findings and insightful comments provide a unique perspective on interpretation of events, the influence of media, and the experiences of those whose profession links them directly to the arena of supernatural belief.

Focusing on the Hawaiian goddess Pele, anthropologist Joyce Hammond explores the concept of Other, something both sought and feared as it applies to the tourist experience, desirable precisely because it is distinct from self and one's typical experiences; Hammond examines the function and value of this distinction. Initially often skeptical, some tourists later place credence in the Pele legends encountered during their visit to Hawaii. Whether they are human fabrications or actual, independently existing figures, substances, or essences, gods like Pele—although conceived of differently by Hawaiian natives and by non-native tourists—become symbolic of the exotic physical environment and culture, and of individual interaction with both.

In Chapter 10, Shelley Adler discusses the vital concept of how belief in the supernatural can affect health and one's sense of well-being.

Working with Hmong immigrants to the United States, Adler investigates their belief in dab tsog, a supernatural nocturnal visitation by an evil presence in which the individual experiences deep fear, an interval of paralysis, and pressure on the chest. Adler speculates about the relationship between this experience, which is attributed to a supernatural force, and the occurrence of sudden unexpected nocturnal death syndrome (SUNDS), found in an unusually high proportion of the male Hmong population living in the United States. She also examines the influence of life in America and acculturation as having positive effects for Hmong when confronting the terror of SUNDS.

8

Bad Scares and Joyful Hauntings: "Priesting" the Supernatural Predicament

Erika Brady

> *"You don't believe in me," observed the Ghost.*
> *"I don't," said Scrooge.*
> *"What evidence would you have of my reality beyond that of your own senses?"*
> *"I don't know," said Scrooge.*
> *"Why doubt your senses?"*
> *"Because a little thing affects them. A slight disorder of the stomach makes them cheats. You may be an undigested bit of beef, a blot of mustard, a crumb of cheese, a fragment of an underdone potato. There's more of gravy than of grave about you, whatever you are!"*
>
> Charles Dickens, *A Christmas Carol*

SCROOGE'S INTERPRETIVE DILEMMA IS A COMMON ONE IN THE NARRATIVE arts—a dilemma faced by fictional characters which extends to include a real-life audience of readers and listeners. Whether the tone of the work is gently facetious, profoundly serious, or calculatingly sensational, the author portrays a character caught in a situation that suggests a supernatural action or presence, while at the same time offering clues to the circumstances, motives, and psychological state of the character that equally suggest a mundane explanation: an interpretive ambiguity that both attracts and repels. "Gravy" or "grave"? The author turns the screw until the tension is—usually—broken by some definitive evidence that either explains away or confirms the supernatural component within the fictional frame.[1]

The structure and strategy of the literary horror story and its relationship to the horror stories common in oral circulation have been ingeniously explored by Susan Stewart, who notes the emphasis on closure as the focus of attention in both types of narrative. Suspense builds with each bit of evidence shared by an authorial voice, which Stewart describes, in terms themselves almost gothic, as a "manager of a theater of fright . . . hold[ing] an absolute, if not cruel, authority over the reader, controlling the flow and juncture of the narrative sequence, manipulating the appearance and disappearance of images."[2] In the world of literary fiction and in stories in oral circulation that are understood by audiences to be a raconteur's fictive tour de force, the success of the supernatural story lies in the artfully combined use and disguise of artifice. Readers or listeners are lured into a temporary suspension of disbelief so that they identify with the central character, forget the theatrical context of presentation and its "manager," and become, in a sense, co-victims in the tale itself and thus relieved participants in the resolution of ambiguity given at the tale's conclusion.

But what of stories in which no closure is yet possible? Some narratives concerning the supernatural are not fictional, but rather are accounts of experience related precisely because the teller—far from a controlling master of ceremonies—is still anxiously "writing the script."

Many people do encounter sights, sounds, and sensations which are interpreted as supernatural. According to a study performed by the National Opinion Research Corporation (NORC) in 1973, more than one out of four Americans have felt that they were at some time "really in touch with someone who has died."[3] A Gallup survey conducted in 1981 found that nearly a third of Americans have had "what they call a religious or mystical experience." Five percent of the scientists queried in the same survey gave a positive response to the more explicit question, "Have you ever had what you consider as an encounter with an angel or a devil or some other kind of supernatural experience?"[4]

The structure of these queries is in two parts. Each inquires about an experience and a subsequent interpretation of that experience: "Have you ever had a . . . which you have interpreted as . . . ?" A positive response indicates both the occurrence of an experience and a degree of certitude concerning its meaning. But it is likely that many more people undergo experiences which might be interpreted as supernatural in nature, but which are complicated by factors that make certainty of interpretation impossible.

Scholarly and journalistic attention to the Gallup and NORC surveys has focused on the positive and negative responses to the queries, but perhaps of equal significance is the proportion of uncertain or withheld responses. Ten percent of the scientists surveyed by Gallup refused to answer with certainty a question concerning any personal encounter with an angel, devil, or the supernatural, and replied "no opinion." Assuming that this answer was not necessarily a contemptuous summary dismissal of the query, we still cannot be sure whether the opinion was withheld with reference to the experience or to the interpretation.[5]

Theologically and philosophically, the evidential force of experience—perceptual or non-perceptual, sensory or cognitive—is a matter of formal dispute still unresolved, although recent discussion suggests a shift from a generalized skepticism to a cautious process of discrimination and selective acceptance of the supernatural possibility.[6] But for those lacking the formal tools of the theologian and philosopher, the process is different, conditioned by cultural frames and constructs involving the delineations of the "possible" and "rational" that are by no means in themselves consistent or unambiguous. Once the possibilities of human hoax, disordered senses, and misinterpretation of sense-data are eliminated, the exceptional remains, begging interpretation. Many feel the need for a supernatural specialist. In such circumstances, Roman Catholic priests are often called upon by Catholics and non-Catholics alike to evaluate the validity of a supernatural interpretation of an experience.

My investigation of the role of Catholic priests as arbiters and mediators in unusual events was prompted by a common pattern I heard in stories from students enrolled in my supernatural folklore class at Western Kentucky University. Students routinely supported secondhand accounts of a supernatural occurrence by reporting "and they were so scared that they went to a priest to find out about it—just like *The Exorcist!*" Further questioning often revealed that neither the narrator nor the participants in the visit to the rectory were Catholic. I wondered if such visits were in fact common, and if so, what priests' narrative accounts of these episodes might reveal concerning the practice.

Previous work as a folklorist with Catholic dioceses located in southern Missouri, southern Illinois, and northern Arkansas had given me an unusually wide acquaintance among priests in the region, enabling me to interview a number of men of diverse age and experience. These interviews confirmed that calls and visits in which a priest is requested to interpret and sometimes intervene in paranormal matters are quite common, at least in this region.[7] This practice is sufficiently widespread to itself qualify as a kind of traditional customary practice: the enactment of the "priesting" of the interpretive dilemma serves to mark the importance of the ambiguous event to the person who experienced it, sometimes (though not always) resulting in an acceptable interpretation of it, and in some cases providing a dramatic flourish to subsequent narrations in which the trip to the rectory is recounted as the denouement of the event, underlining the weight given it by the participant.

According to the priests interviewed, they are consulted concerning a wide range of situations. As one might expect, these include experiences conforming to the classic mystical sense of divine presence. Episodes of this kind do not seem to be recounted to a priest out of need for explanation or clarification—the meaning of the experience itself is apparently self-evident, is often not reported until well after the fact, and is recounted in an almost offhand way in the context of an individual's total spiritual history. More problematic are apparitions of sacred beings actually evident to the senses, such as the appearance of the Virgin Mary or the sound of angelic voices.

Most frequently reported, however, are consultations concerning visitations from more sinister entities. In the case of college students, these occurrences are especially common in connection with the use of a Ouija board or other practices often undertaken to elicit a supernatural thrill. Sometimes participants get more than they had bargained for, as in the following very typical report:

> When I was at St. Agnes [in Springfield, Missouri], I would say in 1975 or so, that's where Southwest Missouri University is, I got a call one evening from some girl from college there, from the University.
>
> She sounded very frightened, and her response was to call a priest, to call St. Agnes Cathedral. She told me that she and her girlfriend were with three boys, and they had—one of the boys, or two of the boys—had been attempting some sort of a seance, and that as they went through this ritual or whatever they were doing, that they suddenly had a great sense of something that was very, very evil. It frightened them so much that they decided to call the rectory and see whether—they called to see if they could have one of us, a priest, pray over them.
>
> I found it rather strange. So I asked them a few questions, and the girl told me that she was Catholic. I don't remember if her companion, the other girl, was Catholic or not. And I don't think the boys were not [?], but I said, "Well, sure, I'll talk with you," although it was probably ten o'clock, ten-thirty at night.
>
> So they came over, and I was surprised down in the parlor to find that not just the two girls were there, but these three boys. There were three of the boys, there might have been more young men there in this, or maybe other girls, but five of them were at our door.
>
> And this was no put-on at all. The boys were sort of sullen, as though they were being blamed by the girls for whatever happened. They didn't say anything at all. But the girls immediately began—they didn't describe exactly what this seance involved, but they said suddenly they had an overwhelming sense of evil present in their room, and they said it frightened them very much. They couldn't describe—it was just a sense of evil. I don't know whether they heard or saw anything, but they [unclear] but I do remember that they said they were very, very frightened.
>
> So I talked with them quite a bit about how God always does keep evil under control, and we don't have to fear it from the devil—in other words, if we asked God to protect us from evil, do that—I probably mentioned the story from our past

histories of saints that the sign of the cross would cause the Devil to flee or whatever, but—we talked a bit, visited a bit, and I didn't want to sit there for the rest of the night, so I said, "Well," to finish the session I said, "Let's go to the church and we'll pray."

And so the two girls, now that I think I remember more, I think the other girl was Catholic, we just went to the church and prayed with them and I think I blessed them; I might have used our traditional "Devil-scatterer" (that's the holy water, I sprinkled them with holy water). And then we went back to the rectory, and the boys were still waiting for them, and then they left.

But the thing that impressed me was that none of them took this in a light way; they were all very serious about it. The boys, as I say, they were somewhat sullen, or as if they were responsible for this, or being accused by these girls, or blamed, for what happened. And the girls were just kind of mystified by what they experienced. So we went back to the rectory, and in a few minutes they were gone, and that was the end of this particular incident.[8]

Also reported with some frequency were consultations concerning uninvited supernatural guests:

> The truth is, I get the occasional one whose house is haunted—and very often a non-Catholic. There's one man down in Hayti [Missouri] who calls regularly, wants me to go down with holy water or something. He wants me to believe, and he wants to believe himself, that this house is haunted. Every once in a while he calls, or he used to, about his friend's apartment, or house, that was haunted. And I can tell, you know, that he wants me to believe that it is, and of course, I'm trying to tell him that in my opinion, more than likely, it's not. And I tell him I'm not going to do an exorcism, and you can tell, you can almost sense the disappointment. He wants something spectacular.[9]

Among the elements that most consistently emerge from these accounts of "priesting" a supernatural experience, the most striking is the frequent reference to William Peter Blatty's best-selling novel *The Exorcist* (1971) and its enormously successful film version released in 1973. Virtually every priest consulted alluded to its influence, although several remarked that they themselves had neither read the book nor seen the movie:

> Around the time of *The Exorcist*, you know, there were always rumors, and people were always looking for the Devil. There was a whole lot of that. People get mad when you don't buy it, you don't react! They want you to say, "Let's get out the ritual here, we'll do an exorcism!" That's what they want to do.[10]
>
> I've had a number of occasions where people think they've gotten that kind of encounter, especially like right after *The Exorcist* came out. The movie, not the book. I think people in every town were contacting their rectory, you know, "Oh, I've got this problem, so-and-so is crazy," and I think that's all it was. Completely induced kind of paranoia.[11]

The plot of *The Exorcist* centers on a young Jesuit psychiatrist embroiled in a crisis of disbelief who nonetheless intervenes in the case of demonic possession of a child. Although the audience is brought to believe that the child is indeed possessed by the Devil, Father Damien clings stubbornly to a medical explanation of her condition—until his desperate final act of self-sacrifice brings about the child's rescue and his own spiritual redemption. Damien is first approached by the child's agnostic mother, who is motivated in part by genuine uncertainty concerning the origin of the child's behavior, and in part by the practical fear that the child may be a suspect in a murder.[12] The immensely affecting character of the tormented Damien Karras, portrayed in the film with astonishing force by playwright Jason Miller, as well as the brief but powerful appearance of Max von Sydow as an experienced older Jesuit, both color the contemporary image of the role of priest as interpreter and mediator in matters concerning the supernatural.

This role predates the book and film, of course. Catholics have been instructed to seek specialized assistance in the interpretation of unexplained spiritual phenomena virtually from the time of the establishment of an organized priesthood—even before. St. Paul warned the members of the church at Corinth not to overvalue the gift of speaking in tongues, because such a gift required a specialist's mediating companion gift of interpretation. Medieval manuals of instruction for priests typically included lists of questions to determine whether voices or apparitions experienced by penitents were natural or supernatural. The sixteenth-century mystic Teresa of Avila listed a series of criteria by which apparently heavenly voices could be tested to determine their origin, whether divine, diabolical, or imaginary, but continued by instructing her readers to resort to a "learned and prudent confessor" for definitive interpretation: obedience to this judgment was, in her opinion, the safest spiritual course, even if the judgment itself was mistaken.[13] Despite historical precept and precedent, however, it is the fictional work *The Exorcist* which offers a model, suggests an incentive, and lends a dramatic tone to most contemporary requests for priestly interpretation and intervention.

Scholars with an interest in beliefs and practices related to the supernatural and sensational have noted the impulse of some individuals to adopt roles originally encountered in narratives of oral legend, fiction, and journalism. Clearly, facts often inspire narratives; and drawing on the vocabulary of semiotics, Linda Dégh and Andrew Vázsonyi have applied the term *ostension* to the process by which narratives also become facts in this process of conscious reenactment.[14] The adolescent practice of "legend-tripping," for example, in which teenagers drive to the scenes of reputed hauntings in order to position themselves as the latest recipients of supernatural experience, has been well-documented and analyzed by Bill Ellis.[15] Since 1973, cases in which individuals consult priests can be assumed to have at least some ostensive component: the fictional horror story has provided a model for a real-life scenario.

Although the plot of *The Exorcist* provides relatively satisfactory closure, in Stewart's terms, with regard to the supernatural for the characters of the possessed child and her mother, as well as for members of the audience, the same cannot be said of the priest characters: one suffers a fatal heart attack and the other throws himself from an upper window to a bloody death. The fact that each priest meets his end in the line of duty, and no doubt thereby merits a martyr's crown, does not inspire a spirit of emulation in the breast of the real-life priest being cast ostensively in the role of exorcist by parishioners or others. Most priests tolerate the inquiry with varying degrees of patience and sympathy, but resist any request for formal ritual action beyond prayer and a bit of holy water. The need felt by some inquirers for *any* authoritatively sanctioned ritual intervention is demonstrated in the following anecdote:

> One of the funniest things I ever remember—I lived in a rectory in Suitland, Maryland, when I was between seminaries. I was working as a [?] and kind of as a youth minister in this parish, not a priest. And they had a secretary who kind of ran things. Whether you liked it or not, she ran things. She was very efficient and everything, but I still—I don't know where I stand on this, but it was funny, though. [Laughs.] Someone called—their house was haunted, his house was haunted or something, so the secretary said, "Oh, the priest is busy, but here's the standard procedure." And she had him hanging up paper clips on the doors, and everything else, and two days later the guy called back and said everything was fine, and thanked her. And that's a true story, I swear! I was there! That was really a true story.[16]

Most priests offer considerably less concrete satisfaction than the church secretary of this anecdote, though with more elevated motives. They frequently disappoint those consulting them by paradoxically acknowledging the existence of the supernatural in general terms, while vigorously urging a non-supernatural explanation of the episode at hand. One priest who is frankly made uncomfortable by such visits remarked:

> I think in general I'm put off by real dramatic stuff. I think that was one thing I learned [in seminary] over in Italy—they overreact to everything! Maybe I just reacted to that.
>
> But the other thing is—the whole working premise is that probably there's nothing to it. It's very, very rare. . . . It's not denying the possibility. There's usually some other explanation.[17]

Some priests deflect the question of objective validity by emphasizing pastoral concerns that privilege psychological well-being over spiritual questions:

> To me, it really doesn't matter that much when somebody calls here and says, "The water's going on and off," and all that. Whether they're telling the truth or not. What does matter to me is those people are definitely hurting. And how do you find peace?[18]

Other priests, more at ease with a possible supernatural explanation, still tend to desensationalize the interpretation of the accounts by placing them in a larger theological context:

> We're comfortable with that [the supernatural]. There's a big leeway in terms of people saying they've seen UFOs. You can think, "Well, that's a possibility!" We don't affirm for sure, because it takes some sort of scientific proof, but at the same time we wouldn't say someone's crazy if they saw a UFO. I'd be comfortable with that, if someday those people were to make themselves visible.
>
> God had created more than one kind of being, of intelligence. We're just one of them. We know that. So that's one thing—it's perfectly comfortable when we start looking at possession, the knowledge of a spiritual being inhabiting another human being, that's possible. Again we say, "Well, from our understanding of Scripture, Jesus apparently freed people from this kind of bondage." It is possible, in looking at a number of experiences over the centuries—because this kind of behavior was present, and an exorcism was performed, and after the exorcism there was a cure— seemingly there was a true possession. Some being able to control another person. So we have a pretty long-standing acceptance of that reality.[19]

There are historical and professional reasons for this cautious deemphasis of the sensational aspect of supernatural experience, especially in the larger context of a predominantly Protestant society that has traditionally tended to equate "Roman Catholic" negatively with "superstitious." As Keith Thomas has pointed out in *Religion and the Decline of Magic*, at the time of the Reformation the issue of interpretation of apparently supernatural events was greatly complicated by the theological teaching and pastoral practice implemented in Protestant communities. Following the teachings of Thomas Aquinas, medieval Catholic belief maintained that the souls of the dead could and did appear to the living, but in light of most post-Reformation Protestant theology, any divine or ghostly manifestation was to be regarded de facto as either diabolical, delusory, or the result of a (probably Papist) hoax.[20] The fact that Protestants in good standing continued to see ghosts and experience demonic presences remained an embarrassment—and no doubt accounts for the number of non-Catholics who consult Catholic priests under such circumstances, even today.

Unbeknownst to most secular inquirers, the situation is further complicated by the fact that priests as a group today represent a kind of intellectual hybridization at least as polarized as that of the general American public. Most subscribe simultaneously to both orthodox Catholic belief in the supernatural and the formal skepticism and generalized secular scientism which predominate in academic training—even in the seminary.[21] Reflecting this sometimes uneasy duality, Blatty astutely modeled the character of the saintly elderly Jesuit Lancaster Merrin on the Jesuit paleontologist Pierre Teilhard de Chardin, whose formal and informal writings propose a reconciliation of science and theology in a kind of evolutionary spiritual physics.[22]

Whether or not rectory visits concerning supernatural experiences are received sympathetically by the priest in question, the very "priesting" of the predicament suggests a yearning for affirmation of belief on the part of the visitor. After all, the question is being referred not to a "ghostbuster" physician or physicist, but rather to the expert who, at least in his popularly ascribed role, is most likely to take the possibility of a supernatural explanation seriously. This affirmation of belief is eagerly sought even if that belief begins painfully with the validation of the palpable presence of evil.

> They kind of . . . they want me to, not necessarily agree with them, but they want me to establish that there is a supernatural. To agree with them: "Yeah, there might be spirits out there. There might be something happening. That's why you've got to be careful with this voice you've been playing with, like a game or something."[23]

Some individuals seem to find transcendent meaning most inescapable when it comes in the form of a thrill or fear. One priest remarked with concern, "All these horror movies, even these sick things—people need something really out of the ordinary, and if all else fails, they feel like they need to be terrified out of their wits."[24]

David Hufford, Carolyn Franks Davis, and others have remarked on the curious evidential relationship between such a powerfully negative experience and the acknowledgment of seemingly more promising possibilities of supernatural love and redemption.[25] Indeed, in describing the process by which he came to write *The Exorcist*, Blatty himself described what might be considered the typical train of thought in such an instance. As a student at Georgetown University, he came across a *Washington Post* account of an exorcism performed on a boy in Mount Rainier, Maryland:

> The article impressed me. And how coolly understated that is. I wasn't just impressed. I was excited. For here at last, in this city, in my time, was tangible

evidence of transcendence. If there were demons, there were angels and probably a God and life everlasting. And thus it occurred to me long afterward, when I'd started my career as a writer, that this case of possession which had joyfully haunted my hopes in the years since 1949 was a worthwhile subject for a novel.[26]

The real-life epiphany underlying Blatty's writing of the novel *The Exorcist* may explain in part the story's power to inspire ostensive behavior—to provide a script in which unresolved encounters with inexplicable experience are resolved by subjecting them to priestly arbitration.

But real-life priests are at best reluctant stand-ins for their iconic mediating counterparts in the fictional realm. Priests, too, have experiences which baffle their interpretive powers, and they do not necessarily turn more readily to supernatural explanations for these episodes than their peers among the laity. The most moving interview I conducted in the course of this research was with a priest who himself initiated the contact. At first he spoke confidently and eloquently of routine "Ouija board" rectory visits typical of those described previously in this article. But something else was on his mind—an experience with which he himself had not yet come to terms.

He had been rector of a church in southwest Missouri when the teenaged son of one of the parishioners was convicted as the ringleader of the savage gang murder of a classmate. The case was highly publicized due to the boys' alleged involvement with satanic cult activity. The priest visited the boy several times in prison, and found the experience profoundly disturbing:

> [This] incident is considerably more troublesome and—upsetting, in some sense, because you see Catholic people involved in—evil, could we call it?—or certainly "non-Gospel acting." It's tragic.
>
> What makes me wonder, makes me put some belief in [his] contact with satanism and that as being a possible explanation for what happened, is that this Jim, being a smart, intelligent young man, that they would do this, that if they would give two thoughts to it, in their right mind, they would have seen, well, there's no chance for them to get away with it. Because they did it in a—there's just no way for them to think that they could get away with it, nobody would ever find out.
>
> It seems to me that perhaps it's, in this situation in which they found themselves in experiencing satanism, that it gave them some false sense or some belief that the Devil would protect them or that evil would be protected in this. It almost—to hear this boy telling it, it reminded me of some of the Nazi philosophy, the SS troops of Hitler. They definitely said, "We'll settle for what we can get here. We don't care about what's going to happen next. We've got power enough so, we'll kill the Jews and do what we want, and that's what we're going to do." Even though there was a—it's like they bought into the forces of evil.
>
> If anyone has any trouble believing there is evil, its mystery, you see it in a situation like this. Not—I'm not saying that they were evil, but evil was in control of a

family with intelligence: the father is a CPA, has a great business [. . .] I just consider evil in some sense took control of those people. And who's responsible for them?[27]

In his prison interviews with the boy, this man experienced a sense of the presence of evil, not as a theological abstraction, but as a reality with which he sat and conversed. The sense of evil inhered not only in his knowledge of the boy's participation in the murder, but also forcefully and tangibly in the boy's very being as the older man experienced it in their talks: in a taped passage so fraught with false starts and qualifications that it defies coherent transcription, he tried to tell me of his sensation of irrational fear and horror at watching the boy calmly pocket a handful of toothpicks that had been left by the jailer on the table. Somehow this simple act, seemingly harmless but enigmatic, conveyed an explicit sense of evil not in the orthodox theological sense of "absence of good," but as a challenging presence in itself.

This priest's insistence on sharing his response to the prison interviews with me curiously recapitulates the many times in which others have approached him as a specialist—as confidante or mediator. Nor was this the first time I had been approached in this manner. I would venture to say that any folklorist who has included a component on supernatural belief and practice in a class, or who has "gone public" with opinion or information on the topic in the media, has been called upon to evaluate ambiguous experience directly or implicitly. Whether by vocation or profession, it appears that all—priests, folklorists, or professional pundits—who undertake to interpret the nature of human belief in the supernatural place themselves willy-nilly in the role of umpires of the empirical, whether or not they claim such authority.

In his article "Satanism: Where Are the Folklorists?" Phillips Stevens Jr. takes the discipline to task for neglecting to debunk the myth of satanic conspiracy so widespread at present in our culture. Certainly it is an important and useful role for folklorists, and for all who are in a position to understand the power of legend and rumor, to encourage more responsible journalism and a more skeptical public response with regard to this mass paranoia. But at the same time, we must be careful to listen sensitively and attentively to the voices of inquiry trying to make sense of individual experiences of the seemingly supernatural.

Thankfully, it is not our task to make a final determination—"gravy or grave?"—by bringing these narratives to a premature interpretive closure. For those who have experienced them, many of these stories must conclude with an unresolved question mark. But we can place these highly personal episodes in a wider context of understanding, social as well as metaphysical: common human experiences framed in cultural terms. If priests play shifting and ambiguous roles in the process of bringing meaning to the inexplicable by virtue of their profession, then by virtue of our avowed intellectual concern with matters out of the ordinary, and our persistent ambivalence concerning supernatural claims, perhaps so, too, do those who study folk belief.

Acknowledgments

A version of this article was delivered at the annual meeting of the American Folklore Society, 1990, held in Oakland, California, at which time it benefited from the comments of David J. Hufford and Leonard J. Primiano.

Endnotes

1. David Hufford had usefully defined the term *supernatural* as referring to "an order of reality that is different from the natural world of matter and energy and also different from purely subjective imagination (that is, has objective reality) that at least occasionally interacts with the natural and subjective worlds (that is, has empirical relevance)." In "Reason, Rhetoric, and Religion: Academic Logic versus Folk Belief," *New York Folklore* 11 (1985): 192.

2. Susan Stewart, "The Epistemology of the Horror Story," *Journal of American Folklore* 95 (1982): 33–50.

3. Andrew M. Greeley, *Sociology of the Paranormal: A Reconnaissance* (Beverly Hills, CA: Sage Publications, 1975), 36. A 1986 follow-up placed the proportion at 42 percent.

4. George Gallup Jr., with William Proctor, *Adventures in Immortality* (New York: McGraw-Hill, 1982), 17.

5. In "Ambiguity and the Rhetoric of Belief," *Keystone Folklore* 21 (1976): 11–24, David J. Hufford has identified three significant forms of ambiguity in communications concerning the experience of the Old Hag phenomenon (sleep paralysis with hypnagogic hallucinations, particularly when associated metaphorically or literally with the sense of a malevolent presence): the use of terms which carry both a descriptive and interpretive complex of meanings, such as *ghost*; the use of terms which have two or more separate meanings, such as *witch*; and the use of terminology which admits of either literal or metaphorical interpretation. Much of his discussion, however, addresses the varying interpretations placed on accounts of the experience by a listener due to intentional or inadvertent ambiguity in forms of expression chosen by the teller, rather than addressing the teller's own ambivalence concerning interpretation.

6. For a particularly impressive formal defense of the validity of religious experience against traditional challenges to it, see Caroline Franks Davis, *The Evidential Force of Religious Experience* (Oxford: Clarendon Press, 1989).

7. Confidentiality was maintained with regard to the identity of the individuals who consulted the priests. Because these consultations were undertaken outside the context of the sacrament of reconciliation, no formal interdiction prevented each

priest from sharing his version of the encounters. The names of individual interviewees are pseudonyms.

Interviews were tape-recorded and later transcribed by the author; the interviews took place during September 1990 at rectories located in southeast Missouri, southern Illinois, and western and south-central Kentucky. The tapes are in possession of the author; tape numbers refer to the author's coding system.

8. Interview, PRST.09.30.90.1.
9. Interview, PRST.09.08.90.1.
10. Interview, PRST.09.08.90.1.
11. Interview, PRST.09.08.90.2.
12. William Peter Blatty, *William Peter Blatty on* The Exorcist *from Novel to Film* (New York: Bantam Books, 1974), 11.
13. Kieran Kavenaugh, OCD, and Otilio Rodriguez, OCD, trans. "The Interior Castle," *The Collected Works of St. Teresa of Avila,* vol. 2 (Washington, D.C.: Institute of Carmelite Studies, 1980), 375.
14. Linda Dégh and Andrew Vázsonyi, "Does the Word 'Dog' Bite? Ostensive Action: A Means of Legend-Telling," *Journal of Folklore Research* 20 (1983): 5–34.
15. Bill Ellis, "Legend-Tripping in Ohio: A Behavior Survey," *Papers in Comparative Studies* 2 (1982–83): 61–73; and "Death by Folklore: Ostension, Contemporary Folklore, and Murder," *Western Folklore* 48 (1989): 201–220.
16. Interview, PRST.09.20.90.1.
17. Interview, PRST.09.08.90.1.
18. Interview, PRST.09.20.90.1.
19. Interview, PRST.09.08.90.2.
20. Keith Thomas, *Religion and the Decline of Magic* (New York: Scribner's, 1971), 131–149. The Aquinian discussion of ghosts is found in *Summa Theologica,* III, supp. q.69.iii.
21. Hufford's provocatively developed discussion of the "tradition of disbelief" that coexists with other forms of conviction in this culture can be found in "Ambiguity and the Rhetoric of Belief," *Keystone Folklore* 21 (1976): 11–24; *The Terror That Comes in the Night: An Experience-Centered Study of Supernatural Assault Traditions* (Philadelphia: University of Pennsylvania Press, 1982); "Traditions of Disbelief," *New York Folklore* 8 (1982): 47–55; "The Supernatural and the Sociology of Knowledge: Explaining Academic Belief," *New York Folklore* 9 (1983): 21–29; and "Reason, Rhetoric, and Religion: Academic Logic versus Folk Belief," *New York Folklore* 11 (1985): 177–194.
22. Blatty, 32; Pierre Teilhard de Chardin, *The Phenomenon of Man,* trans. Bernard Wall (New York: Harper, 1959), and *Toward the Future,* trans. René Hague (New York: Harcourt Brace Jovanovitch, 1975). Of further interest to folklorists is the fact that Swedish actor Max von Sydow, who played Lancaster Merrin in the film, is the son of scholar Carl Wilhelm von Sydow, whose investigations of process and taxonomy of traditional narrative have been of such value in the study of supernatural memorate.
23. Interview, PRST.09.08.90.2.
24. Interview, PRST.09.08.90.1.
25. Hufford, "Reason, Rhetoric, and Religion," 178; and Davis, *The Evidential Force,* 51.

26.   Blatty, 6. A full journalistic account of this exorcism can be found in Thomas B. Allen, *Possessed: The True Story of an Exorcism* (New York: Doubleday, 1993).
27.   Interview, PRST.09.30.90.1.
28.   Phillips Stevens Jr., "Satanism: Where Are the Folklorists?" *New York Folklore* 15 (1989): 1–22.

9

The Tourist Folklore of Pele:
Encounters with the Other

Joyce D. Hammond

Every year hundreds of packages and letters are sent to tourist bureaus, travel agencies, hotels, and national parks in the Hawaiian Islands from people who have visited the islands as tourists. The packages, sent most frequently from the U.S. mainland,[1] contain volcanic rock, sand, or articles made from volcanic material. Many of the packages also contain confessional letters which explain that at the time of their visit, the senders either did not believe in or did not know of the curse attributed to Pele, Hawaiian "goddess of volcanoes." Subsequently, however, the tourists, and sometimes those upon whom they bestowed the souvenirs, suffered a series of misfortunes, often enumerated in great detail in the letters, which confirm the belief that Pele causes bad luck for those who take volcanic rock from her islands. According to the tourist folklore, only by returning the rock to Pele can the negative consequences be arrested or avoided:

> Dear Sir:
> Well, here's another testimonial for your files. In spite of the warnings we read while on the Big Island, we picked up some pieces of volcanic rock at several road cuts on the south and southwestern part of the island. These were to be souvenirs for ourselves and our friends. We were on Hawaii in mid-December. Since we returned home, we've had a monstrous snowstorm which ruined our family reunion here at Christmas. My sister and I had the first big fight of our lives and we are still not speaking to each other. Both my wife and I have had a terrible cold or flue [sic] bug since mid-January. And today another big snowstorm has ruined the grand opening of my wife's new business. WELL, ENOUGH IS ENOUGH! We are returning to Pele all of her rocks. Please entreat her to release us from her terrible spell.[2]

Pele tourist folklore dates to at least the 1940s and may have existed earlier in the history of Hawaiian tourism,[3] but the idea of Pele causing non-indigenous visitors to suffer a revenge for the removal of volcanic rock has no apparent precedent in early Hawaiian folk beliefs.[4] Missionary William Ellis of the London Missionary Society recorded in his 1823 journal that when he visited the active volcano of Kilauea on Hawai'i, the Hawaiian people requested that he and his party "not . . . strike, scratch, or dig the sand, assuring us it would displease Pele, and be followed by an irruption [sic] of lava, or other expression of vengeance."[5] However, the indigenous people thought they would suffer from the desecration of Pele's realm, rather than the foreigners. Ellis wrote: "[W]hen our boys showed them the ohelo berries with the specimens of sulphur and lava that we had brought away, they were convinced that we had been there, but said we had escaped only because we were *haore,* foreigners. No Hawaiian, they added, would have done so with impunity."[6] Some months after Ellis's party visited Kilauea, a priestess of Pele told the principal chiefs of the islands "that, in a trance or vision, she had been with Pele, by whom she was charged to complain to them that a number of foreigners had visited Kirauea [sic]; eaten the sacred berries; broken her houses, the craters; thrown down large stones, &c [sic] to request that the offenders might be sent away; and to assure them, that if these foreigners were not banished from the islands, Pele would certainly, in a given number of days, take vengeance by inundating the country with lava, and destroying the [Hawaiian] people."[7]

While in traditional Hawaiian folklore there was no precedent for foreign visitors to suffer the effects of Pele's wrath, it is possible that as more foreigners visited Hawai'i and removed volcanic rock, indigenous Hawaiians or the visitors themselves might have extended the taboo on disturbance of Pele's domain to include tourists. The notion of magical contagion, a belief that objects once in physical contact with a supernatural force remain in mystical contact after their physical separation, is clearly operative in Pele tourist folklore. Nevertheless, the puzzle remains as to why many Western tourists who subscribe to a monotheistic religious belief in the Bible's God and who in their confessional letters sometimes purport not to be superstitious find the Pele tourist folklore so compelling. Here I argue that the appeal of the tourist folklore (and perhaps its origin) is intimately tied to the tourist experience itself and tourists' ambivalent views toward the Other represented by Pele. My discussion also centers on the ways in which the Pele tourist folklore itself has been subjected to multiple uses which reflect and influence relationships between tourists and their hosts. An analysis of the folklore would not be complete without a consideration of its management by the media, capitalist concerns, and hosting agencies such as the National Park Service.

Pele as Other

The concept of the "Other" has received a great deal of academic attention in the past few decades as scholars have critiqued Western representations of various peoples,[8] explained the past exclusion of certain groups as subjects of academic research,[9] and presented one group's views of another within a given society.[10] Despite the diverse ways in which it is applied, the concept of the Other consistently emphasizes the constructed character of one group/society's views of another group/society (hence the convention of capitalizing Other) and the manner in which the construction reflects and perpetuates power differences and the biases, self-interests, and values of the group defining the Other.

While the concept of the Other has been used primarily to explore relationships among humans, many parallels may be cited in the ways humans regard and interact with the supernatural, other animals, and the natural environment. As some scholars have demonstrated, Otherness is often constructed by combining representations from different categories of phenomena. Much has been written, for example, on the ways women and nature are frequently associated, and women's "naturalistic" qualities are rendered anti-cultural and taboo as a result.[11] Anthropologist Mary Douglas's discussion of the perceived connection between certain animals and the supernatural,[12] and Victor Turner's insights into the manner in which certain groups of people may be placed in anti-structural categorizations by ascribing supernatural and animalistic characteristics to them[13] are instructive of the ways in which different cultural categories may be combined to emphasize Otherness.

The concept of the Other has appeared in discussions of tourism to explain tourists' search for and means of creating differences between themselves and the people, places, and various attractions they seek in their travels.[14] However, few studies focus on the construction of specific tourist Others and the message tourists create through their fabrication of and interaction with their Other. Pele is a tourist Other of mythic proportions. Having supernatural, feminine, ethnic, and natural attributes, Pele originated and persists in tourist folklore, I submit, because she is a powerful symbol of those tourist Others most frequently "encountered" in the tourist quest, particularly in ethnic and environmental tourism.

Pele's supernatural, invisible, and destructive powers are of paramount importance for her status as Other. By contrast to Hawaiians' characterization of Pele as a supernatural with a wide range of powers and many human-like attributes, the tourists' Pele is a one-dimensional invisible figure, who wreaks revenge for a single offense—that of removing volcanic rock from the islands.

As a supernatural figure originally "belonging" to indigenous Hawaiians, Pele is a foreign deity, unfamiliar and distanced from the tourists; her supernatural stature and actions seem credible precisely because of this. The common ascription of supernatural powers, particularly harmful ones, to others who are outside the established structure of society[15] is extended to Pele as a foreign, supernatural power.

The tourists' "leap of faith" is also supported by the association of Pele with the "sacred" time and place of a vacationing destination. Since Pele's domain is in the islands, a place geographically and temporally removed from the profane, work-a-day world of the tourist, she is part of tourists' experience within the sacred state of tourism.[16] While she may use her supernatural powers to track down a tourist anywhere in the world, her home remains in the Hawaiian Islands, outside the location and time of the tourists' ordinary frame of reality and belief.

Further, Pele is most strongly associated with areas of obvious volcanic activity, such as Haleakala National Park and Hawaii Volcanoes National Park. Many people regard "naturally awe-ful places" such as caves, deep lakes, and mountains with a certain amount of ambivalence and fear.[17] The sacred character of such sites arises from their "extra-normal" character as outside of (and unsuitable for) normal living areas. They are often appropriated as places for ritual gatherings and liminality.[18]

While a parallel might be drawn between the feelings of ambivalence and fear felt by tourists and local Hawaiians alike when they visit areas of recent volcanic activity, Western tourists' fear of Pele may be compounded by popular associations of Pele's domains with descriptions of Hell as a place of fire and brimstone. Analogous to the contrast which may be formed of Pele's "hell" to the "paradise" of the islands (heavily promoted by the tourist industry) are Pele's ascribed powers of harming tourists in comparison to the Christian God's beneficence in helping humankind.[19]

Within her own Polynesian domain, Pele is viewed by many Hawaiians as a constructive force, as well as a destructive one. As in traditional Hawaiian folklore, Pele relies on volcano forces, such as lava flows and fires, to achieve her ends. While she may destroy flora, fauna, homes, and other human property, ultimately she is the creative force that adds new land to the islands, providing the basis for new life. Tourists who return volcanic souvenirs to the islands sometimes profess that the rock is Pele's creation, but the tourist folklore highlights Pele's destructive acts directed at offending tourists. The incentive for returning the rock, frequently mentioned in accompanying letters, is to arrest or avoid Pele's vindictive acts: "Dear Madam Pele: I have tasted your wrath and I want to avoid your fury." "I've begun to fear that Pele might be angry with me for stealing these pieces of volcanic rock." "For seven months we lived with the guilt you sent."

A listing of Pele's damage to the tourist is a prominent feature of many letters which accompany packages of returned rock:

Dear Madam Pele,
    I am returning the lava I took from Black Sands Beach in 1969. I hope this pleases you so my husband and I will have better luck in future trips to Hawaii.
    1st time—Cut my foot
    2nd time—Scraped my arm at airport
    3rd time—Lost my hearing and broke eardrum on crater in Maui
    4th time—Sprained two toes on cement steps
    5th time—Cut my finger
    6th time—Husband had heart attack and I fell twice—1st time broke my left elbow; 2nd fall broke my kneecap in two places and crushed it.
    I'm sorry we ever took it, but in 1982 we visited the Volcano House and saw the misfortunes of others [letters in display case]. So please accept this black lava sand.
    From two who love all the islands of Hawaii.[20]

Pele's invisibility to tourists enhances her status as Other by more completely separating her from them. Her invisible powers for sending harm to tourists are mirrored by her concealment from them while they are in the islands. Unlike island folklore which is full of stories of residents' encounters with Pele,[21] tourists' folklore rarely includes any face-to-face contact. The charitable side of Pele, frequently evidenced by her appearing as a woman to residents and warning them of impending volcanic activity, is missing in tourist folklore.[22] To tourists, Pele is always invisible and potentially harmful.

Pele's potency as Other also emanates from her feminine identity, derived from Hawaiian mythology, combined with her ethnic identification as native Hawaiian. While her ethnicity was not at issue in early mythology, Pele is consistently described as native Hawaiian in contemporary island folklore. The tourists' view of Pele as a native Hawaiian female is also reinforced in artists' drawings and paintings of her.[23] While contemporary descriptions and depictions may serve to instill pride in Hawaiian heritage for people of Hawaiian descent, their effect on tourists' assessment of Pele is to support the view of Otherness.[24]

Although Pele's status as Other is undoubtedly tied to the general association of the female as Other in tourists' own societies[25] and the ascription of masculine identity to the Christian God, Pele's power as a symbol of the Other derives most clearly from the replication of Otherness which is constructed for native women. The overwhelming number of photographs of island women in the promotional tourist materials for Hawai'i, as well as the predominant use of "ethnic" women to greet tourists, dance for tourists, and serve tourists, attests to the tourists' equation of the native woman herself with the exoticism sought in the touristic quest.

In their book, *The Wild Woman: An Inquiry into the Anthropology of an Idea*, Sharon Tiffany and Kathleen Adams trace the construction of native woman as a symbol of exploited lands and peoples dominated by colonialist powers.[26] Reflecting the conqueror's views of lands and peoples to be tamed and domesticated for their own use, "wild women" have been alternately characterized as virginal, uncorrupted, and desirable, or dangerous, contaminating, and vengeful. Given the long history of Western characterization of Hawaiian native women as childlike, pleasure-seeking, and sexually desirable, it is perhaps not surprising that tourists, who are frequently urged by the tourist industry to identify with earlier explorers to the islands, have constructed the darker side of the "wild woman" in Pele. Local folk terms identify certain rock formations as Pele's tears, Pele's hair, Pele's diamonds, and the land itself is equated with Pele's body, so the removal of volcanic rock from the islands may serve to reinforce the image of a female who has been violated.[27]

For many tourists to the Hawaiian Islands, Pele may serve as a stand-in for the ethnic Hawaiian Other. Hawaiian tourist institutions sometimes promise the visitor glimpses into Hawai'i kahiko (old Hawai'i) and encounters with authentic, "traditional" Hawaiian culture, but the typical tourist to Hawai'i is unlikely to encounter many "pure" Hawaiians because of a long history of Hawaiian intermarriage with other ethnic groups. Pele's ancestral pedigree as a supernatural figure from indigenous legends, along with her specific alignment to the Hawaiian Islands, lends her authenticity.

Pele is also Other to the tourist because she embodies nature, a cultural category viewed as structurally outside Western society. While indigenous Hawaiian legends placed Pele among a large pantheon of supernatural forces (many of whom were characterized as feminine) who regularly affected or interacted with humans, tourist folklore singles Pele out as the only Hawaiian supernatural who is of direct concern to tourists. Based on a touristic depiction of Polynesian islands as natural settings physically and psychologically removed from tourists' homes, Pele's Otherness in nature builds on a long history of Western ideology which opposes nature and champions culture's dominance and control over nature even as it paradoxically laments its loss.[28]

The feminization of nature, still prevalent in Western thought, lays the foundation for sexual metaphors associated with humans' acts toward nature. As a part of the "virginal" paradise of Hawai'i's nature, Pele attracts and may even be considered "seductive" to those tourists who wish to take new, shiny volcanic rock from recent lava flows or gleaming black sands from beaches.

When tourists seek to exploit Pele by taking that which belongs to her (sexual connotations underlie these actions as well), she shows the dark side of her nature. In her wrath, she destroys parts of tourists' lives. What was taken must be returned. Tourists come to know Pele as the Other who must be feared, avoided, and propitiated. As nature, she is Other because she is wild, unconquerable, and destructive.

Despite Pele's uncontrollable attributes, there is one way in which tourist folklore posits a cultural domination of Pele and keeps her in her place. This is the belief that while Pele's invisible powers may extend worldwide to follow the erring tourist home, her "natural powers," made visible in her volcanic activity, are usually limited to the Hawaiian Islands.[29] Volcanic rock from other parts of the world are not returned to Pele, nor are tourists content with returning Hawaiian volcanic rock to nature outside of the Hawaiian Islands. Pele's Otherness is thereby reinforced, and since some of Pele's domain has been preserved in national park sites, she has become even more effectively removed from tourists and the human realm. Ironically, as MacCannell states, "A preservation of nature serves to separate it from society and elevate society over it."[30]

As this discussion of Pele as Other suggests, the tourists' Pele may serve as a particularly potent symbol of the Other because she encompasses a number of qualities frequently recognized in tourists' Others. Pele's supernatural, natural, and human attributes combine in ways which reinforce and amplify one another. As a female who jealously guards her volcanic creations of nature and is able to supernaturally punish those who violate her, Pele simultaneously represents the host, exploited by outside conquest; the Other, who holds supernatural powers of revenge (even back home in the tourists' own settings); and the female exotic who is equated with nature and non-human animals.

A large part of Pele's "popularity" among tourists may be attributed to the tourist perspective that Pele is an Other *not of their construction.* Because Pele has long existed in Hawaiian tradition and is associated with the Hawaiian Islands, tourists can view her (in a way that might stretch the imagination when viewing "natives" performing the hula at the beach-front hotel) as "pure" Other. By displacing the Other onto a mythological, supernatural figure, the tourist does not have to claim any responsibility for assigning attributes or passing judgments on the Other. In a world where the influence of more powerful societies on those of lesser power is increasingly more visible, the function of an Other of mythic proportions has great appeal and can be viewed as part of a justification for exploitation.

The tourists' Pele is a complex interweaving of Other attributes. She is, nevertheless, much more one-dimensional in character and concerns than the Pele

of indigenous or residential Hawaiian folklore. As previously stated, for indigenous and residential Hawaiians, Pele has been viewed both as a constructive
and destructive force, and while the Pele of indigenous thought combines the
feminine with the supernatural, a parallel between the Western ideology of an
opposition of the natural and the supernatural or the exclusivity of the feminine with the supernatural cannot be drawn. The unique combination of
attributes ascribed to Pele in the tourist folklore reflects the concerns and cultural backgrounds of the tourists themselves. In a manner that resembles many
tourists' narrow view that the "natives" exist primarily as tourist attractions, so
too, Pele is presented in tourist folklore as being singularly concerned with the
tourists and their actions.

Encountering Pele

Some visitors to the Hawaiian Islands find the Pele tourist legend amusing or
irrelevant; other tourists who might consider taking volcanic rock or material
from the islands are deterred; still others are ignorant or dismissive of the folklore and carry out volcanic souvenirs. A few tourists take volcanic rock to
"challenge" the goddess and her alleged powers.

While there is no way to know how many tourists take volcanic rock home,
the number who do and later send them back to the islands is staggering.
Hundreds of letters and packages are delivered annually to the islands, but
most of the mail[31] is sent to Maui and Hawai'i, since these are the islands
which have had the most recent volcanic activity and where tourists are most
likely to learn about Pele and volcanic activity. Haleakala National Park, which
features a volcanic crater, and Hawai'i Volcanoes National Park, the site of the
active volcano Kilauea, receive the bulk of the Pele mail.

Volcanic rock and objects made from volcanic material are acquired by
tourists for their exotic qualities, serving as a reminder of both the islands and
the tourists' experiences of the islands. As Susan Stewart points out,

> The exotic object represents distance appropriated; it is symptomatic of the more
> general cultural imperialism that is tourism's stock in trade. To have a souvenir of
> the exotic is to possess both a specimen and a trophy.[32]

Regardless of whether a tourist associates the volcanic souvenir with Pele at
the time of acquisition or later, the souvenir's possession as a specimen and tro-
phy of exoticism can be viewed as symbolic of Western attitudes toward the
Other revealed both in the Pele tourist folklore and in the actions of tourists
toward such Others as female "ethnics." For those who know the Pele tourist

legend and take volcanic rock in spite of (or to spite?) Pele, taking something of Pele's may be interpreted as an attempt to appropriate the Other for one's own purposes.

The tourists' fascination with the exoticism of the souvenir volcanic rock becomes magnified when the souvenir is linked to the exoticism of Pele as Other. Ironically, it is this quality of the rock that ultimately leads many tourists to reject the rock as souvenir.

> The danger of the souvenir lies in its unfamiliarity, in our difficulty in subjecting it to interpretation. There is always the possibility that reverie's signification will go out of control here, that the object itself will take charge, awakening some dormant capacity for destruction. . . . curiosity is replaced by understanding only at the expense of the possessor's well-being.[33]

The danger of the Hawaiian volcanic souvenir may be linked to the danger associated with Pele herself as Other. However, the link goes beyond the principle of magical contagion; the rock comes to be understood as part of Pele in a literal sense. Metaphorically, as a part of that cultural domain identified as nature, the volcanic rock is part of the Otherness of nature.

Once a tourist experiences misfortunes, he or she may find the Pele legend plausible. The folklore offers an answer to the question of why things have gone wrong. Pele's vengeful, destructive acts to which tourists bear witness or, at least, subscribe, reverse the touristic assumption that the Other (symbolized and embodied by the souvenir) can be used for the tourists' own purposes. The volcanic rock on the coffee table cannot continue to serve as a decorative adornment to the home.

Tourists who come to an understanding that volcanic rock belongs to Pele and cannot be used in ways designated by them gain their knowledge through experiences which serve to deify Pele's attributes of mystery, danger, and destruction. Pele's morality, which revolves around punishing those who seek to violate her integrity and destroy her, "makes sense" to the tourist.

At the core of Pele tourist folklore is a message that counsels tourists to realign their interactions with Others; the Other possesses an authenticity and integrity which cannot be violated without consequence. A quotation from Palikapu Dedman,[34] a Hawaiian who fought to prevent geothermal mining in Hawai'i, provides another example of the link between Pele and Otherness.

> If Pele is recognized by the world [spared the desecration of being violated through exploitive geothermal mining] then you would recognize thousands of Hawaiians with their spiritual beliefs on every island who are keeping (their beliefs) in themselves, and scared to bring it out.

Left in her "natural" setting, Pele will not harm the tourist. It is when the tourist tries to incorporate and appropriate the Other for his or her own purposes (in this case, as a souvenir) that the Other's actions may have direct and undesirable consequences. Pele forces the tourist to recognize her integrity and to return what is rightfully hers.[35]

Pele tourist folklore issues a warning about the exploitive nature of souvenir-seeking and tourism itself through the central message that one will suffer dire consequences if one does not respect Others.[36] As a morality story, the Pele tourist folklore counsels that the actions of tourists toward their Others have consequences for both. The links between tourists and Others may appear to have mysterious and unfathomable dimensions (as in Pele's supernatural connections to tourists' personal lives), but they exist. Acts which destroy Others' integrity and authenticity point out the necessity for tourists to regard and interact differently with their Others.

Paradoxically, however, the very existence of the Pele tourist folklore and its prescriptive formula reinforces the differentiation of the tourists from their Others. Tourists' volcanic souvenirs function best in emphasizing the exoticism of the Other when the tourist or recipient of the rock places credibility in the Pele tourist folklore and sends the rock back to the Hawaiian Islands. The narrative told by tourists of "why I had to send the rock back" widens the distance between the tourist and the Other, and further authenticates the tourists' experience with the exotic. The tourists' negative experiences and their rendition of those experiences come to replace the rocks themselves as souvenirs of the Other.

Pele tourist folklore and its prescriptions work at cross-purposes for the tourist, who simultaneously destroys and creates Otherness. As a text which may engage the tourist personally, the Pele tourist folklore exemplifies and makes concrete the overall contradictions of tourism and the ambivalence tourists exhibit toward their Others.[37]

Managing the Folklore

The tourist folklore about Pele is of major importance to many individuals and institutions that seek to transmit, interpret, or otherwise interact with the folklore for their own purposes. The media, souvenir entrepreneurs, tourist guides, and the National Park Service are most involved with the tourist folklore and, given their various self-interests, respond to it in different ways.

Not surprisingly, the media delights in the tourist folklore. Many newspapers and magazines published both within and outside of the Hawaiian Islands have printed articles about the phenomenon of "Pele's Curse." Journalists' accounts appear in such diverse newspapers as *The National Enquirer* and the *Wall Street Journal.* Television shows such as *That's Incredible* and *Tales of the Unexplained* have also used the tourist folklore for their programming.

For human interest stories, the media almost always emphasize the "bad luck" experienced by tourists who have taken volcanic rock, recounting the problems of named informants in great detail, thereby implying credibility for the folklore's explanations of experiences. The reports appear in the same media that carry news of local, national, and international scope,[38] and while the reporter does not personally assert a link between a supernatural power and tourists' bad luck, a journalist's carefully chosen words may serve to reinforce the causal explanation between Pele and bad luck: "Under National Park regulations, the removal of any natural material from parks is prohibited. But Pele remains the best enforcer of the regulations."[39]

Media coverage of the Pele tourist folklore undeniably serves to perpetuate and disseminate the folklore. Employees of Hawaii Volcanoes National Park assert that the number of packages received is directly affected by the media coverage. Every time *The National Enquirer* reissues its original story from the 1970s, for example, the park receives a marked increase in the number of packages. Alberta de Jetley, a writer for the *Mauian,*[40] reported in 1986 that "Kauai's Mayor Tony Kunimura was on a television program in Los Angeles last year and offered to return lava rocks for people who had taken rocks home. Within days of the program, his office was deluged with lava rocks accompanied by notes and maps for their safe return."

In the recent past, some of the national parks have used media reportage to introduce the Pele tourist folklore to visitors as an interesting phenomenon and, in an effort to preserve the tourist sites, to deter tourists from illegally removing rock from park grounds. At one time, Pu'uhonua o Honaunau Historical Park on Hawai'i, for example, placed one of writer Frankie Stapleton's newspaper articles on its front desk for visitors to view. At the bottom of the photocopied article, which recounted the misfortunes of the Loffert family and their decision to send volcanic rock back to Hawai'i, was an inscription in large letters: "READ THIS BEFORE REMOVING ROCKS FROM THE PARK."[41] Haleakala National Park on the island of Maui likewise utilized a journalist's account of "Pele's Curse" in a display with tourists' letters in their visitors' center.[42]

In addition to the media's influence on the Pele tourist folklore, island tour companies also have pursued their self-interests, with mixed approaches, in responding to the lore. One origin story of the tourist folklore, widely held in the Hawaiian Islands,[43] is that bus tour operators themselves started it to discourage passengers from littering the buses with rocks and sand, a practice which would cause the operators the extra work of cleaning up the debris. Whether or not tour operators played an instrumental role in the origins of the lore, it is to the tour companies' advantage to deter passengers from taking volcanic rock since they, like many other businesses in the islands, often receive packages of the rocks being returned.[44] Tour companies also receive notices from both the national and county park services asking the tour operators to remind visitors that taking rocks and other volcanic material is illegal.

Local guides for tour bus companies are mixed in their response and use of the Pele tourist folklore. From interviews with tour personnel from several leading tour companies on the island of Hawai'i, it appears that tour companies have no established policies as to how their guides should handle the tourist lore. Remarks from the guides themselves reveal a range of different approaches. Many tour guides repeat public laws and do not mention the lore to tourists. One guide said that he discontinued talking about the legends because of tourists' reactions. Some of his passengers were offended by the stories; others were scared and didn't want to get out of the bus. Some tour operators repeat the beliefs but take no personal stance, even when questioned as to their own opinion. Others repeat examples of tourists' bad luck, implying or stating that it is harmful to take volcanic rocks.

The introductions and interpretations of the Pele lore by tour guides are not uniform, and, from a sampling of guides, it appears they do not play a major role in the dispersal of the folklore. However, as hosts to tourists, some bus tour operators have undoubtedly contributed to what H. Arlo Nimmo terms "a growing belief in Hawai'i that Pele brings misfortune to those who carry bits of her lava or sand away."[45] The following story, related by a National Park employee and resident of the islands, is exemplary:

> One of the most interesting stories I did hear was of a bus driver with a bus full of visitors going on a circle island tour, and he came to the park and he did tell the people, "Whatever you do, don't take the rocks. You will get bad luck, and I don't want any rocks on this bus." And one of the visitors said, "Well, I'm a paid customer and I'm going to take this rock." And she went out and she picked up a rock, and she was on the bus and all the other people on the bus were saying, "That's bad luck. Get rid of that. Get rid of that rock. We don't want bad luck on this bus." And she said, "Oh, I don't believe in any of that. I'm going to keep this rock. I want it." You know, for whatever purpose. And so every stop they'd say, "Now get rid of that rock." And they went around the island, down to the black sand beach at Kaimu, and they stopped there and everybody again just on her case, on her case: "Get rid of that rock! Get rid of that rock!" And she looked at them and she said, "You people are—you know, you're out of your minds. You're all superstitious fools." She goes, "OK. Well, I'll get rid of this rock," and she walked up through the aisle of the bus and the bus driver smiled and he opened the door. And she said,

"You see this rock? Are you happy now?" And she took the rock and she threw it out the bus door and it hit the door and it came back and cracked her in the head. And they had to take her into the hospital. The bus driver told me this a day or so after it happened.[46]

In 1988, an Aloha Airlines Boeing 737 traveling between Hilo, Hawai'i, and Honolulu, Oahu, met disaster when a gaping hole opened in the roof of the jet and pressurized air pulled an airline attendant out of the aircraft to her death. Approximately sixty passengers were injured. While transportation experts later placed blame on the commercial airline's neglect of their equipment, a tour guide waiting for his clients in a parking lot of Hawaii Volcanoes National Park told me that the "accident" occurred because some tourists had taken Pele's rocks aboard the jet with the idea of transporting them home as souvenirs.

Some souvenir manufacturers, recognizing the attraction of volcanic rocks, market items made from or incorporating volcanic material. They too may have an interest in the Pele tourist folklore, since it might impact tourists' reactions to their products.[47] In one instance, at least, the manufacturer may have consciously attempted to counter the bad luck stigma associated with the Pele tourist folklore. Cocojoe's black, mostly plastic figures (all are marked as made in Hawai'i; lava by the islands) are fashioned into forms of the goddess Pele, Laki "Lucky" Menehune, Lono Tiki, and other figures of implied legendary stature. The souvenirs have labels affixed which describe the supernatural figure and usually ascribe *good* luck to the owner of the souvenir:

Lucky you, if you get me. I "Laki" Menehune.
In one night I can do wondrous things just for you!
Make a wish and hold me tight.
Rub my "opu," shine it bright.
Whether you be "he" or "she"
Good fortune's yours when you own me.

This souvenir "folklore," created specifically for tourists by marketers, is purchased along with the souvenir and provides an interesting contrast to the Pele tourist folklore that surrounds non-purchased volcanic rock. A concern with the ethics of creating commercialized folklore marketed as Hawaiian folklore for financial gain, or of representing indigenous Hawaiian folk figures for tourist consumption, is lacking in this capitalistic approach.

In contrast to those marketers, who strive to reverse any adverse effects the Pele tourist lore may have on their sale of volcanic materials, two entrepreneurs recently began a novel capitalist scheme of advertising volcanic rocks for sale to people who would like to send someone bad luck.[48] This suggests that commercial enterprises may alternatively reinforce or negate the tourist lore, always with the goal of achieving greater sales.

The National Park Service, particularly on the islands of Maui and Hawai'i where the most recent volcanic activity in the Hawaiian Islands has occurred, is affected by the legends more than any other institution. As one employee of Hawaii Volcanoes National Park stated, "It is a law enforcement problem, an interpretive problem, and a maintenance problem."[49] There has never been an official park policy about how to handle the phenomenon of the Pele lore, but if questioned, park personnel state that there is no reliable basis for the authenticity of the folklore in indigenous Hawaiian belief. However, in their struggle to discourage visitors from removing rocks, park personnel have sometimes utilized the legends as a strategy to persuade tourists to leave volcanic rock alone. Hawaii Volcanoes National Park established a display case in 1982 that featured examples of letters, returned volcanic rock, and other items sent by former visitors. One letter, for example, was accompanied by a photograph of a car totaled in an accident. A pair of shoes, thought to have volcanic rock particles adhering to their soles, was another part of the display.

Despite the fact that the display was one of the most popular sights at the visitors' center and was often remembered as an attraction to see on subsequent trips,[50] it was dismantled in 1988 as a result of its perceived adverse effects to the park's intent. According to one employee, many local people, especially of indigenous Hawaiian descent, were offended by the display because it was often misinterpreted by tourists as an expression of indigenous Hawaiian belief. The display may have deterred some people from taking volcanic rock, but it also disseminated the folklore more widely, inspiring some tourists to write letters entreating park personnel to add their testimonials to the display.

In addition to dismantling the display of tourists' letters, personnel of Hawaii Volcanoes National Park now refuse to aid print and TV journalists interested in doing what park personnel sometimes refer to as "rock stories," which perpetuate the tourist folklore. Their justification is based on practicality, as well as the issue of morality and authenticity, since all packages received at Hawaii Volcanoes National Park—from twelve to twenty packages a week on average—must be opened. Volunteers (and sometimes paid staff) spend a great deal of time opening the packages and letters that are sent directly to the park. In addition to taking time away from other activities, the task involves opening tightly wrapped packages and extracting sharp pieces of volcanic rock from layers of wrapping material. In the past, park employees tried to return rocks to their areas of origin—a task made possible because rocks differ in appearance on the basis of age. However, returned rocks are now usually deposited in a designated pile behind the visitors' center. To return rock to its approximate place of origin is a costly endeavor, and according to park personnel it might also lead future geologists to misidentifications.[51]

The interpretive problem which the Pele lore presents is viewed by many park personnel as their greatest challenge. Park employees say that they strive to provide "authentic and credible information" which relates to indigenous Hawaiian belief and practice associated with a site in order to "interpret it in a respectful and traditional manner."[52] The park interpreters' self-assigned task of presenting "authentic" Hawaiian belief is, of course, part of the ongoing construction of "tradition" in the present.[53] Park personnel avoid mentioning tourist lore unless directly questioned, and then seek to dispel it by citing the lack of scholarly evidence supporting its existence in traditional Hawaiian society. As one park interpreter stated,

> The "folklore" of the misfortune associated with removal of volcanic rocks is not Hawaiian tradition or folklore at all, but rather a recently mistaken or altered perception of the character and characteristics of Pele, the Hawaiian Goddess of the Volcano. Frankly, we are not interested in perpetuating this mistaken view of the Hawaiian's genuine respect for Pele. We would really want to discourage any further publication of this spurious oral tradition.[54]

Dedicated to preserving the authenticity of the islands' natural environment, the park service is also concerned with preserving the authenticity of the indigenous Hawaiian's conceptions of Pele as based on authoritative texts. In the park service's view, removal of volcanic rock destroys the first, but ironically, return of the rock on the basis of the tourist folklore threatens destruction of the second.

The media, tour operators, souvenir entrepreneurs, and the park service take a variety of stances vis-à-vis the Pele tourist folklore based on perceived problems or opportunities. Tour guides, for example, may tell clients about the tourist folklore as a way to avoid legal sanctions and dirty buses. On the other hand, they may avoid discussing the folklore for fear that someone will be offended by the stories. While it may present opportunities or problems for those who have frequent dealings with tourists, the legends will undoubtedly continue to exist as popular and viable for as long as they prove useful to the tourists themselves.

Conclusion

Pele tourist folklore communicates much about tourism and its consequences. Although interested parties such as tour guides and the media may seek to reaffirm, modify, redirect, or ignore it, this lore remains fundamentally generated by and for the tourists themselves. It is at once a descriptive perpetuation of the

Other and a prescriptive formulation for tourists' interaction and realignment with the Other, and it communicates tourists' ambivalence toward the Other.

One significant theme, which is echoed in the perspectives of some who are most affected by the lore, is that tourism has detrimental effects. Although the legends seemingly emphasize the destructive qualities of Pele herself,[55] the foundational message is that it is the destructive nature of the tourists' actions which brings about Pele's actions. The tourist phenomenon of taking volcanic material for souvenirs is utilized within the folklore as an exaggerated sign of the inevitable negative alterations of a touristic presence. The embedded moral message to everyone—tourists and Others alike—is that bad things happen to tourists because of the bad things they do as tourists.

Another significant theme is found in the tourists' search for their own identity and authenticity as reflected in Others.[56] The initial impulse to appropriate some of the Other (by taking a souvenir rock) may be interpreted as a means for tourists to close the distance between themselves and their Others, even though it results in a division between hosts and guests.

In projecting, through the legends, retaliation by the Other in response to their own exploitive acts, tourists signal an awareness that their initial disregard served to distort and violate the integrity of the Other. Within the legends, however, the souvenir rock—although removed from its native environment—ironically reauthenticates the Other when it attracts Pele's vengeance toward the tourist. The tourist, in turn, acknowledges Pele's supernatural powers and recognizes that the Other is, indeed, viable and "real."

The Pele tourist legends invite island visitors to change their treatment of the Other by encouraging respect, and they act as cautionary tales, warning that those who violate, exploit, or otherwise denigrate Others will eventually have to face the consequences of committing such acts.

The legends reflect human desire for transformative relationships with Others, as well as reinforce the mechanisms which limit those relationships. A recognition of the interdependence of people with their Others and the potential for unification that recognition proffers lead to an inevitable paradox—that tourists, in finally finding the Other, simultaneously encounter restrictions limiting their relationship to the Other; and both the encounter and restrictions perpetuate and further reinforce constructions of the Other.

Acknowledgments

Jim Martin, John Wise, James Boll, Carol Beadle, Patty Belcher, DeSoto Brown, Thomas E. White, Lisa Farmer-Edie, Jon Erickson, R. A. Mitchell Jr., Mardie Lane, Adela Fevella, Becky Soglin, Vicki Greive, Joni Mae

Makuakane-Jarrell, Claudine Fujii, and tour guides of Adamai Tours, Jack's Tours, Gray Line Tours, and Robert's Tours.

Endnotes

1. National Park Service personnel and others report that some packages are also sent from Europe, Australia, and Japan.

2. Research for this article was conducted over a several-week period during the late 1980s. In the role of both tourist and researcher, I gathered information by observing displays on the Pele folklore phenomenon, reading both letters from tourists and media reports on the phenomenon, and conducting interviews with National Park personnel, tour operators, tourists, and resident Hawaiians.

    Tourists' complete letters or excerpts used in this paper are from recent correspondence (within the past ten years) sent to Hawaii Volcanoes National Park on Hawai'i or Haleakala National Park on Maui. While almost all the letters are signed and dated in their original form, I have deleted these details to ensure anonymity.

3. The tourist folklore may not have existed prior to 1929. In "A Note on Present Day Myth" (*Journal of American Folklore*, no. 163 [1929]: 73–75), Melville J. Herskovits and Morris J. Rogers Jr. report on Pele folklore of the late 1920s, but do not mention anything resembling the tourist folklore.

4. Martha Warren Beckwith, *Hawaiian Mythology* (Honolulu: University of Hawaii Press, 1970); William D. Westervelt, *Hawaiian Legends of Volcanoes* (Rutland, VT: Charles E. Tuttle, 1963); and Pedraic Colum, *Legends of Hawaii* (1937; New Haven, CT: Yale University Press 1967).

5. William Ellis, *Journal of William Ellis* (Honolulu: Advertiser Publishing, 1963).

6. Ibid., 185.

7. Ibid., 186.

8. Edward Said, *Orientalism* (New York: Pantheon Books, 1978); Johannes Fabian, *Time and the Other: How Anthropology Makes Its Object* (New York: Columbia University Press, 1983); James Clifford and George E. Marcus, eds., *Writing Culture—The Poetics and Politics of Ethnography* (Berkeley and Los Angeles: University of California Press, 1986).

9. Michelle Zimbalist Rosaldo and Louise Lamphere, eds., *Woman, Culture, and Society* (Stanford, CA: Stanford University Press, 1974); Annette Weiner, *Women of Value, Men of Renown* (Austin: University of Texas Press, 1976); Gloria Hull, Patricia Bell Scott, and Barbara Smith, eds., *All the Women Are White, All the Men Are Black, But Some of Us Are Brave: Black Women's Studies* (Old Westbury, CT: Feminist Press, 1982).

10. Edwin Ardener, "Belief and the Problem of Women," in *Perceiving Women*, ed. Shirley Ardener (New York: John Wiley and Sons, 1975), 1–17; T. Minh-ha Trinh, *Woman, Native, Other: Writing Postcoloniality and Feminism* (Bloomington: Indiana University Press, 1989). These references are exemplary; there are many other works which seek to accomplish the same goals. A large body of feminist literature, in particular, speaks to these issues.

11. Sherry B. Ortner, "Is Female to Male as Nature Is to Culture?" in Rosaldo and Lamphere, previously cited; E. Ardener, previously cited; Susan Griffin, *Woman*

and Nature: The Roaring Inside Her (New York: Harper and Row, 1978); Carolyn Merchant, *The Death of Nature: Women, Ecology, and the Scientific Revolution* (San Francisco: Harper and Row, 1980).

12.   Mary Douglas, *Purity and Danger: An Analysis of Concepts of Pollution and Taboo* (New York: Praeger, 1966).

13.   Victor Turner, *The Ritual Process* (Chicago: Aldine, 1969).

14.   Dean MacCannell, *The Tourist, A New Theory of Leisure Class* (New York: Schocken Books, 1976); Erik Cohen, "A Phenomenology of Tourist Experiences," *Sociology* 13 (1979): 179–201; Nelson Graburn, "Tourism: The Sacred Journey," in *Hosts and Guests, The Anthropology of Tourism,* ed. Valene L. Smith (Philadelphia: University of Pennsylvania Press, 1977), 17–31; Susan Stewart, *On Longing: Narratives of the Miniature, the Gigantic, the Souvenir, the Collection* (Baltimore: The Johns Hopkins University Press, 1984).

15.   Turner.

16.   Graburn, 1977, 21.

17.   Nelson Graburn, *To Pray, Pay, and Play: The Cultural Structure of Japanese Domestic Tourism* (Aix-en-Provence: Universite de Droit, d'Economie et des Sciences, Centre des Hautes Etudes Touristiques, 1983).

18.   Turner.

19.   In traditional Hawaiian lore, Pele was frequently destructive, but her acts of violence could be motivated by a desire to aid Hawaiians she favored, as well as to punish those who offended her.

20.   Correspondence between tourist and Hawaii Volcanoes National Park (see Note 2).

21.   In traditional folklore, Pele frequently interacted with mortals, appearing as a beautiful young woman or an older Hawaiian woman. Pele's transformations into human form mirrored the transformative qualities of volcanic activity and matter themselves. Pele still appears in human form to some residents in the islands.

22.   "Pele is a significant ingredient in the culture of the contemporary Hawaiian Islands. Belief in the volcano goddess is widely held by a broad stratum of society—doctors, professors, scientists, writers, housewives, engineers, hotel managers, and countless others." From H. Arlo Nimmo, "Pele, Ancient Goddess of Contemporary Hawaii," *Pacific Studies* 9, no. 2 (1986): 168.
        Many stories told in the islands center on Pele's physical destruction of property if residents don't pass her tests of charity. The tests, administered in Pele's guises as a young or elderly woman, provide opportunities for residents to demonstrate their compassion toward others. If they fail to extend generosity and thoughtfulness, Pele may destroy their homes and land with lava flows and fire. If the residents pass the tests, their property is clearly spared. Still other island legends reflect recent, controversial issues in Hawaiian society. During events surrounding Hawaiians' efforts to thwart geothermal mining operations, for example, stories of Pele's reactions to the mining were told. As Ken Kobayashi reported in *The Honolulu Advertiser* ("High Court Leaning against Pele Worshippers," April 23, 1987, A1), "Dr. Aluli said Pele will have the 'last say. She's already wiped out Kahaualea [an earlier proposed site, destroyed by 1983–84 volcanic eruptions].'"

23.   See, for example, Herb Kane's paintings in Herb Kawainui Kane, *Pele, Goddess of Hawai'i's Volcanoes* (Captain Cook, HI: Kawainui Press, 1987); Gail Ka'uhane's

illustration on the back cover of Margaret Stone's *Supernatural Hawaii: Actual Mysteries, Blessings, Curses, Rituals, and Legends* (Honolulu: Aloha Graphics and Sales, 1979); and Nelson Makua's 1984 illustration and design of Pele, published on a greeting card by Graphic Images Hawaii (Hilo, Hawaii).

24. Mullins.

25. Simone de Beauvoir, *The Second Sex* (New York: Knopf, 1957 [1953]); Rosaldo and Lamphere, previously cited; bell hooks, *Feminist Theory: From Margin to Center* (Boston: South End Press, 1984).

26. Sharon W. Tiffany and Kathleen J. Adams, *The Wild Woman: An Inquiry into the Anthropology of an Idea* (Cambridge, MA: Schenkman Publishing, 1985).

27. The text of an advertisement taken out in a Hawaiian newspaper by activists interested in arresting geothermal operations read: "To violate Pele by drilling [geothermal wells] into her body is as outrageous to us as someone bulldozing the Sistine Chapel would be to Christians." Reported in Rod Stone Thompson, "Activist Fears Desecration of Pele's Spirit," *Honolulu Star Bulletin*, March 14, 1988, A1.

28. Ortner; Merchant; Camille Paglia, *Sexual Personae* (New York: Vintage Books, 1990).

29. In "Mount St. Helens and the Evolution of Folklore," *Northwest Folklore* 4, no. 1 (1985): 43–47, Elizabeth Simpson relates that some people associated Pele with Mount St. Helens in Washington when it erupted in the spring of 1980: "[A] bottle of gin wrapped in ti leaves was sent from Hawaii to appease the goddess, and photographs of the ash plume are said to show her profile." Newspaper articles and oral accounts from 1980 to 1982 also included stories of Pele posing as a hitchhiker and warning travelers of a second eruption. As Simpson points out, "This variation of the traditional tale [of the vanishing hitchhiker; see Jan H. Brunvand, *The Vanishing Hitchhiker: American Urban Legends and Their Meanings* (New York: W.W. Norton and Company, 1981)] may have come to Washington from Hawaii, or may have generated afresh—there is no way of knowing" (p. 46). Certainly, many residents of Washington have traveled to Hawai'i as tourists or have heard Pele lore through the media. However, the association of Pele with Washington volcanic activity and volcanic rock seems confined to Mount St. Helens and limited to a small minority who drew the association around the time of Mount St. Helens' eruption. Simpson reports that "Robert Dunnagan, chief of operations at Mount Rainier National Park said he, too, heard the reports [of a vanishing female hitchhiker warning of an eruption] from his associates. He question[ed] the comparison to Pele" (p. 45). Volcanic rock from other Washington locations has not been associated with Pele. Irwin Slesnick, professor of biology at Western Washington University in Bellingham, reported that he was "really surprised how many people rejected the idea of including samples of black sand from a southeast Hawaiian beach in a sand activity kit. Instead, we had it packed out of a Mount Baker lake beach" (personal communication, January 21, 1991).

30. MacCannell, 84.

31. Repeated questioning revealed that there are no established archives of letters. One collection from Hawaii Volcanoes National Park is said to have been inadvertently destroyed in the 1950s. Some of the national parks unsystematically keep letters for a few years before discarding them. Some of the park employees

and others who receive letters keep those which are of greatest personal interest to them.

32. Stewart.

33. Ibid., 148.

34. Thompson.

35. Pele provides a particularly apt symbol for the Other's integrity because many Hawaiians regard volcanic rock to be Pele's body, as well as her home.

36. In *The Golden Hordes, International Tourism, and the Pleasure Periphery* (New York: St. Martin's Press, 1976), Louis Turner and John Ash say that "tourism is, everywhere, the enemy of authenticity and cultural identity" (p. 197). Those who are concerned with retaining the authenticity of people, places, objects, or mythological figures in the face of tourist visitations are paradoxically involved in preserving and displaying these as tourist attractions.

37. Tourism's paradox arises from what MacCannell (p. 13) cites as tourism's doom to eventual failure: "Even as it tries to construct totalities, it celebrates differentiation."

38. This parallels media reports of urban legends (*cf.* Brunvand).

39. "Madame Pele's Power Reaches Out for Rock," *Hawaii Tribune-Herald,* July 17, 1972, 5:1.

40. Alberta de Jetley, "Maui People," *Mauian* (June/July) 1987, 24.

41. Frankie Stapleton, "Madame Pele, Please Turn Off the Bad Luck," *Hawaii Tribune-Herald,* November 9, 1978, p. 8. The article appeared on the desk in 1986, but had been removed by 1988.

42. This display was exhibited in 1988.

43. Kane, 50; Nimmo, 159.

44. Some guides are very accommodating and will carry rock back to designated areas mentioned in letters accompanying the rock. Such action, however, does not necessarily mean that the bus operators subscribe to the tenets of folklore.

45. Nimmo, 159.

46. Mardie Lane, personal communication with author, Hawaii Volcanoes National Park, December 13, 1988.

47. Nimmo (p. 159) reports, "A Filipino man told me there were many cases of people dying or becoming ill because they took lava to the mainland United States, but the tourist industries have been successful in hushing up the stories because they were afraid it would harm their sales of the many souvenir items made of lava."

48. de Jetley.

49. Mardie Lane, previously cited.

50. Mardie Lane said that many bus tour guides felt the display helped to discourage tourists from bringing rocks aboard their buses. Jon Erickson, another employee of Hawaii Volcanoes National Park, said that many tour bus guides would only encourage the tourists to look at that display in the visitors' center. In 1988, when I talked with different tour operators, several mentioned the exhibit, unaware that it had recently been dismantled. The display case was the way in which I initially learned of the Pele tourist folklore, in 1986. On my subsequent trip to the park in 1988, the case was no longer on display. Reportedly, many tourists returning to the park after earlier visits are disappointed that the display was dismantled.

51.   Jon Erickson, personal communication with author, Hawaii Volcanoes National Park, December 13, 1988.

52.   Mardie Lane, previously cited.

53.   Richard Handler and Joyce Linnekin, "Tradition, Genuine or Spurious," *Journal of American Folklore* 97, no. 385 (July–September, 1984): 273–290.

54.   Thomas E. White, Chief Park Interpreter of Hawaii Volcanoes National Park in 1987, in personal communication with the author, August 31, 1987.

55.   Tourists' recognition of Pele and her supernatural powers reaffirms the characteristics associated with the constructed Other. Yet by displacing the Other onto a supernatural figure, it might be argued that tourists to Hawai'i avoid some of tourism's detrimental effects on human Others.

56.   MacCannell, p. 41.

10

Terror in Transition:
Hmong Folk Belief in America

Shelley R. Adler

WITH THE FALL OF THE CAPITAL CITY OF VIENTIANE IN 1975, THOUSANDS OF Hmong fled their native Laos and, often after extended delays in Thai refugee camps, began arriving in North America. In the West, the Hmong are more widely known than other Laotian ethnic groups because of their efforts during the war in Vietnam, especially after it spread to Laos and Cambodia. Thousands of Hmong were funded directly and secretly by the U.S. Central Intelligence Agency to combat the Communist Pathet Lao. Hmong men served as soldiers, pilots, and navigators, and their familiarity with the mountain terrain helped make them remarkable scouts and guerrilla fighters.[1] By the end of the civil war, the Hmong had suffered casualty rates proportionally ten times higher than those of Americans who fought in Vietnam;[2] it is estimated that nearly one-third of the Laotian Hmong population lost their lives.[3] When the Laotian government changed hands after the departure of American troops, large groups of Hmong were forced to flee Laos rather than chance "reeducation" camps or possible death under the new Communist regime.[4]

There are currently over 110,000 Hmong living in the United States, with 70,000 in California's Central Valley alone.[5] The city of Fresno is now home to the largest single community of Hmong in existence. The transition these refugees from Laos face is an extraordinarily difficult one.

> These displaced and resettled Hmong, while finding welcome freedom from persecution and physical annihilation, are nevertheless going through a grave cultural crisis, immersed as they are, an infinitesimal minority, in overwhelmingly dominant majority modes of living, norms of behavior, beliefs, and values. Everywhere

they face the possibility of cultural annihilation, and struggle to maintain, for themselves and their children, a clear idea of who they are, of their identity as Hmong, of their place in history, and in the cosmic realm of spirits, ancestors' souls, and human societies.[6]

The Hmong who have fled Laos leave behind them a homeland ravaged by war, but in their transition to the West they encounter new and unique problems. Those Hmong who have come to the United States find themselves in a place where their religion, language, and skills are decontextualized and where their previous social support system is greatly weakened.[7] In particular, for many Hmong the move marks the end of the existing form of their traditional religion.

In the traditional Hmong worldview, the natural world is alive with spirits. Trees, mountains, rivers, rocks, and lightning are all animated by distinctive spirits. Ancestor spirits continue to interact with their living descendants, and many animals share and exchange souls with human beings. As Dwight Conquergood explains in his life history of a Hmong shaman:

> The Hmong celebrate their humanity, not as a discrete and impenetrable part of the natural order, but as part of the circle of life of all creation—caught up in the rotation of the seasons, and deeply connected with the configuration of the mountains, and the reincarnation of life from generation to generation, even from species to species. Life, in its myriad forms, is intimately articulated through souls and spirits.[8]

Many Hmong feared that the ancestor spirits who protected them from harm in Laos would be unable to travel across the ocean to the United States. Solace was taken, however, in the conviction that the myriad evil spirits who challenged Hmong well-being in Laos would also be prevented from following the Hmong to their new home. Among these evil spirits assumed to remain behind was the nocturnal spirit *dab tsog* (pronounced *da cho*).[9] It soon became frighteningly apparent, however, that the notorious evil spirit had made the journey to America as well.

The Nightmare

Dab tsog is the Hmong manifestation of the supernatural nocturnal experience that I refer to as the "nightmare."[10] I use the word *nightmare* not in the modern sense of a bad dream, but rather in older traditional terms as the nocturnal visit of an evil being that threatens to press the very life out of its terrified victim.[11]

According to descriptions of the Nightmare spirit, the sleeper suddenly becomes aware of a presence close at hand. Upon attempting to investigate further, the victim is met with the horrifying realization that he or she is completely paralyzed. The presence is usually felt to be an evil one, and often this impression is confirmed by a visual perception of the being, which places itself on the sleeper's chest and exerts a pressure great enough to interfere with respiration. (To avoid confusion, I use *Nightmare* [uppercase] to refer to the spirit or demonic figure to which these nocturnal assaults are attributed, and *nightmare* [lowercase] to refer to the basic experience; that is, the impression of wakefulness, immobility, realistic perception of the environment, and intense fear.[12])

The nightmare syndrome appears to be universal. There are innumerable instances of the nightmare throughout history and in a multitude of cultures. References exist to the Assyrian *alu*,[13] the ancient Greek *ephialtes* ("leap upon"), and the Roman incubus ("lie upon"). Instances of the nightmare are present in many other areas, as evidenced, for example, by terms denoting the experience from the following languages and cultures: Eskimo *augumangia*; Filipino *urum* or *ngarat*;[14] French *cauchemar* (from Latin *calcare,* "to trample upon, squeeze"); German *Alb*,[15] *Alpdruck* ("elf pressure"), *Nachtmahr*,[16] or *Trud*;[17] Newfoundland "Old Hag";[18] Polish *zmora*; Russian *kikimora*; Spanish *pesadilla*.[19]

The Nightmare and Laboratory Sleep Research

The stable features of the nightmare, that is, those that comprise the core experience, are better understood with the assistance of concepts from laboratory sleep research. Current scientific thought on sleep phenomena also offers one explanation for the pervasiveness of the nightmare.[20]

Somnologists distinguish between two major divisions of sleep: active sleep (known as REM because of its characteristic rapid eye movements) and quiet sleep (non-REM or NREM). REM sleep is characterized by brain waves resembling those of wakefulness. In contradistinction to the waking state, however, the body is paralyzed, apparently to keep the sleeper from acting out his or her dreams.[21] In rare instances, this normal muscle inhibition or atonia occurs during partial wakefulness, either during the period of falling asleep (hypnagogic) or, less frequently, the period of awakening (hypnopompic). This condition is known as "sleep paralysis," a stage in which the body is asleep, but the mind is not.[22] Often sleep paralysis is accompanied by hypnagogic hallucinations, which consist of complex visual, auditory, and somatosensory perceptions occurring in the period of falling asleep and resembling dreams.[23]

Sleep paralysis and hypnagogic hallucinations are products of "sleep-onset REM," a REM stage that occurs earlier than normal, when the individual is still partially conscious.[24] Both David Hufford[25] and Robert Ness[26] show convincingly that sleep-onset REM accounts for the subjective impression of wakefulness, the feeling of paralysis, and, as a result, the tremendous anxiety that mark the nightmare experience. I would extend Hufford's and Ness's explanations to include that the sense of oppression or weight on the chest and the attendant feature of lying in a supine position are a result of the fact that when the sleeper is lying on his or her back, the atonic muscles of the tongue and esophagus collapse the airway. The relaxed muscles not only hinder breathing, but actually create a sensation of suffocation, strangulation, or pressure on the chest of the terrified sleeper.[27]

The Hmong Nightmare: *Dab Tsog*

In the Hmong language, the Nightmare spirit is commonly referred to as *dab tsog*. *Dab* is the Hmong word for "spirit" and is often used in the sense of an evil spirit, as opposed to *neeb (neng)*, which is a friendly or familiar spirit. *Tsog* is the specific name of the Nightmare spirit and also appears in the phrase used to denote a Nightmare attack, *tsog tsuam (cho chua)*. *Tsuam*, the Hmong word meaning "to crush, to press, or to smother"[28] is used in conjunction with *tsog* to mean "An evil spirit is pressing down on me!" or to refer generally to a Nightmare attack.[29]

Tsog are evil spirits thought to live primarily in dark, deserted caverns. In Laos, Hmong women and girls of childbearing age avoid going into or near caves because of the danger that the supernatural being will rape them. When a *tsog* rapes a woman, she becomes sterile (or, if she is pregnant at the time of the attack, a miscarriage will ensue and she will subsequently be infertile). These Hmong traditions regarding the effect of Nightmare spirits on childbearing are reminiscent of the widespread European belief that Lilith, as a succubus, poses a danger to pregnant women and newborn children,[30] as well as medieval traditions regarding the rape of women by incubi.[31]

Dab tsog, however, is most widely feared because of its propensity to come in the night to sleeping men and women and sit or lie upon them while pressing down and squeezing them tightly, rendering all movement impossible, and suffocating them.

Case 1: Chue Lor

A typical nightmare experience is recounted by Chue Lor,[32] a fifty-eight-year-old Hmong man from Xieng Khouang province in Laos. He arrived in the United States in 1979, after spending six months in a Thai refugee camp. He experienced his first of four or five Nightmare attacks, which he referred to as *tsog tsuam*, at the age of nineteen or twenty.

Like many who have undergone a Nightmare attack, Chue recounted his personal experience dramatically and with great intensity. Although the supernatural encounter took place more than thirty years earlier, his mannerisms and tone conveyed an immediacy to the event of his retelling. Furthermore, the impact of the nightmare experience, as well as the significance accorded the event, is evident from the fact that Chue was able to recall details with astonishing precision many years after the actual occurrence:

> I was in my bed at night. There were people at the other end of the house and I could hear them talking. They were still talking outside. I heard everything. But I knew that someone else was there. Suddenly there comes a huge body, it looked like, like a big stuffed animal they sell here. It was over me—on my body—and I had to fight my way out of that. I couldn't move—I couldn't talk at all. I couldn't even yell, "No!" By the time it was over, I remember, there were four other people inside the room and they said, "Gee, you made all this noise." I was trying to fight myself against that and it was very, very, very scary. That particular spirit was big, black, hairy. Big teeth. Big eyes. I was very, very scared.[33]

Chue's account not only contains the core symptoms of paralysis and intense fear, but also exemplifies the semiconscious nature of the experience. Most people who have experienced nightmares make an effort to convey the fact that they were not asleep during the encounter. As Chue describes, "There were people at the other end of the house and I could hear them talking." This combination of elements of waking (realistic perception of the environment) and sleeping (paralysis and dreamlike visualizations) is largely responsible for the nightmare's basic impact, not only on the Hmong, but also on people without animist beliefs. The perceived intrusion of a supernatural figure into everyday reality prevents the dismissal of the entire experience as merely an unconscious dream.

The Nightmare and Hmong Sudden Unexpected Nocturnal Death Syndrome

The continuation of terrifying Nightmare attacks after the Hmong departure from Laos is not the only unexpected element of their transition to life in America. Chue's narrative is part of a body of data I collected during an investigation of a mysterious fatal illness that has affected Hmong refugees and, to a lesser extent, other Southeast Asian immigrants.[34] Scores of seemingly healthy male Hmong immigrants in America have died mysteriously and without warning during the night from what has come to be known as Sudden Unexpected

Nocturnal Death Syndrome, or SUNDS.[35] (Only one Hmong woman has died of SUNDS since the first reported death in 1977.) The rate of death from SUNDS among Hmong men has reached alarming proportions, being equivalent to the sum of the rates of the five leading causes of natural death among U.S. males.[36] Despite numerous studies of SUNDS—which have taken into account such varied factors as toxicology, heart disease, genetics, metabolism, and nutrition—medical research has provided no adequate explanation for the Hmong sudden nocturnal deaths.

Based on preliminary fieldwork and a review of previous research, and from my perspective as a folklorist, I undertook a belief-centered investigation of Hmong SUNDS. The case definition presented by epidemiologist Neal Holtan and his associates in the *Final Report of the SUNDS Planning Project* provided further impetus for my approach.[37] Holtan and his colleagues emphasize the need to observe closely people "who fit the demographic characteristics of SUNDS" and who have transient nocturnal events that include "(1) a sense of panic or extreme fear, (2) paralysis (partial or complete), (3) a sense of pressure on the chest, (4) a sense that there is an alien being (animal, human, or spirit) in the room, [and] (5) a disturbance in sensation (auditory, visual, or tactile)."[38]

This list of five symptoms of SUNDS-related events is identical to the characteristics of the nightmare experience as it is known in countless folk traditions, including those of the Hmong. Since the conditions described by Holtan and his colleagues as "SUNDS-related" are consistent with the symptoms of a Nightmare attack, I decided to investigate the possibility that SUNDS is triggered by such a confrontation. Rather than searching for an exclusively pathophysiological etiology for SUNDS, therefore, I explored the role of powerful traditional beliefs in illness causation.

I conducted fieldwork with a representative sample of 118 Hmong in California's Central Valley from January 1990 to March 1991 in order to determine whether there was a connection between Hmong Nightmare attacks and SUNDS.[39] By studying first-person accounts of these nocturnal visitations, I was able to investigate whether the disruption of traditional Hmong culture—evident from factors such as rapid acculturation and changes in religious practice and gender roles—may be responsible for the sudden deaths.[40]

I developed the following hypothesis regarding the etiology of SUNDS: A supranormal nocturnal experience traditionally known as the nightmare and familiar to the Hmong acts as a trigger for the sudden nocturnal deaths. I also determined that, in order for this hypothesis to be proven correct, it was necessary to test the veracity of a series of suppositions:

1. The Hmong supernatural experience that I had isolated is in fact a culture-specific manifestation of the universal nightmare phenomenon.
2. Hmong belief regarding the experience forms a collective tradition (i.e., there is widespread awareness of the nightmare tradition among the Hmong).
3. The nightmare, in specific contexts, causes cataclysmic psychological stress.
4. Intense psychological stress can cause sudden death.

Dab Tsog as a Culture-Specific Nightmare

In his pivotal work on the nightmare, *The Terror That Comes in the Night,* David J. Hufford formulates two opposing ideas regarding the origin of the nightmare (as well as other supranormal experiences): the "cultural source hypothesis" and the "experiential source hypothesis."[41] According to the cultural source hypothesis, supranormal experiences are either fictitious products of tradition or imaginary subjective experiences shaped (or occasionally even caused) by tradition. This is the prevailing view in American society and an example of what Hufford refers to as "traditions of disbelief."[42] The experiential source hypothesis, on the other hand, posits that the supranormal nightmare tradition contains elements of experience that are independent of culture. It is this hypothesis that Hufford confirmed in his investigation of the Old Hag phenomenon in Newfoundland. Rather than assuming that preexisting traditions completely determine the nature of unusual experiences that we have, Hufford shows that it is possible to have real albeit strange experiences that are *subsequently* elaborated upon by culture. By taking the beliefs of his informants seriously, by trusting their perceptive and descriptive capabilities, Hufford is able to present a phenomenology that eluded skeptical investigators. Taken a step further, the methodological stance of accepting informants' beliefs and experiences as rational and plausible allowed me to learn the true role of the nightmare in Hmong culture and as it relates to SUNDS.

Hufford writes that "one check for the cultural shaping of certain perceptions is the determination of whether the same perceptions are found under different cultural conditions."[43] Examples of nightmare traditions and experiences throughout history and from a host of cultures highlight one of the most fascinating aspects of the nightmare experience: its apparent universality. Researchers such as Hufford and Ness have explained that the major factor in the worldwide appearance of the nightmare seems to be its physiological nature. The mechanism of the nightmare experience is found in human physiology, while the Nightmare's manifestation is elaborated upon by each individual's personal and cultural experience.

In my own interviews with Hmong informants I was careful not to bias questions regarding the nightmare *experience* phenomenologically (i.e., sleep paralysis and hypnagogic hallucinations) with inquiries regarding Hmong traditional *belief.* It was essential to separate the core nightmare experience from cultural elaborations in order to determine whether or not the nocturnal phenomenon that I planned to study was, in fact, a type of nightmare experience. To this end, I began the central portion of the interview with the question, "Did you ever wake up during the night and realize that you were unable to move or speak?" Rather than phrase the question in terms of a nocturnal pressing spirit, I intentionally used a vague description of sleep paralysis and hypnagogic hallucinations. By simply outlining a sleep-onset REM experience, I hoped to: (1) elicit responses that were uncolored by my use of a particular, and perhaps not widely known, cultural term, (2) afford informants the opportunity to describe the experience in their own words, (3) provide an opportunity for Christian Hmong, who I assumed might be reticent to discuss the experience in traditional Hmong supernatural terms, to describe their encounters, and finally, (4) replicate Hufford's findings regarding the recognizability of the experience in the absence of cultural elaborations.[44]

I was not optimistic about the number of positive responses to such a vague question, and did not expect that sixty-four from my sample of 118 informants would immediately recognize the experience described in the question and answer affirmatively. Another five people were initially confused by the question, but in subsequent discussion described a Nightmare/*dab tsog* experience that they had had. In total, a remarkable 58 percent of the sample had experienced at least one nightmare. On the basis of the data from this initial question and informants' subsequent narratives, I concluded that the Hmong supernatural experience that I had isolated was in fact a cultural manifestation of the Nightmare phenomenon.

I also elicited the native terms informants used to denote their nightmare experiences. *Dab tsog* and *tsog tsuam* were mentioned almost an equal number of times and were overwhelmingly the most widely known: 115 informants used either *dab tsog* or *tsog tsuam* to denote the nightmare experience. All of the informants who were able to provide a name for the nocturnal encounter could also define it. Thus, 97 percent of the sample interviewed were familiar with the nightmare experience. Also, 76 percent of the informants interviewed knew of at least one other person who had had a nightmare experience. This widespread awareness of the Nightmare tradition among the Hmong clearly establishes that Hmong belief regarding nightmare experience forms a collective tradition.

Case 2: Neng Her

Neng Her is a thirty-three-year-old Hmong man from Louang Prabang province in Laos. He fled Laos in 1979 and after four years in a refugee camp in Thailand finally arrived in America. Neng had only one nightmare—shortly after his arrival in 1983.

> First, I was surprised, but right away, I got real scared. I was lying in bed. I was so tired, because I was working very hard then. I wanted to go to school, but I had no money. I kept waking up, because I was thinking so much about my problems. I heard a noise, but when I turned—tried—I could not move. My bedroom looked the same, but I could see—in the corner, a dark shape was coming to me. It came to the bed, over my feet, my legs. It was very heavy, like a heavy weight over my whole body, my legs, my chest. My chest was frozen—like I was drowning, I had no air. I tried to yell so someone sleeping very close to me will hear. I tried to move—using a force that I can—a strength that I can have. I thought, "What can I do about this?" After a long time, it went away—it just left. I got up and turned all the lights on. I was afraid to sleep again.[45]

Like many of the informants, at one point in the interview, Neng emphasized that recurrent attacks must be prevented—ideally by establishing the reason for the repeated visits (through a shaman) and appeasing the spirit (through animal sacrifice). The problem of recurring Nightmare attacks is exacerbated and their terror intensified because in most cases, as Neng described, people "don't use shamans anymore."

Since Neng had expressed surprise at Nightmare spirits' presence in the United States, I was interested to learn his opinion of how *dab tsog* came to be in America. Neng explained:

> Some people say that someone carries *dab tsog* from Laos to Thailand, and Thailand to America. It's very hard for me to believe that you can carry a *dab tsog* from Thailand to here—when you jump into the jet, it's so noisy. We go through electronic gates, you know, the checking [Neng laughs]. I don't mean to say insulting things to someone who has *dab tsog* a lot. It's terrible to have *dab tsog*—it's very dangerous . . . . I didn't think we would have *dab tsog* here. I thought there would be new spirits—but I guess *dab tsog* also like to live in America.[46]

Neng is in an interesting position since he maintains his identification with traditional Hmong religion while his parents have converted to Christianity. His familiarity with both religions enables him to comment insightfully on the relevance of religious conviction to Nightmare attacks.

SRA: Do Hmong who are Christian still have *dab tsog?*

Neng: Yes, they do. But they believe that somehow God will get rid of those things. They try to change their beliefs and some are devoted to their new religion. It might help [laughs]. If you have a shaman, and you do the rituals, that will help. The problem is that many Christians believe that if you strongly believe in God, the chance that *dab tsog* will disturb you will be lesser. Sure, if you strongly believe in your religion, and you say, "I will believe this until my last breath," it will help you. But many Christian Hmong don't believe this strongly. If you are in a neutral—you know, not there and not there—and you still have a doubt, chances are that *dab tsog* will be dancing around you for quite a while.[47]

* * * * *

The Nightmare and Religious Stress

Since both Christian and traditional Hmong die of SUNDS, the testing of my hypothesis necessitated an exploration of the impact of the Nightmare on Hmong of both religions. In my sample, 54 percent of traditional Hmong and 72 percent of Christian Hmong had experienced at least one nightmare. Of the Christian Hmong who had experienced nightmares, 64 percent had at least one nightmare encounter after their conversion to Christianity.

A few Christian Hmong informants, apparently uncomfortable with the application of the concept of Hmong evil spirits to their own experiences, described the Nightmare as a demon or evil spirit, in the satanic sense. Rather than deny the existence of the Nightmare phenomenon, these informants chose to "demonize" it to be more compatible with their new Christian worldview. (This is reminiscent of the medieval church practice of labeling the former deities of recent converts as demons; an acknowledgment that, ironically, resulted in a certain credibility being lent to those otherwise heretical religious experiences.)

Out of thirty-five Christian Hmong in my sample, eleven had converted to Christianity before arriving in the United States (approximately half of these, however, had converted in Thai refugee camps). Missionary activity, primarily on the part of the French, led to the conversion of some Hmong while still in Laos. Approximately 69 percent of the Christian Hmong I interviewed converted to Christianity after their arrival in the United States.

There are Christian Hmong who converted out of a genuine desire to worship and practice according to Christian doctrine, but there are also Hmong who converted out of a sense of loyalty or obligation to their church sponsors, or for a host of other non-religious reasons. Outward conversion thus is not necessarily an indication of internal conviction.[48] One researcher noted during her study in Philadelphia in 1983, for example, that several hundred Hmong refugees were associated with various Christian churches, but that the "majority of ministers . . . suggest that most of the refugees attend because of a desire for community, not doctrine."[49] As a social worker, himself Hmong, explains:

> It's hard to tell how many Hmong are Christian. They are strong, strong believers in their traditional religion. When they adapt to this society, this new lifestyle, their children go to church—but when they come home, they still worship like before. . . . Some people go to church on Sundays, but when they come home, they still have something on the wall [i.e., an altar] and like that.[50]

Although the more devout Christian Hmong I spoke with denied this ambivalence, many of the Christian Hmong informants described ways in which they combined the two religions in order to prevent incurring the Hmong spirits' wrath.

Sadly, one consequence of these religious conversions has been an increasing rift between traditional and Christian Hmong. Typical of the comments I heard were allegations on the part of Christian Hmong that traditional Hmong were "worshipping evil" and arguments by Hmong who practiced the traditional religion that Christian Hmong have not separated themselves from their native religion as much as they like to think they have.

Not only did both Christian and traditional Hmong in my sample experience Nightmare attacks, but 98 percent of traditional Hmong and 67 percent of Christian Hmong who suggested a cause for Nightmare attacks attributed them either directly to spirits or to the absence of traditional Hmong religious practice in their lives. Additionally, the psychological stress induced by Nightmare attacks affected Hmong irrespective of their religion. Both Christian and traditional Hmong experienced great stress regarding religious conflicts, which appeared to be heightened by the supernatural attacks.

In the insightful work *Hmong Sudden Unexpected Nocturnal Death Syndrome: A Cultural Study,* Bruce Bliatout (himself Hmong) analyzes the role of religious stress in SUNDS. Bliatout comments that in his sample of thirty-eight Hmong (nineteen Christians and nineteen traditional Hmong) in the United States who died of SUNDS:

> [B]oth Christian and non-Christian Hmong were under similar stresses caused by the inability to resolve religious conflicts . . . . many [Christian] families gave up their traditional religion to become Christian without truly taking any comfort from their new religion. Therefore, it seems that peer pressure and lack of understanding of Christianity may cause some Hmong Christians to have anxieties about not fulfilling their expected traditional religious duties, particularly towards their ancestors.[51]

Bliatout also notes a corresponding religious stress in traditional Hmong:

> Of the Hmong families who continued in Ancestor Worship, every one of them expressed the view that they were not able to satisfactorily perform certain religious ceremonies. Reasons for this were that, besides being fearful of the police and breaking public health laws, many complained that since they were not allowed to raise or slaughter animals in their homes, it was difficult to find adequate livestock necessary for Hmong ceremonies. Some families said that due to the disruption of village and clan groups caused by relocation, they were unable to find a Hmong religious leader or other family members to help in the performance of correct ceremonies. Others cited that living in an apartment was not conducive to providing a central pillar for ancestors to live in.[52]

Bliatout asserts that recent converts to Christianity (the group that forms the vast majority of Christian Hmong in my sample) are at greater risk for feelings of religious dislocation and stress from nightmare experiences than those who have practiced Christianity for many years. Recent converts are still very familiar with the tenets of traditional Hmong culture, and Bliatout argues that even for those Hmong who did change religions out of spiritual conviction, feelings of guilt, displacement, and ostracism greatly increase the negative impact of a nightmare encounter.

Case 3: Tong Yee Xiong

Tong Yee Xiong is a forty-year-old Hmong man from Sayaboury province. He fled Laos in 1975 and, after living in a Thai refugee camp for a little less than two years, arrived in the United States in 1977. Tong has had four nightmare experiences, which he refers to as *tsog tsuam*: the first attack occurred in Laos in 1975, and the others occurred after his arrival in the United States in 1979. Tong converted to Christianity in 1988. His Nightmare attacks are particularly interesting because they continued after his conversion to Christianity.

Tong is one of many of the Christian Hmong informants who blended elements of their previous beliefs into their new religion. The meshing of the two religions, however, proved to be complicated and problematic. Tong seemed comfortable including both traditional Hmong and Christian elements in his own religious practice, but he was forced to maintain a distinction when dealing with either traditional Hmong or non-Hmong Christians. An example of this separation is the religious self-consciousness he displays in describing methods of preventing Nightmare attacks.

SRA: How can you stop the attacks from happening?

Tong: A shaman has to do a ceremony. Or you can ask the priest to pray in church for that person. But you don't say, "This person has *dab tsog*—an evil spirit," you have to say, "My cousin is sick." Christians who are not Hmong do not understand. But also some Hmong—Hmong who follow the old way—do not understand.[53]

When I asked Tong about the immediate causes of his recent Nightmare attacks, he responded, "After I became Christian, it usually only happens if I don't go to church or don't pray for a long time." Ironically, Tong has incorporated his traditional Hmong beliefs and experiences into his new religion in such a way as to interpret *dab tsog* attacks as the consequence of his failure to meet his Christian religious obligations. Tong's intense fear of *dab tsog*, however, is consistent with traditional Hmong belief.

Case 4: Cheng Her

Cheng Her is a thirty-one-year-old Hmong man from Vientiane province in Laos. He fled Laos in 1975 and came to the United States three years later, after living in a Thai refugee camp. Cheng had one *tsog tsuam* encounter in 1979, a few months after arriving in the United States. He was initially helped by the Christian Missionary Alliance and he converted to Christianity in 1979. In describing his nightmare encounter, Cheng used the terms *Devil* and *dab* interchangeably, a conflict that is mirrored, on a larger scale, by his ambivalence regarding the true nature of the Nightmare spirit. Cheng is representative of a group of Christian Hmong informants who appear to be struggling with the exclusion of aspects of traditional Hmong religion even years after their conversion to Christianity. His fears of *tsog tsuam* are rooted in Hmong traditional belief, but he responds to the threat of a Nightmare with prayer.

SRA: Did you behave differently because you were Christian?
Cheng: Oh, yes—after that happened, I prayed. I turned on the light and prayed, and then I felt better. When it happened, I tried to forget the old way. We tend to believe that God will help us, that that is nothing—nothing happened. God will help us, and we pray, and we tend to forget, and we act like nothing happened. When Hmong people become Christian, they tend to forget the old beliefs and how the shamans helped, and how their ceremonies saved people's lives. They think, "Well, nothing happened like that, and now God is taking care of us." Now, when we have a bad dream or an evil spirit comes to us, we just pray and try to forget . . . People who do not become Christian, they will worry so much, and they will have to do something—a ceremony. Christians—even though we will think sometimes, "It is an evil spirit," we will try to put it away, to not think about it.[54]

Cheng's comments, in particular his observation that Christian Hmong "try" to forget their old traditions and beliefs, reveal the lingering influence of *dab tsog* on at least some Christian converts. Since both traditional and Christian Hmong have died of SUNDS, in order for my hypothesis of a folk-belief-centered trigger to be proven correct, it was essential that indications of nightmare belief be present among Hmong of both religions. My own research reveals that psychological stress regarding religious practice is present in both groups, and also that this stress is exacerbated in both groups by the supernatural nocturnal assaults.

* * * * *

Cataclysmic Psychological Stress and Sudden Death

Case 5: Chia Xiong

Chia Xiong is a forty-nine-year-old Hmong man from Sayaboury province in Laos. Chia left Laos in 1980 and, after living in a Thai refugee camp for one year, arrived in the United States in 1981. Chia had two episodes of *tsog tsuam* during the years 1981 and 1982. (Chia is one of a few informants who used the English word *nightmare* to label his *tsog tsuam* experiences. His usage parallels my own in adopting the classic "pressing-spirit" definition of the English word, and thus the terms *nightmare* and *tsog tsuam* are interchangeable in his narrative.)

Chia explained that in the first few months after his arrival in the United States, he constantly worried about his family and his own livelihood. On the night of his first *tsog tsuam* episode he was preoccupied with troubling thoughts.

> I remember a few months after I first came here—I was asleep. I turned out the light and everything, but I kind of think about, think about, think about, and then—all of a sudden, I felt that—I cannot move. I just feel it, but I don't see anything, but I—then I tried to move my hand, but I cannot move my hand. I keep trying, but I cannot move myself. I know it is *tsog tsuam*. I am so scared. I can hardly breathe. I think, "Who will help me? What if I die?"[55]

The emotional stress and preoccupation with worrisome thoughts ("think about, think about, think about") that formed the psychic background of Chia's attack are significant in terms of nightmare etiology. (Emotional stress, physical exhaustion, and sleep deprivation have been shown to be predisposing factors for sleep-onset REM.[56]) I have noted an increased incidence of nightmares during informants' times of stress.

Chia continues to describe his personal experience with a description of his second attack:

> The other nightmare I had was also like that. I was sort of sleeping. My eyes were still open and I was still seeing. I felt that I could—could not move. It's like a ghost putting pressure on you. Something like that. I saw someone come to me and start pushing me. I could not breathe, I could not talk, I could not yell. But I can still see the TV, I can still see the light. Like, in my brain, I'm saying, "Move! Move!" but my body cannot. I try—keep trying—to move. I am so frightened. I feel I am alone. But I'm still trying to move—kick this spirit off of me. Finally, I can move my legs, and then my arms. Right away, I can move my whole body—and then the spirit runs away.[57]

Since one of the ultimate goals of my fieldwork was to establish whether the informants themselves perceived a connection between *dab tsog* attacks and SUNDS, I was particularly interested in comments regarding death and dying that were included in informants' personal narratives. It was important for me to learn at what point the traditional Nightmare encounter was considered to be lethal. Chia explained:

> *Chia:* During his lifetime, the person who died of SUNDS usually has at least two nightmares before it really becomes serious.
> *SRA:* Why, after two non-fatal attacks, would it become so much worse?
> *Chia:* It is believed that once you have one of those nightmares—you are visited by one of the *dab tsog* evil spirits—once you are seen by one of those evil spirits, often they will come back to you, until you have the worst nightmare and probably die.[58]

According to the belief Chia described, *tsog tsuam* assaults are rarely, if ever, fatal on the first encounter. Usually the lethal potential manifests only after an individual has been given time to rectify a situation, but chooses not to, or is unable to, appease the intruding spirit. Chia also explains that, because of traditional countermeasures undertaken in Laos, SUNDS did not occur prior to the Hmong exodus: "There were nightmares, but the sudden death was unheard of. It might have happened, but I never heard of it." None of the informants I interviewed recalled incidents of SUNDS in Laos.

* * * * *

As I have stated, my approach to the question of what causes SUNDS differed from that of other researchers in that I focused on the phenomenology of the Hmong nightmare; that is, the nocturnal spirit assault as it is experienced by the victims themselves. This methodology allowed me to learn the reason for the intense fear of the retribution of *dab tsog* from the Hmong perspective. As Chia eloquently explains, most Hmong perceive a direct causal relationship between failure to perform traditional Hmong rituals and Nightmare attacks. (Etiologies related to either traditional spirits or to the lack of traditional religious practice constituted 81 percent of all the nightmare causes suggested.)

> At least once a year those evil spirits must be fed. If someone forgets to feed them, then they will come back and disturb you. If you have *tsog tsuam,* the ancestor spirit is supposed to protect you. If you feed the ancestors regularly, then whenever you have *tsog tsuam,* the ancestor spirits will protect you. Usually the father, the head-of-household, is responsible for feeding the evil spirits. Women have nightmares, too, but not as often as men. The evil spirit would first attack the head-of-household. Coming to this country, people tend to forget to do the rituals. A lot of people either ignore or forget to practice their religious belief . . . . *Tsog tsuam* happens to both people who still believe in ancestors [spirits] and those who have been converted into Christianity. It happens to all . . . . If you have a nightmare, and the spirit intends to make you die, it will simply take your soul away . . . . Men are the ones who are responsible for feeding both the evil spirits and the ancestor spirits. Since they are not doing their part, it is logical that their soul should be taken away.[59]

Chia's explanation (reiterated by the majority of informants) clearly has great significance for my investigation of SUNDS etiology, in that it contains a matter-of-fact description of the precise manner in which a man's failure to fulfill traditional religious obligations can result in his death.

Although such resettlement factors as language and employment problems may not be unique to Hmong immigrants, the particular combination of difficulties involving changing generational and gender roles,[60] the conflict between Hmong traditional religion and Christianity, survivor guilt,[61] and trauma-induced emotional and psychological disorders is unique to the Hmong refugee experience. These changes affect both Hmong men and women to varying degrees, but it is important to keep in mind the ways in which Hmong men and women might experience these difficulties differently. Many of the resettlement problems, particularly conflicts between traditional Hmong religious practice and American society, appear to affect Hmong men most severely given their role as spiritual caretakers of the family. This gender dichotomy is mirrored by the vast discrepancy in the ratio of male to female SUNDS. Interestingly, several informants hypothesized that the one woman who died of SUNDS must have been unmarried or widowed and hence, as the head of her household, the individual held accountable by the spirits.

The Nightmare as the Trigger for Hmong SUNDS

Since I had established that there were Nightmare assaults and other spirit-related problems in Laos but no informants were aware of SUNDS deaths in that country, it was important to learn the reason that so many Hmong refugees in the United States attributed SUNDS to traditional spirits. I believe that the differences between the Hmong way of life in pre-war Laos and their current situation in the United States are responsible for this phenomenon. Traditional Hmong culture has sustained a severe disruption. The Hmong have undergone a seemingly endless series of traumatic experiences: the war in Laos, the Pathet Lao takeover and subsequent Hmong persecution (including the threat of genocide), the harrowing nighttime escapes through jungles and across the Mekong River, the hardships of refugee camps in Thailand, and finally resettlement in the United States, with not only housing, income, language, and employment concerns, but the inability to practice traditional religion, and hasty conversions to Christianity. Additionally, in a shortsighted federal effort to avoid "overburdening" individual communities with new immigrants, refugee resettlement officials dispersed sections of Hmong clans through the country. This policy effectively shattered the clan and extended family structure that had been an important source of emotional and economic support in Laos. I believe that these recent changes account for the fact that SUNDS occurs in the United States while no informant I interviewed was aware of SUNDS in pre-migration Laos.

As I have indicated, *dab tsog* did torment sleepers in the Hmong homeland, but in that cultural and social context there existed a fundamental structure of support. Hmong shamans conducted prescribed rituals designed to ascertain the nature of the individual's transgression and sought to appease the angry spirits in order to prevent the possibility of the sleeper's death during a subsequent nocturnal encounter. In the United States, while the majority of Hmong retain many of their traditional beliefs, in many instances they have lost their religious leaders and ritual responses. The insular communities that characterized Hmong life in Laos appear to have fostered traditional cultural practices whose presence alleviated, but whose subsequent loss provokes, feelings of terror and impending death associated with negative supernatural encounters. The folk beliefs regarding Nightmare attacks and their causes are still very much a part of Hmong collective tradition. What has eroded are the means for dealing with the assaults. Therefore, although the *dab tsog* attack in Laos was akin to the worldwide Nightmare tradition, the peculiar stresses of the recent Hmong experience have transformed its outcome.

The fact that SUNDS affects men almost exclusively has been one of its most perplexing aspects. The inability to fulfill roles and responsibilities with regard to religion (as well as in their lives generally) has had a calamitous impact on the psyche of many Hmong males. As many of the Hmong informants repeatedly explained, it is the male, as head-of-household, who is responsible for religious duties. Chief among these obligations is the care of the ancestor spirits and appeasement of evil spirits. When an evil spirit (primarily an untamed evil spirit, such as *dab tsog*) is angered or offended, it is the Hmong man who is sought for retribution. In the event that the individual's protective ancestor spirits have not been properly cared for and the ancestors desert him, he is particularly vulnerable to spirit attack and consciously aware of this vulnerability. Although Hmong women do experience Nightmare attacks and are aware of the roles of both spirits and the absence of traditional religious practices in SUNDS, they also know that *dab tsog* will seek out their husbands, fathers, or brothers as the individuals held accountable. As one Hmong informant recalled of her own nightmare experience, "Even though I was very, very scared, I thought it was good my husband wasn't there, so the spirit wouldn't hurt him."[62]

Although both Hmong men and women have sustained enormous difficulties as a result of their disruptive relocation to the United States, it is the Hmong male who—faced with the breakdown of traditional gender and age hierarchies, and the sudden inability to provide for himself and his family both financially and spiritually—appears particularly susceptible to "stress related to the trauma of cultural dislocation."[63]

Since both traditional and Christian Hmong men have died of SUNDS, it was essential to learn whether Nightmare attacks and the interpretations of them were religion-specific. I discovered that, despite the fact that *dab tsog* is a supranormal figure in traditional Hmong religion, both Nightmare attacks and the psychological stress they engender affect Hmong men and women irrespective of individuals' religious convictions. Ninety-eight percent of the traditional Hmong and 67 percent of the Christian Hmong who suggested a cause for their Nightmare attacks attributed them either directly to traditional spirits or to the absence of traditional Hmong religious practice from their lives. Thus, Nightmare attacks exacerbate stress regarding religious practice for both Christian Hmong and traditional Hmong.

The subject of intense emotional stress as the cause of sudden death is a motif well-represented in world folklore throughout history and has also been a topic of serious biomedical investigation. A number of anthropological and biomedical studies suggest a link between psychological stress and sudden death.[64] In the medical anthropological and ethnomedical literature, the notion of beliefs playing a significant role in illness causation (nocebo effect) or its remedy (placebo effect) is widely held.[65] Significantly, the concept of ethno-medicogenic illness and healing, with its emphasis on the relationship between the mind/spirit and body, is compatible with the holistic traditional Hmong worldview regarding health.

The Hmong informants that I interviewed made it clear that in the context of recent and severe sociocultural change, *dab tsog* attacks on Hmong men can result in cataclysmic psychological stress on the part of the victim. The analysis of the interview data confirms that the power of traditional belief in the Night-mare—compounded with factors such as the trauma of war, migration, rapid acculturation, and the inability to practice traditional healing and ritual—causes cataclysmic psychological stress that can result in the deaths of male Hmong refugees from SUNDS.

The incidence of SUNDS deaths peaked in 1981. Since that time the num-ber of deaths and the crude death rate has more or less fallen steadily. This pattern appears to be directly affected by the stress of relocation and resettle-ment. The number of deaths of Hmong refugees in the United States rises and falls in response to the amount of time that individuals have been in this coun-try. The various stresses I have discussed manifest most strongly during the ini-tial arrival period, which is characterized by the greatest change and often the least amount of readily available support. Therefore, a likely reason for the decline in the number of deaths appears to be the fact that subsequent cohorts of new Hmong immigrants have many more possibilities to receive various forms of support (e.g., close-knit communities, restored clan ties, greater opportunity for traditional religious practice).

Through the phenomenon of "secondary migration," the majority of Hmong families have moved from their initial cities of resettlement to reunite as clans and extended families in large, more rural communities, such as those of California's Central Valley. Just as the disruption of traditional Hmong cul-ture appears to have created the context for the devastation of Hmong SUNDS through *dab tsog* attacks in the United States, the rebuilding of many traditional Hmong sociocultural supports has apparently formed the remedy.

Acknowledgments

A version of this chapter with a more medical focus has been published under the title "Ethnomedical Pathogenesis and Hmong Immigrants' Sudden Noc-turnal Deaths," in *Culture, Medicine and Psychiatry* 18 (1994): 23–59.

Endnotes

1. Keith Quincy, *Hmong: History of a People* (Cheney: East Washington University Press, 1988).

2. Joseph Cerquone, *Refugees from Laos: In Harm's Way* (Washington, D.C.: U.S. Committee for Refugees, 1986).

3. Quincy, *Hmong: History of a People.*

4. Ibid.

5. *Profiles of the Highland Lao Communities in the United States* (Washington, D.C.: U.S. Department of Health and Human Services, 1988).

6. Charles Johnson, *Dab Neeg Hmoob: Myths, Legends, and Folktales from the Hmong of Laos* (St. Paul, MN: Macalester College, 1985).

7. Marjorie A. Muecke, "In Search of Healers: Southeast Asian Refugees in the American Health Care System," *The Western Journal of Medicine* 139 (1983): 835–840.

8. Dwight Conquergood, *I Am a Shaman: A Hmong Life Story with Ethnographic Commentary* (Minneapolis: University of Minnesota, Southeast Asian Refugee Studies Project, Center for Urban and Regional Affairs, 1989).

9. Hmong was an exclusively oral language until the 1950s when Christian missionaries in Laos developed a written form using the Roman alphabet. In this essay, terms in the Hmong language are written in the Romanized Popular Alphabet (RPA). For ease of pronunciation, I provide an English transliteration in parentheses.

10. The word *mara*, from which *nightmare* is derived, can be traced to a proto-Indo-European root that most likely referred to a nocturnal pressing spirit; see Friedrich Kluge, *Etymologisches Wörterbuch der Deutschen Sprache* (Berlin: Walter de Gruyter, 1960). The Old English *nihtmara*, which is the antecedent to the modern English word, and the German *Mahr* (masculine) or *Mahre* (feminine) (Old High German *Mara*) are related examples of this root; see Johannes Hoops, ed., *Reallexikon der Germanischer Altertumskunde* (Strassburg: Karl J. Trubner, 1916), 172; Kluge, 454.

11. David J. Hufford, "A New Approach to the 'Old Hag': The Nightmare Tradition Reexamined," in *American Folk Medicine: A Symposium*, ed. Wayland D. Hand (Berkeley and Los Angeles: University of California Press, 1976), 73–85; Hufford, *The Terror That Comes in the Night* (Philadelphia: University of Pennsylvania Press, 1982); Donald Ward, "The Little Man Who Wasn't There: Encounters with the Supranormal," *Fabula: Journal of Folklore Studies* 18 (1977): 213–225.

12. I am indebted to David J. Hufford for his characterization of the nightmare in *The Terror That Comes in the Night*. Although I have altered his configuration slightly (based on the results of my own fieldwork in Jerusalem [1987–88] and Los Angeles [1986–87]), Hufford's criteria, which are unique in the literature on the subject, remain the foundation of the minimal requirements for the nightmare experience as I present them.

13. R. Campbell Thompson, *Semitic Magic: Its Origin and Development* (New York: Ktav Publishing, 1971).

14. Ronald C. Simons and Charles C. Hughes, eds., *The Culture-Bound Syndromes: Folk Illnesses of Psychiatric and Anthropological Interest* (Dordrecht: D. Reidel, 1985).

15. Kurt Ranke, *Enzyklopodie des Marchens*, vols. 1ff (Berlin and New York: de Gruyter, 1977).

16. Donald Ward, *The German Legends of the Brothers Grimm* (London: Millington Books, 1981).

17. Lutz Röhrich, *Probleme der Sagenforschung* (Freiburg im Breisgau: Deutsche Forschungsgemeinschaft, 1973).

18. Hufford, "A New Approach"; Hufford, *The Terror*; Robert Ness, "The Old Hag Phenomenon as Sleep Paralysis: A Biocultural Interpretation," *Culture, Medicine, Psychiatry* 2 (1978): 15–39.

19. George M. Foster, "Dreams, Character, and Cognitive Orientation in Tzintzuntzan," *Ethos* 1 (1973): 106–121.

20. Hufford, *The Terror*.

21. William C. Dement, Shervert H. Frazier, and Elliot D. Weizman, *The American Medical Association Guide to Better Sleep* (New York: Random House, 1984).

22. Although in the biomedical literature sleep paralysis is commonly associated with narcoleptics, this phase of sleep has a significant rate of occurrence among people without narcolepsy as well, as has recently been convincingly demonstrated (Yasuo Hishikawa, "Sleep Paralysis," in *Narcolepsy: Proceedings of the First International Symposium on Narcolepsy, Advances in Sleep Research*, vol. 3, eds. Christian Guilleminault, William C. Dement, and Pierre Passouant [New York: Spectrum Publications, 1976], 97–124; Hufford, "A New Approach" and *The Terror*; Ness, "The Old Hag Phenomenon."

23. Ernest Hartmann, *The Nightmare: The Psychology and Biology of Terrifying Dreams* (New York: Basic Books, 1984).

24. Ibid.; Hufford, *The Terror*; J. D. Parkes, *Sleep and Its Disorders* (London: W. B. Saunders, 1985).

25. Hufford, "A New Approach" and *The Terror*.

26. Ness, "The Old Hag Phenomenon."

27. Henry Kellerman, *Sleep Disorders: Insomnia and Narcolepsy* (New York: Brunner/Mazel, 1981); Emery Zimmerman, M.D., Ph.D., personal communication with the author, Los Angeles, California, 1987.

28. Ernest E. Heimbach, *White Hmong–English Dictionary* (Ithaca: Cornell University Press, 1979).

29. Johnson, *Dab Neeg Hmoob*.

30. Joshua Trachtenberg, *Jewish Magic and Superstition: A Study in Folk Religion* (New York: Atheneum, 1984).

31. For example, Chaucer, "The Wife of Bath's Tale," III, 878–881.

32. In order to protect the anonymity of the informants, all names used in this chapter are pseudonyms.

33. Chue Lor, personal communication with the author, Stockton, California, 1990.

34. Individuals belonging to other groups—notably Filipinos, Thai, Khmu, Japanese, and Cambodians—have also died of what appears to be SUNDS. A detailed analysis of these potentially parallel phenomena is beyond the scope of this paper, but my preliminary investigation of the Khmu and Thai sudden

deaths indicates that individuals of both groups perceive a connection between Nightmare spirit attacks and the fatal outcomes. Interviews with Khmu men regarding SUNDS reveal the presence of the belief that the Khmu Nightmare spirit, *hrooy kheut*, is responsible for the deaths. Thai laborers in Singapore and Saudi Arabia have also been victims of what appears to be SUNDS. Suffering from tremendous physical exhaustion and psychological stress, some Thai men have taken steps to thwart the succubus-like spirit they believe is responsible for the deaths: "Blaming female spirits for the killings, the men have begun wearing dresses and red nail polish—apparently to fool the spirits into thinking they're women. A few also have posted wooden replicas of male genitals in front of their homes" (Steve Johnson, "Strange Malady Killing Asian Men," *San Jose Mercury News*, February 18, 1991). Any definitive statement regarding these Nightmare spirits and sudden deaths, however, requires an in-depth study of the type presented here.

35. The disorder is also known by the acronym SUDS, Sudden Unexplained Death Syndrome. I feel that both the unpredictable nature of the syndrome and the fact that 98 percent of the deaths occurred between 10:00 p.m. and 8:00 a.m. (R. Gibson Parrish et al., "Sudden Unexplained Death Syndrome in Southeast Asian Refugees: A Review of CDC Surveillance," *Morbidity and Mortality Weekly Review* 36 [1987]: 43–53) warrant the inclusion of both the words *unexpected* and *nocturnal* in the label. Thus, Sudden Unexpected Nocturnal Death Syndrome is a more accurate description of the disorder. My use of the term SUNDS is consistent with that of the SUNDS Planning Project at St. Paul-Ramsey Medical Center.

36. Roy C. Baron et al., "Sudden Deaths among Southeast Asian Refugees: An Unexplained Nocturnal Phenomenon," *Journal of the American Medical Association* 250 (1983): 2947–2951.

37. Neal Holtan et al., *Final Report of the SUNDS Planning Project* (St. Paul, MN: St. Paul-Ramsey Medical Center, 1984).

38. Ibid.

39. For a detailed description of the research approach and methods, see Shelley R. Adler, "The Role of the Nightmare in Hmong Sudden Unexpected Nocturnal Death Syndrome: A Folkloristic Study of Belief and Health," Ph.D. diss., University of California–Los Angeles, 1991, 48–61.

40. Shelley R. Adler, "Sudden Unexpected Nocturnal Death Syndrome among Hmong Immigrants: Examining the Role of the 'Nightmare'," *Journal of American Folklore* 104 (1991): 54–71; Adler, "The Role of the Nightmare"; Adler, "The Role of Supranormal Nocturnal Encounters in Ethnomedicogenic Illness and Hmong Immigrants' Sudden Nocturnal Deaths" (presentation at the annual meeting of the American Anthropological Association, San Francisco, California, 1992).

41. Hufford, *The Terror*, 14–15.

42. David J. Hufford, "Traditions of Disbelief," *New York Folklore* 8 (1982): 47–55.

43. Hufford, *The Terror*, xvi.

44. Hufford, *The Terror*.

45. Neng Her, personal communication with the author, Stockton, California, 1990.

46. Ibid.

47. Ibid.
48. Adler, "Sudden Unexpected," 63.
49. Christine Desan, "A Change of Faith for Hmong Refugees," *Cultural Survival Quarterly* 7 (1983): 45–48.
50. Male Hmong social worker from Stockton, California, personal communication with the author, Stockton, California, 1990.
51. Bruce Thowpaou Bliatout, *Hmong Sudden Unexpected Nocturnal Death Syndrome: A Cultural Study* (Oregon: Sparkle Publishing, 1982), 90.
52. Ibid., 91.
53. Tong Yee Xiong, personal communication with the author, Stockton, California, 1990.
54. Cheng Her, personal communication with the author, Stockton, California, 1990.
55. Chia Xiong, personal communication with the author, Stockton, California, 1990.
56. See Hishikawa, "Sleep Paralysis"; Ness, "The Old Hag Phenomenon"; Allan Rechtschaffen and William C. Dement, "Narcolepsy and Hypersomnia," in *Sleep: Physiology and Pathology,* ed. Anthony Kales, (Philadelphia and Toronto: Lippincott, 1969), 119–130; Terence C. Riley, *Clinical Aspects of Sleep and Sleep Disturbances* (Boston: Butterworth Publishers, 1985).
57. Chia Xiong, previously cited.
58. Ibid.
59. Ibid.
60. Nancy Dorelle Donnelly, "The Changing Lives of Refugee Hmong Women," Ph.D. diss., University of Washington (Michigan: University Microfilms International, 1989).
61. Joseph Jay Tobin and Joan Friedman, "Spirits, Shamans, and Nightmare Death: Survivor Stress in a Hmong Refugee," *American Journal of Orthopsychiatry* 53 (1983): 439–448.
62. Soua Vang, personal communication with the author, Stockton, California, 1990.
63. Burt Feintuch, *The Conservation of Culture: Folklorists in the Public Sector* (Lexington: University Press of Kentucky, 1988).
64. See, for example, Michael A. Brodsky et al., "Ventricular Tachyarrhythmia Associated with Psychological Stress: The Role of the Sympathetic Nervous System," *Journal of the American Medical Association* 257 (1987): 2064–2067; Walter Cannon, "Voodoo Death," *American Anthropologist* 44 (1942): 169–181; George L. Engel, "Sudden and Rapid Death during Psychological Stress: Folklore or Folk Wisdom?" *Annals of Internal Medicine* 74 (1971): 771–782; William A. Greene, Sidney Goldstein, and Arthur J. Moss, "Psychosocial Aspects of Sudden Death: A Preliminary Report," *Archives of Internal Medicine* 129 (1972): 725–731; Bernard Lown, "Mental Stress, Arrhythmias, and Sudden Death," *American Journal of Medicine* 72 (1982): 177–180; Richard H. Rahe et al., "Recent Life Changes, Myocardial Infarction, and Abrupt Coronary Death," *Archives of Internal Medicine* 133 (1974): 221–228.
65. Robert A. Hahn and Arthur Kleinman, "Belief as Pathogen, Belief as Medicine: 'Voodoo Death' and the 'Placebo Phenomenon' in Anthropological Perspective," *Medical Anthropology Quarterly* 14 (1983): 3, 6–19.

Selected Bibliography

Adler, Shelley R. "Ethnomedical Pathogenesis and Hmong Immigrants' Sudden Nocturnal Deaths." *Culture, Medicine, and Psychiatry* 18 (1994): 23–59.

—————. "The Role of the Nightmare in Hmong Sudden Unexpected Nocturnal Death Syndrome: A Folkloristic Study of Belief and Health." Ph.D. dissertation, University of California–Los Angeles, 1991.

—————. "Sudden Unexpected Nocturnal Death Syndrome among Hmong Immigrants: Examining the Role of the 'Nightmare.'" *Journal of American Folklore* 104 (Winter 1991): 54–71.

Allen, Thomas B. *Possessed: The True Story of an Exorcism.* New York: Doubleday, 1993.

Anderson, Joan Webster. *Where Angels Walk: True Stories of Heavenly Visitors.* Sea Cliff, NY: Barton & Brett, 1992.

Ardener, Edwin. "Belief and the Problem of Women." In *Perceiving Women,* edited by Shirley Ardener, 1–17. New York: John Wiley and Sons, 1975.

Audi, Robert. *Belief, Justification, and Knowledge.* Belmont, CA: Wadsworth, 1988.

Barbanell, Maurice. *This Is Spiritualism.* London: Spiritualist Press, 1959.

Barnes, Peggy. *The Fundamentals of Spiritualism.* Chesterfield, IN: Psychic Observer Book Shop, no date.

Barrow, Logie. *Independent Spirits: Spiritualism and English Plebians, 1850–1910.* London: Routledge and Kegan Paul, 1986.

Bateson, Gregory. *Mind and Nature: A Necessary Unity.* New York: Dutton, 1979.

Baughman, Ernest W. *Type and Motif-Index of the Folktales of England and North America.* The Hague: Mouton, 1966.

Bauman, Richard. *Story, Performance, and Event: Contextual Studies of Oral Narrative.* Cambridge: Cambridge University Press, 1986.

Beaumont, John. *An Historical Physiological and Theological Treatise of Spirits, Apparitions, Witchcrafts, and Other Magical Practices.* London: D. Browne, 1705.

Becker, C. B. "The Centrality of Near-Death Experiences in Chinese Pure Land Buddhism." *Anabiosis: The Journal of Near-Death Studies* 1 (1981): 154–170.

Beckwith, Martha Warren. *Hawaiian Mythology.* Honolulu: University of Hawaii Press, 1970.

Bednarowski, Mary Farrell. "Nineteenth-Century American Spiritualism: An Attempt at a Scientific Religion." Ph.D. dissertation, University of Minnesota, 1973.

Bennett, Gillian. "'Belief' Stories: The Forgotten Genre." *Western Folklore* 48 (1989): 289–311.

———. "Legend: Performance and Truth." In *Monsters with Iron Teeth: Perspectives on Contemporary Legends,* Volume 2, edited by Gillian Bennett and Paul Smith, 13–36. Sheffield: Sheffield Academic Press, 1988.

———. "Narrative as Expository Discourse." *Journal of American Folklore* 99 (1986): 415–484.

———. Review of *Vision Narratives of Women in Prison,* by Carol Burke. *Folklore* 105 (1994): 110–112.

———. *Traditions of Belief: Women and the Supernatural.* Harmondsworth, England: Penguin, 1987.

Berger, Peter L. *A Far Glory.* New York: Free Press, 1992.

———. *A Rumor of Angels: Modern Society and the Rediscovery of the Supernatural.* 1969. Reprint, with a new introduction by the author, New York: Anchor Books, 1990.

Blatty, William Peter. *The Exorcist.* New York: Bantam Books, 1971.

———. *William Peter Blatty on* The Exorcist *from Novel to Film.* New York: Bantam Books, 1974.

Bliatout, Bruce Thowpaou. *Hmong Sudden Unexpected Nocturnal Death Syndrome: A Cultural Study.* Oregon: Sparkle Publishing, 1982.

Bowlby, John. *Attachment and Loss.* Volume 3. New York: Basic Books, 1980.

Brandon, Ruth. *The Spiritualists: The Passion for the Occult in the Nineteenth and Twentieth Centuries.* New York: Knopf, 1983.

Braude, Ann. *Radical Spirits: Spiritualism and Women's Rights in Nineteenth-Century America.* Boston: Beacon Press, 1989.

Britten, Emma Hardinge. *Modern American Spiritualism: A Twenty Years' Record of the Communion between Earth and the World of Spirits.* London: J. Burns, 1869.

———. *Nineteenth Century Miracles: Spirits and Their Work in Every Country of the Earth.* 1884. Reprint, New York: Arno Press, 1976.

Brunvand, Jan Harold. *The Vanishing Hitchhiker: American Urban Legends and Their Meanings.* New York: Norton, 1981.

Bullard, Thomas E. "Folklore Scholarship and UFO Reality." *International UFO Reporter* 13 (July/August 1988): 9–13.

———. "UFO Abduction Reports: The Supernatural Kidnap Narrative Returns in Technological Guise." *Journal of American Folklore* 102 (1989): 147–170.

Bultmann, Rudolf. "A Reply to the Theses of J. Schniewind." In *Kerygma and Myth: A Theological Debate,* edited by Hans Werner Bartsch; translated by Reginald H. Fuller. London: S.P.C.K., 1953.

Burke, Carol. *Vision Narratives of Women in Prison.* Knoxville: University of Tennessee Press, 1992.

Burnham, Sophy. *A Book of Angels.* New York: Ballantine Books, 1990.

Butler, Jonathan M. 1991. "Prophecy, Gender, and Culture: Ellen Gould Harmon [White] and the Roots of Seventh-Day Adventism." *Religion and American Culture: A Journal of Interpretation* 1 (1991): 3–29.

Capron, Eliab Wilkinson. *Modern Spiritualism: Its Facts and Fanaticism, Its Consistencies and Contradictions.* 1855. Reprint, New York: Arno Press, 1976.

Clifford, James, and George E. Marcus, editors. *Writing Culture-- The Poetics and Politics of Ethnography.* Berkeley and Los Angeles: University of California Press, 1986.

Cohen, Erik. "A Phenomenology of Tourist Experiences." *Sociology* 13 (1979): 179–201.

Colum, Pedraic. *Legends of Hawaii*. 1937. Reprint, New Haven, CT: Yale University Press, 1967.

Conquergood, Dwight. *I Am a Shaman: A Hmong Life Story with Ethnographic Commentary*. Minneapolis: University of Minnesota, Southeast Asian Refugee Studies Project, Center for Urban and Regional Affairs, 1989.

Crowe, Catherine. *The Night-Side of Nature: Or Ghosts and Ghost-seers*. 1848. Reprint, Wellingborough, Northamptonshire: Aquarian Press, 1986.

Davenport, Reuben Briggs. *The Death-Blow to Spiritualism: Being the True Story of the Fox Sisters as Revealed by Authority of Margaret Fox Kane and Katherine Fox Jencken*. 1888. Reprint, New York: Arno Press, 1976.

Davis, Caroline Franks. *The Evidential Force of Religious Experience*. Oxford: Clarendon Press, 1989.

D;aaegh, Linda, and Andrew V;aaazsonyi. "Does the Word 'Dog' Bite? Ostensive Action: A Means of Legend-Telling." *Journal of Folklore Research* 20 (1983): 5–34.

DeGeorge, Richard T. *The Nature and Limits of Authority*. Lawrence: University Press of Kansas, 1985.

Dewey, D. M. *History of the Strange Sounds or Rappings, Heard in Rochester and Western New-York, and usually called The Mysterious Noises! which are supposed by many to be Communications from the Spirit World, together with all the Explanation that can as yet be given of the matter*. Authorized edition. Rochester: D. M. Dewey, 1850.

Dods, John Bovee. *Spirit Manifestations Examined and Explained: Judge Edmonds Refuted*. New York: DeWitt and Davenport, 1854.

Douglas, Mary. *Purity and Danger: An Analysis of Concepts of Pollution and Taboo*. New York: Praeger, 1966.

Doyle, Arthur Conan. *The History of Spiritualism*. 2 volumes. New York: George H. Doran, 1926.

Eidelberg, Ludwig, editor. *The Encyclopedia of Psychoanalysis*. New York: Free Press, 1968.

Ellis, William. *Journal of William Ellis*. Honolulu: Advertiser Publishing, 1963.

Emmons, Charles F. *Chinese Ghosts and ESP: A Study of Paranormal Beliefs and Experiences*. Metuchen, NJ: Scarecrow Press, 1982.

Evans-Wentz, W. Y., translator. *The Tibetan Book of the Dead; or, the After-Death Experiences on the Bardo Plane*. Commentary by C. G. Jung. New York: Oxford University Press, 1957.

Fabian, Johannes. *Time and the Other: How Anthropology Makes Its Object*. New York: Columbia University Press, 1983.

Festinger, Leon, Henry W. Riecken, and Stanley Schachter. *When Prophecy Fails: Social and Psychological Study of a Modern Group That Predicted the Destruction of the World*. Minneapolis: University of Minnesota Press, 1956; New York: Harper and Row, 1964.

Fornell, Earl Wesley. *The Unhappy Medium: Spiritualism and the Life of Margaret Fox*. Austin: University of Texas Press, 1964.

Foster, Genevieve. *The World Was Flooded with Light: A Mystical Experience Remembered*. With "Commentary: Mystical Experience in the Modern World" by David J. Hufford. Pittsburgh: University of Pittsburgh Press, 1985.

Freud, Sigmund. *Civilization and Its Discontents*. Revised and edited by James Stachey. Translated by Joan Riviere. International Psychoanalytic Library, No. 17. London: Hogarth Press, 1972. Originally published in English in 1930 by Hogarth Press.

Gallup, George, Jr., with William Proctor. *Adventures in Immortality.* New York: McGraw-Hill, 1982.

Gallup, G. H., and F. Newport. "Belief in Paranormal Phenomena among Adult Americans." *Skeptical Inquirer* 15 (1991): 137–146.

Goffman, Erving. *Frame Analysis: An Essay on the Organization of Experience.* New York: Harper and Row, 1974.

Goldfarb, Russell M., and Clare R. Goldfarb. *Spiritualism and Nineteenth-Century Letters.* London: Associated University Presses, 1978.

Gould, Stephen Jay. "Ten Thousand Acts of Kindness." *Natural History* (December 1988): 12–17.

Graburn, Nelson. "Tourism: The Sacred Journey." In *Hosts and Guests, The Anthropology of Tourism,* edited by Valene L. Smith, 17–31. Philadelphia: University of Pennsylvania Press, 1977.

———. *To Pray, Pay, and Play: The Cultural Structure of Japanese Domestic Tourism.* Aix-en-Provence: Universite de Droit, d'Economie et des Sciences, Centre des Hautes Etudes Touristiques, 1983.

Greeley, Andrew M. "Mysticism Goes Mainstream." *American Health* 6 (January/February 1987): 47–49.

———. *Sociology of the Paranormal: A Reconnaissance.* Beverly Hills, CA: Sage Publications, 1975.

Grice, H. Paul. "Logic and Conversation." In *Syntax and Semantics,* Volume 3, edited by Peter Cole and J. L. Morgan, 41–58. New York: Aademic Press, 1975.

Griffin, Susan. *Woman and Nature: The Roaring Inside Her.* New York: Harper and Row, 1978.

Groot, Jan Jakob Maria de. *The Religious System of China.* 6 volumes. Taipei: Ch'eng Wen Publishing, 1972.

Grose, Francis. *A Provincial Glossary with a Collection of Local Proverbs and Popular Superstitions.* London: S. Hooper, [1787] 1790.

Hahn, Robert. "Understanding Beliefs: An Essay on the Methodology of the Statement and Analysis of Belief Systems." *Current Anthropology* 14 (June 1973): 207–229.

Hand, Wayland D., editor. *Popular Beliefs and Superstitions from North Carolina. The Frank C. Brown Collection of North Carolina Folklore.* 7 volumes. Durham, NC: Duke University Press, 1952–64.

Handler, Richard, and Joyce Linnekin. "Tradition, Genuine or Spurious." *Journal of American Folklore* 97 (July–September 1984): 273–290.

Hare, Robert. *Experimental Investigation of the Spirit Manifestations.* New York: Partridge and Brittan, 1855.

Henderson, William. *Notes on the Folk Lore of the Northern Counties of England and the Borders.* 1866. Reprint, Wakefield: E.P. Publishing, 1973.

Herskovits, Melville J., and Morris J. Rogers Jr. "A Note on Present Day Myth." *Journal of American Folklore,* no. 163 (1929): 73–75.

Hilgard, E. R. *Divided Consciousness.* New York: Wiley, 1977.

hooks, bell. *Feminist Theory: From Margin to Center.* Boston: South End Press, 1984.

Hopkins, Budd, David Michael Jacobs, Ron Westrum, et al. *Unusual Personal Experiences: An Analysis of Data from Three National Surveys Conducted by the Roper Organization.* Las Vegas: Bigelow Holding Corporation, 1992.

Houdini, Harry. *A Magician among the Spirits.* New York: Harper and Brothers, 1924.

Hoyt, Michael F. "Clinical Notes Regarding the Experience of 'Presences' in Mourning." *Omega* 11 (1980–81): 105–111.

Hufford, David J. "Ambiguity and the Rhetoric of Belief." *Keystone Folklore* 21 (1976): 11–24.

———. "Awakening Paralyzed in the Presence of a 'Strange Visitor.'" In *Alien Discussions: Proceedings of the Abduction Study Conference, Held at MIT, Cambridge, MA*, edited by Andrea Pritchard et al., 348–354. Cambridge, MA: North Cambridge Press, 1994.

———. "Commentary: Mystical Experience in the Modern World." In *The World Was Flooded with Light: A Mystical Experience Remembered*, by Genevieve Foster. Pittsburgh: University of Pittsburgh Press, 1985.

———. "Epistemologies of Religious Healing." *Journal of Philosophy and Medicine* 18 (1993): 175–194.

———. "Humanoids and Anomalous Lights: Epistemologic and Taxonomic Problems." *Fabula: Journal of Folktale Studies* 18 (1977): 234–241.

———. "A New Approach to the 'Old Hag': The Nightmare Tradition Reexamined." In *American Folk Medicine: A Symposium*, edited by Wayland D. Hand, 73–85. Berkeley and Los Angeles: University of California Press, 1976.

———. "Reason, Rhetoric, and Religion: Academic Logic versus Folk Belief." *New York Folklore* 11 (1985): 177–194.

———. "The Supernatural and the Sociology of Knowledge: Explaining Academic Belief." *New York Folklore* 9 (1983): 47–56.

———. *The Terror That Comes in the Night: An Experience-Centered Study of Supernatural Assault Traditions*. Philadelphia: University of Pennsylvania Press, 1982.

———. "Traditions of Disbelief." *New York Folklore* 8 (1982): 47–55.

Huguenin, Charles A. "The Amazing Fox Sisters." *New York Folklore Quarterly* 13, no. 4 (1957): 241–276.

Hull, Gloria, Patricia Bell Scott, and Barbara Smith, editors. *All the Women Are White, All the Men Are Black, But Some of Us Are Brave: Black Women's Studies*. Old Westbury, CT: Feminist Press, 1982.

Hymes, Dell. "Ways of Speaking." In *Explorations in the Ethnography of Speaking*, edited by Richard Bauman and Joel Sherzer. Cambridge: Cambridge University Press, 1974.

Iwasaka, Michiko, and Barre Toelken. *Ghosts and the Japanese: Cultural Experience in Japanese Death Legends*. Logan, Utah: Utah State University Press, 1994.

Jahoda, Gustav. *The Psychology of Superstition*. Harmondsworth, England: Penguin, 1970.

Johnson, Charles. *Dab Neeg Hmoob: Myths, Legends, and Folktales from the Hmong of Laos*. St. Paul, MN: Macalester College, 1985.

Kakar, Sudhir. *Shamans, Mystics, and Doctors*. New York: Knopf, 1982.

Kane, Herb Kawainui. *Pele, Goddess of Hawai'i's Volcanoes*. Captain Cook, HI: Kawainui Press, 1987.

Katz, Richard. *Boiling Energy: Community Healing among the Kalahari Kung*. Cambridge: Harvard University Press, 1982.

Katz, Steven T. "Language, Epistemology, and Mysticism." In *Mysticism and Philosophical Analysis*, edited by Steven T. Katz, 22–74. New York: Oxford University Press, 1978.

Kavenaugh, Keiran, O.C.D., and Otilio Rodriguez, O.C.D., translators. *The Interior Castle.* In *The Collected Works of St. Teresa of Avila.* Volume 2. Washington, DC: Institute of Carmelite Studies, 1980.

Kellenberger, J. *The Cognitivity of Religion: Three Perspectives.* Berkeley and Los Angeles: University of California Press, 1985.

Kerr, Howard. *Mediums, and Spirit-Rappers, and Roaring Radicals: Spiritualism in American Literature, 1850–1900.* Chicago, IL: University of Chicago Press, 1972.

La Barre, W. *The Ghost Dance: Origins of Religion.* Revised edition. New York: Delta Books, 1972.

Lawless, Elaine. "Rescripting Their Lives and Narratives: Spiritual Life Stories of Pentecostal Women Preachers." *Journal of Feminist Studies in Religion* 7 (1991): 53–71.

Lèvi-Strauss, Claude. *Tristes Tropiques.* Translated by John Weightman and Doreen Weightman. New York: Atheneum, 1975.

Lewis, E. E. *A Report of the Mysterious Noises Heard in the House of Mr. John D. Fox.* Canandaigua, New York, 1848.

Lloyd, Timothy C., and Patrick Mullen. *Lake Erie Fishermen: Work, Identity, and Tradition.* Urbana: University of Illinois Press, 1990.

MacDonald, W. Scott, and Chester W. Oden Jr. "Case Report: Aumakua--Behavioral Direction Visions in Hawaiians." *Journal of Abnormal Psychology* 86 (1977): 189–194.

Marcus, George, and Michael Fischer. *Anthropology as Cultural Critique.* Chicago: University of Chicago Press, 1986.

Matchett, William Foster. "Repeated Hallucinatory Experiences as a Part of the Mourning Process among Hopi Women." *Psychiatry* 35 (May 1972): 185–194.

McClenon, James. "Chinese and American Anomalous Experiences: The Role of Religiosity." *Sociological Analysis* 51 (1990): 53–67.

———. *Deviant Science: The Case of Parapsychology.* Philadelphia: University of Pennsylvania Press, 1984.

———. "The Experiential Foundations of Shamanic Healing." *Journal of Medicine and Philosophy* 18, no. 2 (1993): 107–127.

———. "Near-Death Folklore in Medieval China and Japan: A Comparative Analysis." *Asian Folklore Studies* 50, no. 2 (1991): 319–342.

———. "A Preliminary Report on African-American Anomalous Experiences in Northeast North Carolina." *Parapsychology Review* 21 (1990): 1–4.

———. "A Survey of Chinese Anomalous Experiences and Comparison with Western Representative National Samples." *Journal for the Scientific Study of Religion* 27 (1988): 421–426.

———. "A Survey of Elite Scientists: Their Attitudes toward ESP and Parapsychology." *Journal of Parapsychology* 46, no. 2 (1982): 127–152.

———. *Wondrous Events: Foundations of Religious Belief.* Philadelphia: University of Pennsylvania Press, 1994.

Merchant, Carolyn. *The Death of Nature: Women, Ecology, and the Scientific Revolution.* San Francisco: Harper and Row, 1980.

Miska, Maxine. "The Dramatic Structure of a Hakka Seance: On Being Convinced." Ph.D. dissertation, University of Pennsylvania, 1990.

Moody, Raymond A. *Life after Life: The Investigation of a Phenomenon--Survival of Bodily Death.* With an introduction by Elisabeth Kubler-Ross. Atlanta: Mockingbird Books, 1975.

Moore, R. Laurence. *In Search of White Crows: Spiritualism, Parapsychology, and American Culture.* New York: Oxford University Press, 1977.

Morse, Melvin. *Transformed by the Light: The Powerful Effect of Near-Death Experiences on People's Lives.* New York: Villard Books, 1992.

Morse, Melvin, with Paul Perry. *Closer to the Light: Learning from Children's Near-Death Experiences.* New York: Villard Books, 1990.

Mullins, Joe. *The Goddess Pele.* Honolulu: Aloha Graphics and Sales, 1977.

Munger, Ronald G. "Sleep Disturbances and Sudden Death of Hmong Refugees: A Report of Fieldwork Conducted in the Ban Vinai Refugee Camp." In *The Hmong in Transition,* edited by Glenn L. Hendricks et al., 379–398. Staten Island: Center for Immigration Studies of New York, 1986.

Nelson, Geoffrey K. *Spiritualism and Society.* New York: Schocken Books, 1969.

Ness, Robert. "The Old Hag Phenomenon as Sleep Paralysis: A Biocultural Interpretation." *Culture, Medicine, Psychiatry* 2 (1978): 15–39.

Nimmo, H. Arlo. "Pele, Ancient Goddess of Contemporary Hawaii." *Pacific Studies* 9, no. 2 (1986): 121–179.

Oppenheim, Janet. *The Other World: Spiritualism and Psychical Research in England, 1850–1914.* Cambridge: Cambridge University Press, 1985.

Osis, Karlis, and Erlendur Haraldsson. *At the Hour of Death.* New York: Avon Books, 1977.

Owen, Alex. *The Darkened Room: Women, Power, and Spiritualism in Late Victorian England.* Philadelphia: University of Pennsylvania Press, 1990.

Owen, Robert Dale. *Footfalls on the Boundary of Another World.* Philadelphia: Lippincott, 1860.

Paglia, Camille. *Sexual Personae.* New York: Vintage Books, 1990.

Parkes, Colin Murray. *Bereavement: Studies of Grief in Adult Life.* New York: International Universities Press, 1972.

Pimple, Kenneth D. "Folk Beliefs." In *The Emergence of Folklore in Everyday Life: A Fieldguide and Sourcebook,* edited by George H. Schoemaker. Bloomington, IN: Trickster Press, 1990.

Podmore, Frank. *Modern Spiritualism: A History and a Criticism.* 2 volumes. London: Methuen, 1902.

Poloma, Margaret. *The Charismatic Movement: Is There a New Pentecost?* Social Movements Past and Present Series. Boston: Twayne, 1987.

Porter, Katherine H. *Through a Glass Darkly: Spiritualism in the Browning Circle.* Lawrence: University Press of Kansas, 1958.

Postman, Neil. *Technopoly: The Surrender of Culture to Technology.* New York: Vintage Books, 1992.

Proudfoot, Wayne. *Religious Experience.* Berkeley and Los Angeles: University of California Press, 1985.

Puckett, Newbell Niles. *Folk Beliefs of the Southern Negro.* Chapel Hill: University of North Carolina Press, 1926.

Randolph, Vance. *Ozark Superstitions.* New York: Dover, 1964.

Rees, W. Dewi. "The Hallucinations of Widowhood." *British Medical Journal,* October 1971, 37–41.

Ring, Kenneth. *Life at Death: A Scientific Investigation of the Near-Death Experience.* New York: Coward, McCann, and Geoghegan, 1980.

————. *Heading toward Omega: In Search of the Meaning of Near-Death Experience.* New York: W. Morrow, 1984.

Rojcewicz, Peter M. "The Boundaries of Orthodoxy: A Folkloric Look at the 'UFO Phenomenon.'" Ph.D. dissertation, Folklore and Folklife Program, University of Pennsylvania, 1984.

————. "The 'Men in Black' Experience and Tradition." *Journal of American Folklore* 100 (1987): 148–160.

Rosaldo, Michelle Zimbalist, and Louise Lamphere, editors. *Woman, Culture, and Society.* Stanford, CA: Stanford University Press, 1974.

Said, Edward. *Orientalism.* New York: Pantheon Books, 1978.

Saler, Benson. "Supernatural as a Western Category." *Ethos* 5 (1977): 31–53.

Schulz, Richard. *The Psychology of Death, Dying, and Bereavement.* Reading, PA: Addison-Wesley, 1978.

Simons, Ronald C., and Charles C. Hughes, editors. *The Culture-Bound Syndromes: Folk Illnesses of Psychiatric and Anthropological Interest.* Dordrecht: D. Reidel, 1985.

Simpson, Elizabeth. "Mount St. Helens and the Evolution of Folklore." *Northwest Folklore* 4 (Spring–Summer 1985): 43–47.

Spiro, Melford E. "Religion: Problems of Definition and Explanation." In *Anthropological Approaches to the Study of Religion,* Volume 3, edited by Michael Banton. Edinburgh: Tavistock, 1966.

Stace, W. T. *Religion and the Modern Mind.* Philadelphia: Lippincott, 1960.

Starr, Paul. *The Social Transformation of American Medicine.* New York: Basic Books, 1982.

Stevens, Phillips, Jr. "Satanism: Where Are the Folklorists?" *New York Folklore* 15, nos. 1–2 (1989): 1–22.

Stevenson, Ian. *Children Who Remember Previous Lives: A Question of Reincarnation.* Charlottesville: University of Virginia Press, 1987.

Stewart, Susan. *On Longing: Narratives of the Miniature, the Gigantic, the Souvenir, the Collection.* Baltimore: The John Hopkins University Press, 1984.

Stone, Margaret. *Supernatural Hawaii: Actual Mysteries, Blessings, Curses, Rituals, and Legends.* Honolulu: Aloha Graphics, 1979.

Teilhard de Chardin, Pierre. *The Phenomenon of Man.* Translated by Bernard Wall. New York: Harper, 1959.

————. *Toward the Future.* Translated by Ren;aae Hague. New York: Harcourt Brace Jovanovitch, 1975.

Teresa of Avila. *The Interior Castle, or the Mansions.* Introduction and notes by Father Benedict Zimmerman, O.C.D. 1577; translated by a Benedictine monk of Stanbrook Abbey, this translation first published 1912. Reprint, Union City, NJ: John J. Crawley, 1980.

Thomas, Keith. *Religion and the Decline of Magic.* New York: Scribner's, 1971.

Thompson, Keith. *Angels and Aliens: UFOs and the Mythic Imagination.* New York: Fawcett Columbine, 1991.

Thompson, R. Campbell. *Semitic Magic: Its Origin and Development.* New York: Ktav Publishing, 1971.

Thompson, Stith. *Motif-Index of Folk Literature: A Classification of Narrative Elements in Folktales, Ballads, Myths, Fables, Medieval Romances, Exempla, Fabliaux,*

Jest-Books, and Local Legends. 5 volumes. Revised and enlarged edition. Bloomington: Indiana University Press, 1966.

Tiffany, Sharon W., and Kathleen J. Adams. *The Wild Woman: An Inquiry into the Anthropology of an Idea.* Cambridge, MA: Schenkman Publishing, 1985.

Tillhagen, Carl Herman. "The Conception of the Nightmare in Sweden." In *Humaniora: Essays in Literature, Folklore, and Bibliography Honoring Archer Taylor.* Edited by Wayland D. Hand and Gustave O. Arlt. New York: J. J. Augustin, 1969.

Titon, Jeff Todd. "The Life Story." *Journal of American Folklore* 93 (1980): 276–292.

Tobin, Joseph Jay, and Joan Friedman. "Spirits, Shamans, and Nightmare Death: Survivor Stress in a Hmong Refugee." *American Journal of Orthopsychiatry* 53 (July 1983): 439–448.

Toelken, Barre. *The Dynamics of Folklore.* Boston: Houghton Mifflin, 1979.

———. "Folklore, Worldview, and Communication." In *Folklore, Performance, and Communication,* edited by Dan Ben-Amos and Kenneth Goldstein, 265–286. The Hague: Mouton, 1975.

Towler, Robert, et al. "Conventional Religion and Common Religion in Great Britain." Religious Research Papers, No. 11. University of Leeds, Department of Sociology, 1981–84.

Trachtenberg, Joshua. *Jewish Magic and Superstition: A Study in Folk Religion.* New York: Atheneum, 1984.

Trinh, T. Minh-ha. *Woman, Native, Other: Writing Postcoloniality and Feminism.* Bloomington: Indiana University Press, 1989.

Turner, Victor. *Dramas, Fields, and Metaphors: Symbolic Action in Human Society.* Ithaca: Cornell University Press, 1974.

———. *The Forest of Symbols: Aspects of Ndembu Ritual.* Ithaca: Cornell University Press, 1967.

———. *The Ritual Process: Structure and Anti-Structure.* Chicago: Aldine Press, 1969.

Underhill, A. Leah. *The Missing Link in Modern Spiritualism.* 1885. Reprint, New York: Arno Press, 1976.

Virtanen, Leea. *"That Must Have Been ESP!": An Examination of Psychic Experiences.* Bloomington: Indiana University Press, 1990.

Wallace, Anthony F. C. *The Death and Rebirth of the Seneca.* New York: Vintage Books, 1969.

———. *Religion: An Anthropological View.* New York: Random House, 1966.

Weber, Max. *The Sociology of Religion.* Translated into English from the 4th Edition by Ephraim Fischoff. Boston: Beacon Press, 1963.

Weiner, Annette. *Women of Value, Men of Renown.* Austin: University of Texas Press, 1976.

Weller, Robert P. *Unities and Diversities in Chinese Religion.* Seattle: University of Washington Press, 1987.

Westervelt, William D. *Hawaiian Legends of Volcanoes.* Rutland, VT: Charles E. Tuttle, 1963.

Wilson, William A. "The Deeper Necessity: Folklore and the Humanities." *Journal of American Folklore* 101 (1988): 156–167.

Zaleski, Carol. *Otherworld Journeys: Accounts of Near-Death Experiences in Medieval and Modern Times.* New York: Oxford University Press, 1987.

Editor

BARBARA WALKER is assistant director of the Folklore Program at Utah State University where she teaches and is director of the Fife Folklore Archives; each year she coordinates the annual Fife Folklore Conference on a variety of topics ranging from ethnicity to material culture to belief. She is author of the *Index to the Austin and Alta Fife Fieldwork Recordings of Cowboy and Western Songs.*

Contributors

SHELLEY R. ADLER is Assistant Research Medical Anthropologist at the University of California, San Francisco. She holds a Ph.D. in Folklore and Mythology from the University of California, Los Angeles, and completed a postdoctoral fellowship in sociocultural gerontology at the University of California, San Francisco. Her research has concerned the relationship between folk belief/folk medicine and biomedicine as it affects health behavior in different ethnic groups and age cohorts. She is currently engaged in research into the reasons behind folk medical and/or biomedical treatment choices made by women with breast cancer.

GILLIAN BENNETT has a Ph.D. in Language and Folklore, and is an honorary research associate at the Centre for English Cultural Tradition and Language at the University of Sheffield in the United Kingdom. Her book *Traditions of Belief: Women and the Supernatural* is an excellent examination of contemporary beliefs in premonitions, dreams, ESP, and other paranormal and psychic phenomena. As a folk narrative scholar, she actively engages in popular belief and oral narrative research, and she lectures in both Europe and the United States.

ERIKA BRADY is an associate professor in Programs in Folk Studies at Western Kentucky University, where she also edits the journal *Southern Folklore*. She holds degrees in folklore from Indiana University, UCLA, and Harvard College. She has served as a consultant to the Vincentians of the Midwestern Province and the Diocese of Springfield-Cape Girardeau on matters concerning regional folklife. Formerly employed by the American Folklife Center, she has undertaken research on early ethnographic methods, as well as trapping in the Missouri Ozarks.

DR. JOYCE D. HAMMOND is an associate professor of anthropology at Western Washington University in Bellingham, Washington. She researches and teaches courses on expressive culture, gender roles, and visual anthropology. She is the author of *Tifaifai and Quilts of Polynesia* and has written a number of articles on contemporary Polynesian expressive forms.

DR. DAVID J. HUFFORD is Director of The Doctors Kienle Center for Humanistic Medicine and professor of Medical Humanities, Behavioral Science, and Family and Community Medicine at The Pennsylvania State University College of Medicine in Hershey, Pennsylvania. He is a nationally recognized scholar and lecturer, and is author of *The Terror That Comes in the Night: An Experience-Centered Study of Supernatural Assault Traditions* and numerous articles on folk belief and topics relating to the supernatural.

TIMOTHY LLOYD is director of the folklife program at Cityfolk, a public-sector folklife center in Dayton, Ohio. He has served as the assistant to the director of the American Folklife Center at the Library of Congress, as the director of the Ohio Arts Council's folk arts granting and research programs, and as secretary- treasurer of the American Folklore Society. His research interests include American foodways, occupational culture, and public-sector folklore. He is the author, with Patrick Mullen, of *Lake Erie Fishermen: Work, Identity, and Tradition.*

JAMES MCCLENON, Ph.D., is associate professor of sociology at Elizabeth City State University in North Carolina, and the author of *Deviant Science: The Case of Parapsychology* and *Wondrous Events: Foundations of Religious Belief.* He has investigated anomalous phenomena in the United States, Japan, Korea, Philippines, Sri Lanka, Thailand, Taiwan, and the People's Republic of China.

MAXINE MISKA is a free-lance folklorist with a doctorate from the University of Pennsylvania. She specializes in Asian folklore, urban folklore, and public sector projects. Her publications include *Tradition and Community in the Urban Neighborhood: Making Brooklyn Home,* with I. Sheldon Posen. She is presently engaged in a research project concerning Chinese popular religion.

KENNETH D. PIMPLE, Ph.D., is a Research Associate at the Poynter Center for the Study of Ethics and American Institutions and a Visiting Lecturer in American Studies, both at Indiana University. He has recently published articles on Herman Melville's *The Confidence-Man* and Edith Wharton's *The Age of Innocence.*

BARRE TOELKEN is professor of English and History at Utah State University where he directs the American Studies graduate program and the Folklore Program. He has published and lectured widely on folklore and related topics, and has an international reputation as a scholar in Native American culture and ballad studies. His textbook *The Dynamics of Folklore* has been used in folklore courses throughout the United States. His recent book *Ghosts and the Japanese: Cultural Experience in Japanese Death Legends,* with Michiko Iwasaka, is also published by USU Press.

Index